From a Broken Covenant to Circumcision of the Heart

SOCIETY
OF BIBLICAL
LITERATURE

DISSERTATION SERIES
Saul Olyan, Old Testament Editor
Mark Allan Powell, New Testament Editor

Number 175
FROM A BROKEN COVENANT TO
CIRCUMCISION OF THE HEART
Pauline Intertextual
Exegesis in Romans 2:17–29

by
Timothy W. Berkley

Timothy W. Berkley

FROM A BROKEN COVENANT TO CIRCUMCISION OF THE HEART
Pauline Intertextual
Exegesis in Romans 2:17–29

Society of Biblical Literature
Atlanta, Georgia

From a Broken Covenant to Circumcision of the Heart
Pauline Intertextual Exegesis in Romans 2:17–29

by
Timothy W. Berkley
Ph.D., Marquette University, 1998
Carol Stockhausen, Advisor

Library of Congress Cataloging-in-Publication Data

Berkley, Timothy W.
    From a broken covenant to circumcision of the heart : Pauline
intertextual exegesis in Romans 2:17–29 / Timothy W. Berkley.
        p. cm. — (Dissertation series / Society of Biblical Literature ; no. 175)
    Includes bibliographical references and indexes.
    ISBN 0-88414-015-6 (hardcover : alk. paper)
    1. Bible. N.T. Romans II, 17–29—Criticism, interpretation, etc. 2. Bible.
N.T. Romans—Relation to the Old Testament. 3. Bible. O.T. Relation to
Romans II, 17–29. I. Title. II. Dissertation series (Society of Biblical
Literature) ; no. 175.

BS2665.2.B465   2000
227'.1077—dc21   99-087044

08 07 06 05 04 03 02 01 00   5 4 3 2 1

Printed in the United States of America
on acid-free paper

Contents

Preface

The research which led to this dissertation began with an assignment to present a paper on Rom 2:17–29 for a Romans seminar at Marquette University led by Dr. Carol Stockhausen in the spring of 1992. I approached that seminar with a certain amount of apprehension, having previously regarded Romans as difficult and enigmatic. Thanks to that seminar, however, my judgment about Romans has changed. In any case, whenever I reflect on my choice of topic, it is not without a bit of irony.

As part of the seminar, Dr. Stockhausen presented a paper and her thoughts on the use of the OT in the NT in uncited material. I was not entirely convinced, but found the subject intriguing because it made sense to me that Paul the Pharisee would rely heavily upon scripture as a basis for his theology. Still somewhat skeptical concerning the method, I decided to investigate the application of intertextual methodology to the passage which had been assigned to me. To my surprise, evidence of Paul's reliance on OT references in Rom 2:17–29 became apparent when I applied the method in the limited fashion in which I then understood it. The paper was well received, and two succeeding papers I produced for that seminar also dealt with Paul's use of the OT in Romans. In two other seminars I produced papers on the intertextual uses of the OT both in 1 Corinthians and the Judas traditions in Matthew and Acts, which were also well received. I became more and more intrigued by the possibilities for fruitful exegesis in this field.

Through these projects, and as I was deciding on Rom 2:17–29 for the topic of my dissertation, the need for methodological definition and clarification became more and more evident. The research process itself has refined the methodology and its application. The evidence presented in that first paper is largely confirmed, but there have been modifications which strengthen the thesis of Paul's reliance on specific OT texts, and which eliminate some weaknesses and earlier conclusions. Important new insights which had previously been

x

overlooked became apparent at every stage which lend further support to the thesis. I am increasingly hopeful that continued development of this methodology and application to other texts will provide results as positive as those evident in this research, giving a greater understanding of the presence of scripture within the NT.

I wish to express my thanks and appreciation to my dissertation director, Carol Stockhausen. Her encouragement, insight, and help through every stage of the work brought this project to fruition. I also thank the members of my dissertation defense committee, Michél Barnes, Julian Hills, Bradford Hinze, and John Schmitt for their comments, suggestions, and corrections both material and editorial. The dissertation is greatly improved as a result of their help and direction. Perhaps most importantly, I thank my wife, Judi, who encouraged me to start, supported my continuation, and looked forward to the end of this endeavor almost as much as I did. Finally, I thank my daughter Laurelin, who displayed uncommon patience and self-reliance in the first three and a half years of her life and allowed me to study.

Introduction

Rom 2:17–29 is in many respects treated as a passage peripheral to the overall argument of Romans. Although it is part of what has been called "the theological epistle *par excellence*,"[1] and a "letter of instruction,"[2] it has nothing directly to say concerning justification by faith, the gospel of Christ, or any other Christian teaching purported to be central to the book of Romans.[3] The passage deals primarily with Jewish identity and guilt, in the process touching on the possibility of

---

[1]Matthew Black, *Romans* (NCB; London: Oliphants, 1973) 18.

[2]"Lehrbrief" (Otto Michel, *Der Brief An Die Römer* [KEK; 14th ed.; Göttingen: Vandenhoeck & Ruprecht, 1978] 6).

[3]A failure to find theologically significant material in the passage stems many times from false expectations and assumptions about the nature of the epistle as a whole. Stendahl's observation is instructive: "Lutheran tradition just knows that the purpose of Romans is to teach justification by faith without the works of the law. Calvinists just know that it is the chief text from which to get the proper doctrine of predestination, and Catholic tradition takes the second chapter as its chief text for substantiating its glorious and correct doctrine of natural law" (Krister Stendahl, *Final Account: Paul's Letter to the Romans* [Minneapolis: Fortress, 1995] 10). Those expectations and assumptions have undergone significant change, however. "It is generally acknowledged that Romans represents the latest extant statement of Paul and that it is, therefore, a summary of Paul's mature thinking. But the importance of Romans can be misleading, for nothing in the letter suggests that Paul means it to resolve or replace his earlier thought....Though Romans may reflect his latest apostolic thinking, the situation to which it was written is also most pressing, so it is as occasional as the other letters, not a systematic theology" (Alan F. Segal, *Paul the Convert: The Apostolate and Apostasy of Saul the Pharisee* [New Haven: Yale University Press, 1990] 255).

gentiles "keeping the law." In this respect it does not appear to address what have historically been treated as the most important issues of Romans, an epistle which to some "approximates so closely a theological treatise...."[4] Like many passages, it has offered little to the development of Christian theology or doctrine, and has not contributed much that is of historical significance. For these reasons it has generated little exegetical interest.[5]

Such supposedly insignificant texts have more to offer, however, and would benefit from closer inspection. Intertextual studies have opened new possibilities for understanding the exegetical background and theological foundation of many passages in both Pauline and non-Pauline studies.[6] As texts

---

[4]Emil Brunner, *The Letter to the Romans: A Commentary* (Philadelphia: Westminster, 1959) 9.

[5]Points of significant debate continue to center around the questions of whether gentiles who "keep the law" refers to gentile Christians or gentiles in general, and whether or not Paul is only speaking hypothetically (2:14–15, 26–27). Most of that discussion is held in connection with 2:14–15, rather than 2:26–27. See, e.g., Richard H. Bell, "Extra ecclesiam nulla salus? Is there salvation other than through faith in Christ according to Romans 2.12–16?" *Evangelium-Schriftauslegung-Kirche: Festschrift für Peter Stuhlmacher zum 65. Geburtstag* (eds. Jostein Adna, Scott J. Hafemann, and Otfried Hofius; Göttingen: Vanderhoeck & Ruprecht, 1997) 31–43. While a debated issue, it is tangential to the point of the passage. There has been very little interest in the issues that are central to the passage itself. The question of a Pauline contradiction in the statement of 2:13 that one is justified by keeping the law, in contrast to the seemingly opposite statement of 3:20 that no one is so justified continues to be debated as well, but does not address 2:17–29 directly.

[6]Chap. 1 will provide extensive examples beyond the few mentioned here. C. H. Dodd is one of many who address NT use of scripture in general (*According to the Scriptures: The Sub-Structure of New Testament Theology* [London: Nisbet, 1952]). Studies dealing with specific non-Pauline texts include those of Krister Stendahl (*The School of St. Matthew and Its Use of the Old Testament* [2nd ed.; Philadelphia: Fortress, 1968]; first published as ASNU 20 [Lund: Gleerup, 1954]), Joel Marcus (*The Way of the Lord: Christological Exegesis of the Old Testament in the Gospel of Mark* [Louisville: Westminster/John Knox, 1992]), and Timothy W. Berkley ("OT Exegesis and the Death of Judas," *Proceedings, EGL & MWBS* 14 [1994] 29–45). Some examples in general

are reexamined with attention to intertextual considerations, new insights are gained even into texts previously considered obscure. Intertextual studies of scripture, although not always under that name, have developed to a point where the exegetical benefits of such research are producing reevaluation of many texts and of presuppositions concerning the exegetical task. The interest of earlier studies was in author-initiated intertextual allusion. That interest has expanded in some more recent studies to include an emphasis on more reader or text-generated allusion. It has extended the range of possibilities for dealing with intertextual material.

There remains, however, room for further definition in intertextual methodology. From a historical-critical standpoint it may still be deemed profitable to establish means to distinguish between author-generated and reader-generated intertextual allusions in NT texts. Greater methodological definition may also help to establish a basis for evaluation and differentiation between subtle types of intertextual allusion, identifying instances where an author has actually engaged in intertextual exegesis of OT texts. Methodological development may also refine the process of identifying those passages containing author-generated intertextual material in cases other than citation, quotation, or overt intertextual allusion.

Recognizing the presence of intertextual exegesis in texts where it has not previously been apparent will provide greater understanding of their background and foundation. That understanding will have an impact on determining the

---

Pauline studies include E. Earl Ellis (*Paul's Use of the Old Testament* [London: Oliver and Boyd, 1957]), Richard B. Hays (*Echoes of Scripture in the Letters of Paul* [New Haven: Yale University Press, 1989]), and Ben Witherington III (*Paul's Narrative Thought World: The Tapestry of Tragedy and Triumph* [Louisville: Westminster/John Knox, 1994]). Among a number of others, Carol Kern Stockhausen (*Moses' Veil and the Glory of the New Covenant: The Exegetical Substructure of II Cor 3:1–4, 6* [AnBib 116; Rome: Pontifical Biblical Institute, 1989]) and Gail R. O'Day ("Jeremiah 9:22–23 and 1 Corinthians 1:26–31: A Study in Intertextuality," *JBL* 109 [1990] 259–67) deal with specific Pauline passages.

place of those passages in shaping an author's overall argument. In particular, the application of such a methodology offers new insight into some of the overlooked texts in the NT like Rom 2:17–29. By applying a refinement of one branch of existing intertextual methodology, this study will test the thesis that Pauline intertextual exegesis of OT texts provides the basis for his conclusions in Rom 2:17–29.

ROMANS 2:17–29

A broad understanding of Rom 2:17–29 already exists without the aid of any significant intertextual analysis. The point of this passage in the argument of Romans may be put fairly concisely. Rom 2:17–29 is part of Paul's developing argument establishing the guilt of all people, placing them in need of God's salvation on the basis of faith.[7] In these verses Paul specifically addresses the guilt of the Jews, alleging that they are guilty of violating the law. He contends that this renders circumcision valueless as a mark of salvation from wrath for disobedient Jews while obedient gentiles may be considered circumcised. He concludes the section with a redefinition of Jewish identity and circumcision based on internal heart circumcision. The course of the argument on these points is not in significant dispute.[8] What Paul is saying and where he is going are fairly clear. Perhaps for this reason these verses have attracted little attention from those engaged in the exegesis of Romans, even though some exegetical difficulties remain. The fact that the passage deals with the supposedly obscure subject of Jewish guilt may also account for the limited attention it has received.

Rom 2:17–29 generally receives only cursory treatment in commentaries, and there are few articles or monographs

---

[7]See, e.g., the statement of E. P. Sanders, "There is general agreement on the purpose of the section [1:18–2:29]. It is intended to demonstrate (or illustrate) the universal sinfulness of all (3:9, 20), so as to lay the ground for Paul's solution: righteousness by faith in Christ" (*Paul, the Law, and the Jewish People* [Philadelphia: Fortress, 1983] 123).

[8]Except for the debate about Paul's references to gentiles keeping the law, mentioned above.

which deal specifically with these verses.[9] Klyne Snodgrass has called attention to this deficiency, commenting, "the commentaries become very brief or evasive and obtuse in their treatments [of chapter 2], particularly for 2:6, 7, 10, 13, and 25–27. It is not uncommon to find explanations of these verses completely omitted. In addition, there are relatively few articles and technical studies of chapter two, especially in English."[10] Studies of vv. 17–29 are even more rare than those of vv. 1–16.

It appears that the passage is so thoroughly understood as to make further comment unnecessary, or is so singularly Jewish in its concerns that it has been the object of little interest for Christian exegetes.[11] Perhaps the treatment of

---

[9]Notable exceptions include the following: A. Fridrichsen, "Der wahre Jude und sein Lob: Röm 2:28 f," *Symbolae Arctoae* 1 (1927) 39–49; Stanislas Lyonnet, "'La circoncision du coeur qui relève de l'Esprit et non de la lettre" (Rom.2:29)," *L'Evangile, hier et aujord'hui. Mélanges offerts au professeur Franz-J. Leenhardt* (Geneva: Labor et Fides, 1968) 87–97; Heinrich Schlier, "Von den Juden. Röm 2:1–29," *Die Zeit der Kirche* (Frieburg: Herder, 1956) 38–47; L. Goppelt, "Der Missionar des Gesetzes: Zu Röm 2,21 f," *Christologie und Ethik; Aufsatze zum Neuen Testament* (Göttingen: Vandenhoeck und Ruprecht, 1968) 137–46; Eduard Schweizer, "'Der Jude im Verborgenen..., dessen Lob nicht von Menschen, sondern von Gott kommt.' Zu Röm 2,28 f. und Matt 6,1–18," *Neues Testament und Kirche: fur Rudolf Schnackenburg [z. 60. Geburtsag am 5. Jan. 1974 von Freunden u. Kollegen gewidmet]* (ed. J. Gnilka; Freiburg: Herder, 1974) 115–25; Klyne Snodgrass, "Justification by Grace—To the Doers: An Analysis of the Place of Romans 2 in the Theology of Paul," *NTS* 32 (1986) 72–93; G. Lafon, "La production de la loi. La pensée de la loi in Romains 2,12–27," *RechSR* 74 (1986) 321–40; Lafon, "Les poètes de la loi. Un commentaire de Romains 2,12–27," *Christus* 134 (1987) 205–14; Don Garlington, "ΙΕΡΟΣΥΛΕΙΝ and the Idolatry of Israel," *NTS* 36 (1990) 142–51; Edgar Krentz, "The Name of God in Disrepute: Romans 2:16–29 [22–23]," *CurTM* 17 (1990) 429–39; J. Duncan M. Derrett, "'You Abominate False Gods; But Do You Rob Shrines?' (Rom 2:22b)," *NTS* 40 (1994) 558–71; Jean-Noël Aletti, "Romains 2: Sa cohérence et sa fonction," *Bib* 77 (1996) 153–77.

[10]Snodgrass, "Justification by Grace—To the Doers," 73. Romans 2 is "a text that has received far too little attention in modern analyses of the Epistle to the Romans" (ibid., 72).

[11]E.g., Glenn N. Davies's study of Romans 1–4, of which Davies says, "the study is primarily exegetical." However, Rom 2:17–24 is

chapter 2 is best explained by Stanley K. Stowers, who recognizes a desire on the part of commentators to get to what may be regarded as more important portions of the epistle: "Commentators are so clear about their destination at 3:9 ('all are sinners in need of Christ') that they tend to fly over chapter 2 quickly and at a high altitude."[12] This has resulted in misunderstanding the foundation for Paul's statements in 2:17–29 and discounting the place of the passage in the larger argument of Romans.

While Paul's central thesis in the passage is not generally in dispute, occasionally the question of the propriety of Paul's harsh indictment of the Jews is raised.[13] To this point no one has offered a satisfactory explanation as to how Paul can have defended his accusations of gross failure to keep the law as more than an arbitrary or prejudicial assertion, or as hyperbole. Paul also makes the radical and unprecedented claim that being a Jew offers one no better a position before God regarding salvation from wrath than that of a gentile (2:1, 27–29; 3:9–18). A failure to take into account Paul's intertextual exegesis leads commentators to inadequate explanations for the bases of Paul's claims. An understanding of Paul's OT references shows that the question of the status of the covenant with Israel is a key to understanding Paul's charges. Most of the discussion of Israel's status is usually sought in chaps. 9–11, when in fact it is central to chap. 2.

---

treated in one brief five sentence paragraph as introduction to a three page overview of 2:25–29 (*Faith and Obedience in Romans: A Study in Romans 1–4* [JSNTSup 39; Sheffield: JSOT, 1990] 18, 67–70).

[12]Stanley K. Stowers, *A Rereading of Romans: Justice, Jews, and Gentiles* (New Haven: Yale University Press, 1994) 126.

[13]Goppelt asks, "But how can one of the Jews...pass off this kind of massive indicting?...It is still in the commentaries not satisfactorily answered..." ("Der Missionar des Gesetzes," 139). C. H. Dodd assumes that a "degradation of Jewish morals" accounts for the "startling" charges (*The Epistle of Paul to the Romans* [MNTC; London: Hodder and Stoughton, 1954] 39). See also C. E. B. Cranfield, *A Critical and Exegetical Commentary on the Epistle to the Romans* (2 vols.; ICC; 6th ed.; Edinburgh: T. & T. Clark, 1975) 1.168.

UNANSWERED QUESTIONS

The charges of 2:17–29 are dealt with by commentators in a variety of ways. In some instances, Paul's assertions are not really dealt with at all. In those cases there appears to be an assumption that the indictment is true and universally applicable to all Jews with little attempt to understand how this may be so.[14] The radical and strenuous nature of the indictment does not capture the attention of these commentators. Whether this stems from an acceptance of Paul's judgment, a determination that the question is not relevant to the exegesis of the passage, or simple oversight is not clear. The issue in these cases simply is not raised.

Others do address the propriety of the indictments. Some refer to traditional parallels, and find similar charges in contemporary writings. The parallels in some cases are valid, but fail to account for Paul's radical conclusions regarding the result of Jewish disobedience.[15] Barrett and Cranfield understand the necessity and the difficulty of seeing the indictment as universally applicable to Jews, or at least nearly so. However, they view the charges as condemnation for Jewish failure to perceive that lesser or inward breaches of the law imply the breaking of the whole law, as in the Sermon on the Mount.[16] There is no indication in anything Paul says that minor violations of the law imply the breaking of the whole law by individuals in the way it is indicated in the Sermon on the Mount. Even though it may be credible that Paul is fa-

---

[14]E.g., Hans Lietzmann, *Die Briefe des Apostels Paulus an die Römer* (HNT; Tübingen: Mohr-Siebeck, 1933) 43–44; John Murray, *The Epistle to the Romans* (NICNT; Grand Rapids: Eerdmans, 1968) 1.83–85; Joseph A. Fitzmyer, *Romans* (AB 33; New York: Doubleday, 1993) 315–19. Fitzmyer, however, assumes a figurative meaning for temple-robbery, and does recognize some OT and traditional basis for Paul's assertions. He does not go into sufficient detail to connect Paul's argument to the OT or the tradition in any meaningful way. Goppelt takes much the same approach ("Der Missionar des Gesetzes," 145).

[15]E.g., Dodd, *Epistle*, 38–39.

[16]C. K. Barrett, *A Commentary on the Epistle to the Romans* (Black's New Testament Commentaries; London: Black, 1991) 53–54; Cranfield, *The Epistle to the Romans*, 1.169.

miliar with that traditional material in some form, he draws no such correspondence between pedestrian violations of the law and the serious charges he makes in Rom 2:21–22. Such explanations do not provide sufficient argumentative justification for Paul's radical assertion that Jews and gentiles alike stand condemned.

A number of commentators do make mention of the fact that in chap. 2 Paul is making the broader claim that being a Jew has no specific advantage in saving one from wrath. They often present correct interpretations of what Paul is alleging and conclude that Paul understands a change in the covenantal status of the Jews. Unfortunately, very little is offered which might explain why or upon what basis Paul makes his statements. These scholars will also give passing mention of Paul's reliance upon a tradition of prophetic rebuke and exhortation. A number of OT examples and possible allusions are often mentioned as background sources for Paul's language or thought. Attention is usually given to the quotation of Isa 52:5 as a proof-text for Paul's conclusion.[17]

However, the OT allusions receive little attention and are not pursued to any meaningful extent. Among these, Dunn believes Paul is "pricking the balloon of Jewish pride," and the belief that Jews are morally superior to gentiles.[18] This much is certainly true if a very inclusive definition of what can be called Jewish in the first century is adopted which does not rely on narrow stereotypes stemming from a legalistic view of Judaism. Dunn recognizes that the argument is more complex than that. Yet the intertextual argument is not addressed. Käsemann understands Paul's position as consonant with a Jewish apocalyptic view wherein the exceptional cases of lawbreaking are treated as representing the entire Jewish community.[19] Others maintain that the charges are not universally true of every Jew, but that Jewish knowl-

---

[17]E.g., James D. G. Dunn, *Romans 1–8* (WBC 38a; Dallas: Word, 1988) 113–14; Fitzmyer, *Romans*, 318; Ernst Käsemann, *Commentary on Romans* (Grand Rapids: Eerdmans, 1980) 69.

[18]Dunn, *Romans 1–8*, 108, 114–15.

[19]Käsemann, *Commentary on Romans*, 69.

edge of the law does not correspond to Jewish action as a whole.[20] Snodgrass makes the important point that Paul is not arguing against works, but against those who have failed to do the works which accompany faithfulness.[21]

Many of these interpretations are correct as far as they go. They point out important aspects of the passage and draw proper inferences from Paul's argument. However, these explanations are inadequate to account for the genesis of the radical Pauline assumption that Jews have no better standing before God regarding salvation from wrath than do gentiles, and that obedient gentiles may in fact be in a position superior to that of Jews. Nor do they give sufficient reasoning to explain why in Paul's mind apparently the covenant with national Israel is no longer in force, at least in the manner previously understood.[22] An understanding of Paul's assumptions and conclusions regarding Israel's covenant status requires further attention to Paul's intertextual exegesis of OT texts.

---

[20]E.g., Schlier, *Der Römerbrief: Kommentar*, (HTKNT 6; Freiburg: Herder, 1977) 45.

[21]Snodgrass, "Justification by Grace—To the Doers," 78–81.

[22]Some do recognize that this assumption has its basis in OT texts, but no detailed examination is presented. See, e.g., Fitzmyer, *Romans*, 318, 320; Dunn, *Romans 1–8*, 114. Scott J. Hafemann does understand the indictments to stem from Paul's view of Israel's history of disobedience to the covenant ("The Spirit of the New Covenant, the Law, and the Temple of God's Presence: Five Theses on Qumran Self-Understanding and the Contours of Paul's Thought," *Evangelium-Schriftauslegung-Kirche*, 174).

When speaking of a change in Israel's covenantal status, or of a broken covenant as I do, there are a number of points to keep in mind. E. P. Sanders notes that the implementation of the curses of the covenant brings about punishment or wrath not removal from a state of election (*Paul and Palestinian Judaism: A Comparison of Patterns of Religion* [Minneapolis: Fortress, 1977] 84–182). Paul assails the idea that Jews are in a better position than gentiles regarding God's wrath. He places them on equal footing requiring justification. Yet, there is advantage in being a Jew (Rom 3:1–2, 9:1–5) and "all Israel will be saved" (Rom 11:26; see also the statement "all Israelites have a share in the world to come" in *Sanh.* 10:1 as discussed by Sanders, *Paul and Palestinian Judaism*, 147–50).

To this point no study has adequately examined those aspects of the passage.

INTERTEXTUAL EXEGESIS

It is not uncommon for commentators to mention a number of intertextual allusions in discussions of Rom 2:17–29.[23] In most instances the mere presence of similar language is noted, or a passage is simply said to provide the language used by Paul. Evaluation of the relative strength or purposefulness of the allusions is seldom provided. Rarely is a text alleged to be a source for the formation of Paul's argument. Hays did provide a useful analysis which gave new insight into the part intertextual allusions play in these verses. He went a step further than previous studies in describing the presence of intertextual echo in Rom 2:17–29, by examining in more detail how images from the echoing texts are woven together into the fabric of Paul's argument.[24]

However, in his broad treatment Hays did not give a full explanation of the function of the intertextual allusions in the formation of Paul's conclusions. His concern was more toward providing a number of examples where Paul's recourse to intertextual echo may be discerned. His analysis also provided little evidence or methodology for a definitive identification of intentional allusions on the part of the author.[25] He left unanswered, and in fact is not interested in, the question of whether or not any of the purported allusions or echoes might appear in Rom 2:17–29 because those passages form an exegetical basis for Paul's argument.

---

[23]See, e.g., Michel, *Römerbrief*, 86–93; Dodd, *Epistle*, 46; Lietzmann, *An die Römer*, 44; Schweizer, "'Der Jude im Verborgenen,'" 118–21; Cranfield, *The Epistle to the Romans*, 1.164–75; Dunn, *Romans 1–8*, 110–14, 123–24, Fitzmyer, *Romans*, 316–18. The allusions mentioned vary widely. Likewise, a fair amount of attention is given to the modification of the quotation from Isa 52:5 at Rom 2:24.

[24]Hays, *Echoes*, 44–45.

[25]See the critique on this point by William Scott Green, "Doing the Text's Work for It: Richard Hays on Paul's Use of Scripture," *Paul and the Scriptures of Israel* (JSNTSup 83; ed. Craig Evans and James A. Sanders; Sheffield: JSOT, 1993) 59–61.

While Hays has given greater attention to the role intertextual echo plays in Paul's epistles, like other commentators
he has not addressed the possibility of Pauline intertextual
exegesis, defined as intentional interpretation done to explain
the meaning of scripture for application to a contemporary
situation or to make sense of human experience. Treatments
of Rom 2:17–29 which do not adequately account for the presence of intertextual exegesis—rather than merely allusion or
echo in Paul's argument—are in some of the more recent
cases a result of the emphasis on reader-centered interpretation in many intertextual studies. These interpreters are not
interested in authorial intent or historical considerations. In
historical-critical treatments of the passage, the lack of attention to author-generated allusion or even intertextual exegesis can be traced in part to the lack of sufficient
methodological tools. There is a need for further methodological development.

The definition and refinement of existing intertextual
methodology in this study will allow the identification of
Pauline intertextual exegesis of OT texts in Rom 2:17–29. It
will show that Paul's exegesis of OT texts lays a foundation
for his argument in these verses, and provides justification for
his conclusions. Paul relies on references from prophetic texts
in Jer 7:2–11, 9:23–26, and Ezek 36:16–27 to interpret the
narrative texts of Deuteronomy 29–30 and Genesis 17. These
interpretations form the basis for Paul's attack upon Jewish
assurance of salvation from wrath and his understanding of a
spiritual obedience based upon faith which can result in salvation for gentiles as well as Jews. These conclusions are an
integral part of the foundation for Paul's defense of God's
righteousness in dealing with both Jews and gentiles, as this
study will confirm the point of the epistle to be.[26]

---

[26]For the useful argument that Paul defends God's righteousness
concerning who is saved, or "soteric domain," rather than how people
are saved, see, Lynn L. Martin ("The Righteousness of God: A Study in
Paul's Use of Jewish Tradition" [Ph.D. diss. Marquette Univ., 1991] 3–4,
154–55, 291, 359, 428–29). I do not, however, concur with Martin's conclusion that Paul addresses judaizing opponents in Rome (ibid., 44, 291,

A FRESH APPRAISAL

As a necessary preliminary step, in chapter 1 this study will first address the question of methodology and the requirement for greater definition. A review of the historical development of intertextual method will demonstrate an existing foundation for the current research. It will outline relevant conclusions already existing in the field which form a basis for such work, and provide points of reference for understanding the current state of varying emphases in intertextual scriptural studies. This review will include an analysis of the progression from works examining OT quotation to modern intertextual scriptural analysis. It will also address research on the relationship between NT use of the OT and contemporary Jewish exegetical practice.

The survey will include varied approaches to dealing with intertextual questions in scripture. This will provide a background for identifying relative strengths and weaknesses in the current state of intertextual scriptural studies.[27] A definition of the task undertaken here in comparison with other intertextual scriptural research will place this study in the broader world of intertextual analysis, outlining what it is and is not intended to produce. Conclusions relevant to this work concerning the methodology of Pauline exegesis in its contemporary setting will be presented.[28] The discussion will conclude with a definition of the current method to be applied to Paul's intertextual exegesis in Rom 2:17–29.

302–3).

[27]For examples of variety in a reader-centered approach, see, e.g., David Penchansky, "Staying the Night: Intertextuality in Genesis and Judges," *Reading Between Texts: Intertextuality and the Hebrew Bible* (ed. Danna Nolan Fewell, Louisville: Westminster/John Knox, 1992) 77–88; Deborah Krause, "A Blessing Cursed: The Prophet's Prayer for Barren Womb and Dry Breasts in Hosea 9," *Reading Between Texts*, 191. Variation exists in more text-centered approaches as well. See, e.g., the essays in Evans and Sanders, *Paul and the Scriptures of Israel*.

[28]The methodology employed by Paul is distinguished from the methodology employed to study Paul's exegesis.

The application of the defined methodology to Rom 2:17–29 will be taken up in chapter 2. A brief discussion of context and intertextual connections bridging between passages will assist in establishing the validity of studying Rom 2:17–29 as an individual unit. Having defined the limits of the passage, the process of identification of intertextual references in the passage will be undertaken in two stages. In the first stage candidate references which do not adequately meet the methodological criteria established for this study will be eliminated from consideration. This process not only narrows the field of possible references, but provides a set of test cases to demonstrate the effectiveness of the methodology. These test cases illustrate the way in which the different methodological criteria are evaluated in any particular text. The process also provides some standard for comparison of the relative strength of the various proposed references. This will be useful since the line between the strongest cases which are rejected and the weakest of those accepted as Pauline references will not always be easily agreed upon.[29] This first stage will assist the reader in understanding the basis for the evaluative decisions made in this study.

The second stage in the process will involve the identification of those intertextual references meeting the methodological criteria and recognized as part of Paul's intertextual exegesis underlying Rom 2:17–29. The context of each reference will be discussed to determine possible applicability to Paul's argument in Romans. Themes and vocabulary significant to Paul's argument will receive additional attention. Thematic and vocabulary connections between OT texts will also be pointed out. The identification of individual reference texts and the recognition of links between them will establish the presence of a mutually interpretive web of linked texts to which Paul has had reference in the formation of his argument in Rom 2:17–29.

---

[29]The methodological criteria are intended to assist in the identification of OT texts serving specifically as Pauline intertextual references. However, variation in the strength with which the various proposed references meet those criteria will of course be evident.

This study will continue its primary focus with the intertextual analysis of Rom 2:17–29 in chapter 3. This analysis will detail the way in which the identified intertextual references inform Paul's argument on the basis of his exegesis of those texts.[30] This will begin with a brief discussion of the epistolary setting of the passage; the probable audience, course of the argument to 2:17, and the diatribal interlocutor. There will be a review of the relevant themes in Paul's reference texts which have a bearing upon his argument in Rom 2:17–29. The following exegesis of the passage will focus upon Paul's own intertextual interpretation, but will necessarily engage the historical-critical exegetical issues and literature relevant to a study of Rom 2:17–29.

The intertextual assessment of the passage will shed light on a number of exegetical difficulties which have not been addressed adequately up to this point. The analysis will confirm that the references identified by the application of the defined methodology account in large part for the final form of the Pauline text. The references will be seen to function as exegeted texts informing and shaping Paul's argument in Rom 2:17–29. The intertextual analysis will reveal a scriptural basis founded in Pauline exegesis for the radical conclusions Paul presents regarding the sinfulness of the Jews, the possibility of gentile inclusion among the circumcised, and the redefinition of a Jew in spiritual terms as one who is circumcised inwardly.

In chapter 4 a brief summary examination of the place of Rom 2:17–29 in the intertextual and epistolary context of Romans will offer an opportunity to evaluate the results of the intertextual analysis of the preceding chapters. Not only must an interpretation make sense of the passage as it stands

---

[30]Such a study may be thought of as having certain elements analogous to source and redaction criticism, although "reference integration criticism" or "allusion analysis" or some such phrase will more accurately define the difference. For a comparison of intertextuality and redaction criticism, see Willem S. Vorster, "Intertextuality and Redaktionsgeschichte," *Intertextuality in Biblical Writings: Essays in Honour of Bas van Iersel* (ed. Sipke Draisma; Kampen: J. H. Kok, 1989) 15–26.

alone and adequately address exegetical difficulties, but it must also make sense of the passage in the context of the epistle. This subsidiary step will be undertaken to test whether the validity of the preceding analysis is confirmed by integration of the proposed interpretation of Rom 2:17–29 into its larger context. This contextual evaluation is not intended to address every issue in Romans, but in two steps will confirm the integration of this analysis of the passage into the epistle according to two different criteria.

First, an overview of the intertextual substructure of Romans will identify themes which are central to Paul's argument, particularly in Romans 2–4 and 9–11. These themes will be seen to derive from an intertextual web of mutually interpreted and linked OT texts upon which Paul is dependent for a number of his conclusions and assumptions. An evaluation of the references, vocabulary, and themes identified in Rom 2:17–29 in comparison with this larger intertextual web will be offered. Analysis will confirm that the intertextual references identified in Rom 2:17–29 are an integral part of the larger web of texts and themes underlying the entire epistle.

The second step will briefly evaluate the proposed interpretation of Rom 2:17–29 in the context of Romans. Relevant exegetical issues and literature will be engaged in an effort to provide an understanding of Romans which adequately takes into account the impact of Paul's intertextual exegesis. The contextual analysis will provide a comprehensible framework for understanding Romans as a tightly woven and cohesive epistle.[31] It will also confirm that Rom 2:17–29 and its intertextual references are an integral part of that cohesive whole.

While the brief overview of Romans in chapter 4 is not intended as a commentary addressing every exegetical issue involved in the interpretation of Romans, it will point to conclusions regarding what is to be understood as the point of the epistle and the central issue Paul is seeking to address. It will

---

[31]For a brief survey on this question, see James D. G. Dunn, "The Formal and Theological Coherence of Romans," *The Romans Debate: Revised and Expanded Edition* (ed. Karl Donfried; Peabody, MA: Hendrickson, 1991) 247–48.

also provide an indication of whether the occasion and purpose of the epistle center more in the situation of the Roman church or in Paul's own plans. It suggests implications for Pauline studies as a whole and for studies of Romans in particular. Some of those issues and implications will be discussed in the concluding chapter.

The core of this study rests, however, in Rom 2:17–29. This study will apply a refinement of intertextual methodology demonstrating that Pauline intertextual exegesis informs Paul's argument in Rom 2:17–29. Paul's own exegesis of OT texts provides the foundation for his indictment of Jewish disobedience, undercutting Jewish identity as God's people. This complex of interwoven texts also gives Paul his understanding of an inward spiritual obedience based upon faith redefining Jewish identity as people of God in such a way that gentiles may also be included in God's salvation. These conclusions are a necessary part of Paul's argument in the epistle to the Romans.

1
Methodology for the Study of Intertextual Exegesis

A missing element in previous studies of Rom 2:17–29 has been an adequate refinement of intertextual methodology to identify and interpret Paul's exegesis of OT texts which are not obviously alluded to or quoted. Methods to study the exegesis Paul and other NT writers engaged in do exist, and have been developing for much of this century. In order to describe the place of this study in the methodological history it is expedient both to recount that development and describe the methodological clarification to be incorporated into this exegesis of Rom 2:17–29. The first section of this chapter will provide a methodological history tracing the development of intertextual method from foundational works to the present. The second section will first examine where this study fits into the broader world of intertextual studies. Second, it will present an analysis of Pauline exegesis in the context of contemporary Jewish exegesis, a summary of the principles of Pauline exegesis, and a description of the method to be employed in this study.

METHODOLOGICAL HISTORY
METHODOLOGICAL FOUNDATIONS

It is interesting, but not surprising given their historical proximity, that many post-canonical Christian writers of the early centuries handled scripture in a manner much nearer to that of Jewish interpreters and biblical writers than did their

17

followers. Ancient Jewish and Christian exegesis was generally not what would later be called historical-critical.[1] In some instances it had no concern for textual and historical context, in contrast to more modern exegesis.[2] However, methodologies which evolved into modern exegesis acquired an overriding concern for the surrounding textual and historical context of a passage. In the process, earlier methods came to be viewed as inferior.

For this reason an understanding of the interpretive method or exegesis done by the biblical writers and early rabbis has not received much attention from Christian exegetes until recently. An added historical consideration is the fact that the split between church and synagogue became so pronounced and hostile, and remained so for such a long time, that connections of method and content between biblical material and rabbinic material were lost.[3] J. W. Doeve's analysis

---

[1]See, e.g., K. Froelich, ed., *Biblical Interpretation in the Early Church* (Sources of Early Christian Thought; Philadelphia: Fortress, 1984); J. L. Kugel and R. A. Greer, *Early Biblical Interpretation* (Library of Early Christianity 5; Philadelphia: Westminster, 1986); J. W. Trigg, *Biblical Interpretation* (Message of the Fathers of the Church 9; Wilmington, DE: Glazier, 1988).

[2]Some modern literary approaches to exegesis, to be discussed, again move away from contextual and historical-critical concerns.

[3]For discussion of the widening gap between the church and Judaism in the early centuries of Christianity in what he calls the "de-Judiazation of Christianity," see Jaroslav Pelikan (*The Emergence of the Catholic Tradition (100–600)*, vol. 1 of *The Christian Tradition: A History of the Development of Doctrine* [Chicago: University of Chicago Press, 1971] 15–27). "Virtually every major Christian writer of the first five centuries either composed a treatise in opposition to Judaism or made this issue a dominant theme in a treatise devoted to some other subject" (ibid., 15). "Christian theologians...no longer gave serious consideration to the Jewish interpretation of the Old Testament or to the Jewish background of the New" (ibid., 21). Notable exceptions are Origen and Jerome, who engaged in dialogue with the rabbis and mastered Hebrew. For most of Christian history rejection of Jewish theology included rejection or ignorance of Jewish exegetical methods and materials. Terence L. Donaldson addresses how the supposed "replacement ecclesiology" of Romans 11 has contributed to the continuance of an "*adversus Judaeos* tradition" ("'Riches for the Gentiles' (Rom 11:12): Israel's Rejection and Paul's Gentile Mission," *JBL* 112 [1993] 82).

of Jewish exegetical technique reflected in the NT begins with a summary of the renewed interest in rabbinic material in relation to the NT which began in the 17th century.[4] This marks the beginning of a new interest in Jewish exegesis which eventually leads to modern NT intertextual studies. Various attempts to collect rabbinic material which related to the NT were made, sometimes with polemical intent.[5] Other scholarly enterprises, however, were founded on the belief that such comparisons could yield exegetical fruit, since most of the NT writers were, after all, Jews. Though many of those attempts were marred by anachronism in the naive attribution of traits and customs of medieval and modern Jewish scholarship to the first century, or by simply presenting rabbinic material alongside NT material without attention to chronology, there were many positive contributions.[6]

---

[4]*Jewish Hermeneutics in the Synoptic Gospels and Acts* (Assen: Van Gorcum, 1954).

[5]The polemical intent of the works of Johann Andreas Eisenmenger (*Entdecktes Judentum* [2 vols.; Frankfurt, 1700; reprinted, Dresden: Brandner, 1893) and August Rohling (*Der Talmudjude; zur Beherzigung fur Juden und Christen aller Stande* [Münster: Russell, 1871]) are mentioned in particular by H.L. Strack and G. Stemberger: "Pretending to seek conversion to Judaism, Eisenmenger spent years studying rabbinic literature under Jewish mentors; but in reality he compiled all the references which were intended to prove Jewish errors or attacks on the Christian religion" (Strack and Stemberger, *Introduction to the Talmud and Midrash* [Minneapolis: Fortress, 1992] 243).

[6]E.g., J Buxtorf, *Lexicon chaldaicum, talmudicum et rabbinicum* (Basle: Konig, 1639; reprinted, New York: Olms, 1977); John Lightfoot, *Horae Hebraicae et Talmudicae* (Cambridge: Field, 1658; reprinted ET, Peabody, MA: Hendrickson, 1989); Christian Schoettgen, *Horae Hebraicae et Talmuicae in universum Novum Testamentum* (2 vols.; Dresden and Leipzig: Hekel, 1733); Johann Jacob Wetstein, *Novum Testamentum Graecum* (2 vols.; Amsterdam, 1751–1752; reprinted, Graz, Austria: Akademische Druck- u. Verlatsanstalt, 1962); F. Nork, *Rabbinische Quellen und Parallelen zu neutestamentlichen Schriftstellen* (Leipzig: Schumann, 1839). Except in the case of Wetstein I rely on the assessments of Doeve (*Jewish Hermeneutics*, 8–9) and Strack and Stemberger (*Introduction*, 243). For comment on anachronism, see Jacob Neusner, "The Mishna in Philosophical Context and Out of Canonical Bounds," *JBL* 112 (1993) 291–304; and "The Use of Later Rabbinic Evidence for the Study of First Century Pharisaism," *Approaches to Ancient Juda-*

Defining Relevant Materials:

Early attempts reached their zenith early in this century with Strack and Billerbeck's massive *Kommentar zum Neuen Testament aus Talmud und Midrasch*,[7] which catalogued rabbinic parallels to material found in the NT. On a different path, J. Rendel Harris hypothesized that the NT writers drew their OT quotations from a book of "testimonies," or passages recognized as suitable and applicable to the gospel message, used and taken out of context.[8] On the one hand were those who were beginning to investigate how the rabbinic traditions might be paralleled in the NT, on the other were those making new inroads into the methodological questions of the use of the OT in the NT.

The question of anachronism, so prevalent in earlier works, continued to be a problem in succeeding decades, and still crops up occasionally.[9] Those working in the area of OT and Jewish exegetical influences on the NT provided legitimate identification of parallels in tradition and method be-

---

ism: Theory and Practice (ed. William Scott Green; Brown Judaic Studies 1; Missoula: Scholars Press, 1978) 215–25. See also Neusner's extensive comments in Strack and Stemberger (*Introduction*, vii–xx).

[7](6 vols.; München: Beck, 1922–61). In discussion of the problem of anachronism, Alan Segal suggests that rather than using Talmudic and Mishnaic sources in Strack and Billerbeck to validate and illuminate NT material, "the converse methodology actually seems more reliable...In spite of the handbook's sometimes unappreciated erudition, its methodology is entirely suspect. Rather, a commentary to the Mishnah should be written, using the New Testament as marginalia that demonstrates antiquity" (Segal, *Paul the Convert*, xv).

[8]*Testimonies* (2 vols.; Cambridge: Cambridge University Press, 1916–1920).

[9]E.g., C. G. Montefiore, *Judaism and St. Paul: Two Essays* (New York: Dutton, 1915). The problematic presentation of undated rabbinic quotations in parallel with NT material in Strack and Billerbeck, and in word studies in Kittel (*TWNT/TDNT*) is addressed by Doeve (*Jewish Hermeneutics*, 22–23). Along with Strack and Billerbeck, the work of E. E. Urbach (*The Sages: Their Concepts and Their Beliefs* [2 vols.; Jerusalem: Magnes, 1975]) is mentioned in Strack and Stembereger as a Jewish study of rabbinic material presenting "an unhistorical description," although the work as a whole is called "excellent" (*Introduction*, 52).

tween the NT and the later rabbis. Yet some of them often erroneously assumed the NT writers' dependence upon mishnaic material. Many of the scholars mentioned below take up this question and provide support for the antiquity of traditions and methods present in both the NT and rabbinic writings.

Identifying Relevant Exegetical Traditions:
In the mid-1930s Joseph Bonsirven wrote several works on Jewish influences on Christianity, the most important of which for intertextual biblical studies is *Exégèse Rabbinique et Exégèse Paulinienne*.[10] Bonsirven outlined rabbinic exegetical methodology, showing that Paul employed very similar methods. Bonsirven analyses explicit Pauline quotations of the OT, but also makes mention of "implicit citations" wherein scriptural language is incorporated into Paul's writing without formula or reference.[11] He notes the difficulty of determining when such language is accidental and when it is intended. For that reason, as others do later, he focuses his attention on explicit or clearer citations.

While Bonsirven was hesitant to attribute to Paul what he considered arbitrariness and imagination in exegesis to the same degree as in rabbinic material, his work was nevertheless groundbreaking. He provided evidence in greater detail than previous studies that rabbinic methods were employed by Paul.[12] He finds great similarity between rabbinic and Pauline exegesis in the areas of homiletic development, attention to text form, modifications of the text, attempts to justify, illustrate, or confirm a position on the basis of scriptural citation, and attention to historical considerations.

While many of Bonsirven's observations are more general than those of later studies, he showed that Paul approached scripture with substantially the same attitude as did the rabbis. The OT was taken as the Word of God given by divine revelation. Scripture "procured a primary and authen-

---

[10](Bibliothèque de Théologie Historique; Paris: Beauchesne, 1939).
[11]Ibid., 276.
[12]Ibid., 324.

tic 'access' to God.'" These conceptions were reinforced by the belief that illumination by Christ and the spirit enabled Christians to comprehend scripture's true meaning.[13] Bonsirven was not troubled about the historical difficulty that the rabbinic writings of the Mishnah and Talmud are later than Paul. He noted the book of Ezra and other pre-mishnaic material as evidence of pre-Christian midrash, or interpretation of scritpture, attempting to show that general principles of midrash later extended and codified by the rabbis were in use before the time of Paul.[14]

Shortly after this, David Daube undertook a study focusing on rabbinic theological themes and content under the categories of types, forms, and concepts.[15] In the same way that Bonsirven demonstrated Pauline use of rabbinic methods, Daube demonstrated NT use of rabbinic themes, with additional references to Philo and other first-century writers, and to the newly-discovered Dead Sea Scrolls. While Daube also falls into anachronism, his work's importance on the whole is not weakened since the thematic parallels do exist regardless of the later date of the rabbinic sources.[16]

W. D. Davies's *Paul and Rabbinic Judaism*, originally published in 1948, did much the same thing as Daube but with specific reference to Pauline literature.[17] The work relies heavily upon what Davies regarded as Paul's major themes. In that sense it was limited by preconceptions about those

---

[13]Ibid., 206–7.

[14]Ibid., 11–14. Bonsirven refers in the canonical scriptures to the study and interpretation of scripture (דרש) spoken of in Ezra 7:10, as well as the explanation of the Law to the people in Neh 8:1–8.

[15]*The New Testament and Rabbinic Judaism* (Jordan Lectures in Comparative Religion 2; London: Athlone, 1956; reprinted, 1973). This work was first published as a series of articles beginning in the late 1930s.

[16]More methodologically rigorous in this regard is the study of Morton Smith (*Tannaitic Parallels to the Gospels* [SBLMS 6; Philadelphia: Society of Biblical Literature, 1951]). Smith acknowledges less in common between NT and rabbinic material than does almost anyone else.

[17] (2nd ed.; London: S.P.C.K., 1955).

themes, but was useful for demonstrating that Paul's major themes had Jewish parallels.
Refining the Methodological Questions:
In J. W. Doeve's 1953 doctoral dissertation, already mentioned, he examined the method and content of the synoptic gospels and Acts, and found that Jewish exegetical methods were used to connect OT passages to important gospel themes such as kingdom of god, the messiah, and the resurrection. He found that Jewish conceptions of those themes were sometimes adopted as well.[18]

Doeve also addresses the question of anachronism, pointing out that though rabbinic material itself post-dates the NT, it makes constant reference to its dependence upon earlier exegetical tradition going back to the time of Hillel and Akiba:

> The period from Hillel to the time of Akiba includes the years from 30 B.C. to 110 A.D. So that is just the time which embraces the appearing of Jesus, the work of the apostles and the formation of the New Testament writings.... it is the period of a few Old Tannaites, of the first generation of the Tannaites, and of the elder group of the second generation.[19]

But Doeve's most important contribution for this study was his emphasis on method. He points out in particular the NT use of the rule of *gezerah shevah*. Most scholars to this point, and even after, seemed to envision a formal halakic relationship between two passages of scripture where a common

---

[18]*Jewish Hermeneutics.*
[19]Ibid., 63. As Jacob Neusner repeatedly points out, not everything in rabbinic material which makes the claim can be assumed to originate from more ancient sources (*The Rabbinic Traditions about the Pharisees before 70* [3 vols.; Leiden: Brill, 1971]; "The Use of Later Rabbinic Evidence"; and "The Rabbinic Traditions About the Pharisees Before 70 AD: The Problem of Oral Tradition," *Kairos* 14 [1972] 57–70). See also, Smith, *Tannaitic Parallels.* But that material which is paralleled by the NT and which is ascribed to a source contemporary with or predating the NT is likely to derive from an early source. Historical source investigation of any given saying may be required to establish its antiquity where extra-mishnaic parallels are doubtful. See also, Strack and Stemberger, *Introduction to the Talmud,* 52–66.

word or phrase shared by the passages makes both passages applicable to a given case. As many have noted, the halakic rule does not function in the free fashion seen in the NT. However, Doeve has shown that haggadic exegesis is less rigid. The liberty of haggadic exegesis is far greater, the creativity of the exegete more important, and the identification of systematic exegetical norms more difficult than in halakic exegesis.[20] Much NT exegesis has more in common with haggadic than with halakic exegesis. Doeve pointed out that in NT usage, as in haggadic exegesis, the presence of linking vocabulary in two passages, sometimes called hook-words, enabled the interpreter to employ one of the passages in the interpretation of the other.[21]

Doeve is aware that a great difficulty for modern interpreters in piecing together the methods used by NT writers is the lack of any descriptive NT material about that methodology or any comparative literature:

> The way the results were obtained does not seem to have been considered of sufficient importance by the first Christian authors for them to communicate it. The results themselves were what mattered to them. But if one is acquainted with the theoretical approach to Scripture and the way of operating with it customary in Judaism as delivered to us by rabbinic literature, then one not only discovers the earliest Christians handled Scripture in the same manner, but also that such Christian midrash lies hidden beneath passages where one would not at first sight expect it.[22]

This is an important observation for the present study. Pauline exegesis in Romans 2 lies below the surface of the text, and is not set out for the readers' inspection. This raises the question of the rhetorical function and effect of Paul's exegesis, which will be discussed later. For now it is enough

---

[20]*Jewish Hermeneutics*, 64.

[21]The phrases "Stichwort" or "catchword" (Rudolf Bultmann, *The History of the Synoptic Tradition* [tr. John Marsh; Oxford: Blackwell, 1963] 325) and "hook word" (Stockhausen, *Moses' Veil*, 26) are sometimes used to describe verbal links between texts.

[22]Doeve, *Jewish Hermeneutics*, 114.

to note that in order to deduce Pauline exegesis of OT texts it is not necessary, nor is one likely, to find Paul explaining the exegetical method he has used. He is not interested in displaying his methodology, but in the results of his exegesis.[23] The exegesis he has done is the "homework" that does not overtly appear in the finished project. It must be reconstructed.

More than others, Doeve saw NT writers moving between OT texts by means of hook-words to weave together a complex of interpretive texts. On the other hand, Doeve sometimes overstates the parallels between rabbinic and NT exegesis. There are similarities which make it certain that NT exegesis has a place in the evolution of rabbinic exegesis, but Doeve gives little attention to the fact that it is a development, and not entirely identical. Doeve's attention to the variation in Jewish exegesis itself is a clue to the impossibility of identifying identical methodologies. Doeve speaks of NT authors employing "the procedure of midrash" as though midrash itself were made up of sharply defined characteristics.[24] This does not appear to be the case.[25] For the purposes of this study the establishment of a relationship of similarity

---

[23]This involves two distinct issues. Not only is Paul's exegetical theory substructural, but as will be discussed later, sometimes only the results of his exegesis, not even the exegesis itself, is on the surface of the text.

[24]*Jewish Hermeneutics*, 109.

[25]The statement by James L. Kugel is becoming a stock joke about the definition of midrash: "since these studies have already not defined midrash in ample detail, there is little purpose in our not defining it again here" ("Two Introductions to Midrash," in *Midrash and Literature* [ed. Geoffrey Hartman and Sanford Budick; New Haven: Yale University Press, 1986] 91). For broad descriptions of midrash see the discussion of the work of Bloch, below. Jacob Neusner (*What is Midrash?* [Philadelphia: Fortress, 1987] 7–8) describes three categories of midrash under the broad definition of "systematic interpretation of Scripture" in Judaism. "It is difficult to specify what the word 'Midrash' in Hebrew expresses that the word 'exegesis' in English does not. How 'exegesis' in English differed from 'Midrash' in Hebrew, or why the Hebrew word will serve better than the more familiar English, I do not know" (ibid., 8).

between Jewish and NT exegesis which points toward dependence is sufficient.[26]

At about the same time, the question of sources which Harris raised was being pursued by C. H. Dodd. While essentially modifying, and in the process refuting, Harris's thesis of a "testimony book," in *According to the Scriptures* Dodd provided a work demonstrating that the NT writers had several *large passages* of scripture, notably from Isaiah, Jeremiah, the minor prophets, and Psalms, which were regarded as foundational for explaining and understanding the Christian gospel.[27] When a text was quoted by a NT author, it often was not as a non-contextual isolated proof-text alone. The writer instead often had the larger context surrounding the quoted material in mind.[28] These portions of scripture (if not always with the same specific application) are found throughout the range of NT writings.

METHODOLOGICAL DEFINITION

Some of the contributors to the definition and refinement of intertextual studies which represent a second stage in methodological development are chronologically coincident with previously mentioned works.

Establishing the Antiquity of Jewish Exegesis:

In two articles, "Midrash," and "Methodological Note for the Study of Rabbinic Literature,"[29] Renée Bloch not only defines midrash but points to its origins in post-exilic OT inner-

---

[26]A distinction is being maintained here between Jewish exegesis in general and the primarily halakic rabbinic exegesis as typified by the Mishnah and Talmud. A distinction is also maintained between rabbinic exegesis and the haggadic midrash of the Midrash Rabbah.

[27]*According to the Scriptures*.

[28]Discussion of the dispute about this claim will be taken up later.

[29]"Midrasch," *Dictionaire de la Bible* Supplement 5 (eds. L. Pirot and H. Cazeues, Paris: Letousey et Ane, 1957) 1263–81; ET in Green, *Approaches*, 29–50; "Note méthodologique pour l'étude de la littérature rabbinique," *RSR* 43 (1955) 194–227; ET in Green, *Approaches*, 51–76

biblical exegesis and emphasizes the importance of haggadic material.[30]

Bloch describes the following characteristics of midrash:

1. Its point of departure is scripture. It is therefore peculiar to Israel as a reflection upon, or a searching of, the scriptures.

2. It is homiletical; a popular genre rather than the genre of the academy.

3. It is attentive to the text, in order to understand it and to illuminate any obscurities found there. Scripture interprets scripture whenever possible by recourse to parallel passages.

4. It adapts the text to the present. Its concern is practical, not purely theoretical. This concern led midrash to reinterpret scripture, to 'actualize' it. Nothing is more characteristic in this regard than the use of the OT in the NT: it always involves midrashic actualization.

5. The nature of the text determines whether the midrash is: halakic, attempting to discover the principles underlying legal sections for application to contemporary problems; or haggadic, attempting to discover the true meaning of events in the narrative passages.[31]

In addition she places the beginning of midrashic exegesis in post-exilic biblical literature, notably in Wisdom litera-

---

[30]"Midrash," 34–44. "[I]t designates an edifying and explanatory genre closely tied to Scripture, in which the role of amplification is real but secondary and always remains subordinate to the primary religious end, which is to show the full import of the work of God, the Word of God" (ibid., 29).

[31]Ibid., 31–34.

ture, post-exilic prophets, and Chronicles. She traces its developmental branches in apocalyptic, Qumran literature, the various versions, the Targums, and finally the NT, where "all the forms of midrash are found." Paul, especially, engages in what Bloch calls "the most authentic form of midrash, what might be called the great midrash."[32] He searches the scriptures to find answers when confronted with shifting realities.

Her work establishing the antiquity of midrashic forms addressed the question of anachronism. While comparison of NT exegesis to rabbinic methods in sources centuries later might be questionable, Bloch demonstrated the use of many of those methods and the development of a broad category of Jewish interpretation of the OT centuries before the writing of the NT. While discussion concerning the fluidity of the definition of midrash continues, these characteristics clearly delimit a class of exegesis to which NT interpretation of the OT belongs.

Bloch's work illuminates the development of tradition as well as methodology. To trace the development of haggadic tradition she proposed a comparative method whereby Palestinian midrash and NT exegesis of the OT are compared with sources outside the rabbinic tradition such as Philo, Josephus, translations, and the Dead Sea Scrolls.[33] A second step would trace a single tradition from the biblical text through the midrashic material of the translations, the Targums, the Talmud, etc. Such a method was intended to help place the origin of traditions (and, it might be said, methods) in a historical context, and to trace the development of individual traditions. Bloch's death prevented further work, but she did show NT use of midrashic traditions.[34]

Geza Vermes, in *Scripture and Tradition in Judaism*, studied the transmission of haggadic tradition.[35] Vermes examined in parallel the various targumic renderings, the Genesis apocryphon, Philo, and other early "rewritings" of

---

32Ibid., 48.
33"Methodological Note," 56–61.
34Ibid., 66–67.
35(SPB 4; ed. P. De Boer; Leiden: Brill, 1961).

various traditions. He employed a modified form of Bloch's comparative method to show how the traditions had developed, and to organize the Targums and related material chronologically. His work illustrated the vitality and the antiquity of haggadic interpretation, and its appearance in the NT.[36]

John W. Bowker, Roger Le Déaut, and Martin McNamara built on the earlier foundation of intertextual studies with concentration on the Targums. Bowker studied targumic exegesis of scripture. He verified the early, though very limited, development of traditions of "rewriting" scripture which were later promulgated by the rabbis.[37] The Targums were not merely translations into Aramaic; instead, "the purpose of the Targum was to make the text meaningful and to bring home its significance to the congregation."[38] The Targum incorporated explanation and interpretation the nature of which is characteristic of later Jewish exegesis. Vermes had already demonstrated the transmission and variation of tradition through the Targums. Bowker's work helped show the development of methodology as well.[39]

Many of these points had already been made convincingly by Le Déaut in 1965. That work was continued and de-

---

[36]Ibid., 176–77, 191, 218–20.

[37]*The Targums and Rabbinic Literature; an Introduction to Jewish Interpretations of Scripture* (Cambridge: Cambridge University Press, 1969).

[38]Ibid., 13. I have sometimes encountered the misconception that the Targums are simply a translation. Martin correctly stresses the fact that the Targums represent an interpretive tradition rather than simply a translation ("The Righteousness of God," 30–31).

[39]E.g.: explanation or exploitation of significant, difficult or odd words or phrases; interpretive paraphrase based upon other passages with verbal similarity; resolution and/or exploitation of perceived contradiction or inconsistency; filling narrative gaps. The greatest element missing from the Targum which is found in most other Jewish exegesis is application to a contemporary situation. This exemplifies the "halfway" position of the Targum as more than a strict translation, yet closely tied to the text itself without a significant concern for application to a specific contemporary circumstance. "Interpretive paraphrase" is an appropriate definition.

veloped in a revision and translation which serves as a concise introduction to the relationship of the Targums to the NT.[40] Like others, Le Déaut argues for the antiquity of targumic material and the haggadic rather than halakic sources of some NT exegesis as exemplified particularly in the Palestinian Targum.[41] Le Déaut points out the exploitation of translational ambiguities, supplying of missing details such as names, explanation of perceived inconsistencies, and a tendency to interpret the Torah through the prophets as characteristics of targumic exegesis.[42] Le Déaut does not emphasize similar exegetical methodologies in the NT, but provides numerous examples of NT dependence upon targumic traditions.

McNamara, while continuing to define methodological procedures, looked to the Targums as sources for several NT themes.[43] McNamara argues, like Vermes and Le Déaut, for the antiquity of at least the oral traditions behind the Targums, and very possibly the written Targums themselves in some form.[44] NT writers reflect a common tradition with the Palestinian Targum on the Pentateuch.[45] McNamara showed that oral use of the Targumic translations and interpretations in the synagogue had to influence Jewish NT writers. All of these works address NT writers' use of rabbinic methods of exegesis by showing the development of those methods from an early date.

---

[40]*The Message of the New Testament and the Aramaic Bible (Targum)* (Subsidia Biblica 5; Rome: Pontifical Biblical Institute, 1982).

[41]Ibid., 7–8, 25.

[42]Ibid., 8–15.

[43]*The New Testament and the Palestinian Targum to the Pentateuch* (AnBib 27; Rome: Pontifical Biblical Institute, 1966); *Targum and Testament. Aramaic Paraphrases of the Hebrew Bible: A Light on the New Testament* (Grand Rapids: Eerdmans, 1972).

[44]*Targum and Testament*, 79–85. He dates some written targumic traditions to pre-Christian times (*The New Testament and the Palestinian Targum*, 35–36).

[45]*The New Testament and the Palestinian Targum*, 70–256; *Targum and Testament*, 93–169.

Michael Fishbane's *Biblical Interpretation in Ancient Israel* provides the most comprehensive survey of Jewish exegetical methods.[46] He proves the antiquity of rabbinic and midrashic exegetical principles and sources by showing the extent and development of OT inner-biblical and intertestamental exegesis. While writers as early as Bonsirven and Bloch had given some evidence of later OT writers exegeting earlier OT books, Fishbane gives extensive and compelling evidence. He also formulates intriguing hypotheses regarding the preservation of oral exegetical tradition not found in the biblical text but surfacing in later exegesis of the DSS and the Pharisees. Fishbane confirms biblical precursors to the exegetical practices of later Jewish interpreters.[47]

David Instone Brewer, although not dealing with NT writers in particular, offers greater insight into Paul's contemporary exegetical milieu.[48] Instone Brewer defines categories of Jewish exegesis, and demonstrates differences and similarities between pre- and post-70 CE Jewish exegesis in the scribal/rabbinic tradition and non-scribal traditions. For his purposes Instone Brewer defines "scribes" as authorities who were the predecessors of the rabbis before 70 CE.[49] He concludes that their exegesis is "nomological," which "regards Scripture as a legal document written by God."[50] The nomological approach of the scribes rests on five assumptions:

1. Scripture is totally self-consistent.

---

[46](Oxford: Clarendon, 1985).

[47]Less comprehensive and detailed on method, but broadly dealing with the spectrum of inner-biblical exegesis from the OT through the NT is the collection of essays edited by D. A. Carson and H. G. M. Williamson (*It is Written: Scripture Citing Scripture. Essays in Honour of Barnabas Lindars* [Cambridge: Cambridge University Press, 1988]). This collection summarizes the evidence of methodological development in Jewish exegesis to the NT period.

[48]*Techniques and Assumptions in Jewish Exegesis before 70 CE* (Texte und Studien zum Antiken Judentum 30; Tübingen: Mohr, 1992).

[49]*Techniques and Assumptions*, 2. Pharisaical exegesis is included in the scribal tradition, which may speak to Paul's training (ibid., 159–60).

[50]Ibid., 15, 163.

2. Every detail in scripture is significant.
3. Scripture is understood according to its context.
4. Scripture does not have any secondary meaning.
5. There is only one valid text form of scripture.[51]

Instone Brewer compares scribal exegesis with the exegesis of the rabbis after 70 CE, concluding that rabbinic exegesis incorporated changes from scribal exegesis. In particular, the rabbis used scripture out of context, derived multiple meanings from one text (particularly in the case of prophecy), and provided interpretations based upon variant readings (although they agreed that there was only one valid text).[52]

Finally, Instone Brewer compares the scribal exegetical tradition with non-scribal exegesis of predecessors and contemporaries of the scribes in the MT, LXX, Targums, Josephus, Qumran, and Philo. He concludes that non-scribal exegesis preceding and contemporary with the scribes is "inspirational." The inspirational approach of non-scribal exegesis rests on five assumptions somewhat different than those of scribal exegesis:

1. Scripture is totally self-consistent.
2. Every detail in scripture is significant.
3. Scripture may be interpreted contrary to or without regard to context.
4. Scripture has secondary meaning(s) independent of its plain meaning.
5. Variant texts and translations are valid forms of scripture.[53]

---

[51]Ibid., 165–71.
[52]Ibid., 173.
[53]Ibid., 212–14. The statements of Steven Scott Alt, "Instone Brewer recently published a book demonstrating that Jewish exegesis in the first century always adhered to the context and never sought a secondary meaning in the text," and "Instone Brewer concluded that exegesis before 70 CE was always contextual, and sought the 'plain' meaning of the texts, while post-70 exegetes were often non-contextual and sought deeper, secondary meanings in the text," are incorrect ("Early

In addition, non-scribal exegesis tends to regard all scripture as prophecy.[54] Instone Brewer also concludes that scribes and their contemporaries were aware of one another's types of exegesis, and that examples of nomological exegesis are found in non-scribal material. Without going into detail, Instone Brewer indicates that the NT is influenced by both nomological and inspirational exegesis.[55]

This is certainly the case for Paul. In fact, the entire argument of Romans is in one sense an argument for the consistency of scripture with itself, and with God's action in the gospel. Like his contemporaries, Paul finds significance in minor details of the text, and while he is contextually aware he can also employ scripture without regard to context. Paul at times derives secondary christological readings from scripture and relies on variant readings and amalgamation of texts to reach his conclusions. On the other hand, Paul can deal with scripture as though interpreting a legal document. Like non-scribal predecessors and contemporaries, Paul employs a variety of exegetical techniques.[56]

Establishing NT Parallels to Jewish Exegesis:

Krister Stendahl refined and defined intertextual biblical studies on another front.[57] His analysis showed that the Gospel of Matthew includes scholarly exegetical work in scriptural interpretation analogous to that done by contempo-

---

Tannaitic Exegesis and Modern Hermeneutics: A Study of Paul's Exegesis of Scripture in Romans and its Repeatability in the Twenty First Century" [M.A. Thesis, Regent University, 1997] v, 3). Instone Brewer did reach those conclusions regarding scribal exegesis, but also gives examples mentioned above of non-scribal "inspirational" exegesis before and contemporary with the scribes.

[54]Instone Brewer, *Techniques and Assumptions*, 215.

[55]Ibid., 224.

[56]If Paul was trained in exegesis as a Pharisee, he not only left Pharisaical Judaism "unconditionally" (Segal, *Paul the Convert*, xv) but he also departed from strictly Pharisaical/scribal exegetical principles. An interesting study might investigate the possibility that Paul intentionally presents his exegesis in contrast to and in competition with the Pharisaical/scribal exegetical tradition.

[57]*The School of St. Matthew.*

rary Jewish exegetes. Whatever one may think of Stendahl's hypothesis of a "school" behind Matthew's Gospel, he made important contributions by his detailed grammatical analysis of the form of Matthean quotations, their introductory formulae, and changes within quotations in comparison to the *pesher* exegesis of Qumran, the rabbinic exegetical tradition of midrashic literature, and the Targums. His demonstration that systematic exegesis was done, and his reliance on Qumran literature and the Targums, provided a foundation, like Bloch's work, that others soon began to build upon.

In 1957 E. Earl Ellis made a comparison of Pauline and rabbinic exegesis.[58] While Pauline exegesis exhibits many of the methodological and topical characteristics as well as some of the content of rabbinic exegesis, Ellis says that its purpose is different in that Paul "did not cite the Scriptures from a sense of duty or love of theology or tradition, but because of their witness to Christ."[59] On the other hand, Ellis relies on Stendahl in seeing elements of Pauline exegesis in common with the *midrash pesher* of the DSS.[60] In both cases exegesis determines the form of the text through:

> (1) merging the pertinent verses onto one strongly expressive 'proof-text', (2) adapting the grammar to the NT context and application, (3) choosing appropriate renderings from known texts or Targums, and (4) creating *ad hoc* interpretations.[61]

---

[58]*Paul's Use of the Old Testament.*

[59]Ibid., 115. It might be noted that Bloch's article on midrash was just becoming available. Ellis gives little consideration to Pauline parallels with haggadic exegesis. To describe Paul's purpose in exegesis as only related to the scriptures' witness to Christ is to underestimate Paul's relationship to scripture as a Jew.

[60]Ibid., 139–47. Again, Bloch did not distinguish the varieties of midrash as clearly as others did. It is difficult to categorize Pauline exegesis as *pesher* rather than rabbinic when neither is easily defined or entirely separable from the other. Certainly Ellis is correct, however, in noting some of the more characteristically *pesher* elements in some Pauline exegesis.

[61]Ibid., 149.

Ellis shows that Paul adheres significantly to the historical and grammatical meanings of the text, at least within the constraints of the contemporary exegetical system. He points out that many of the specifically rabbinic characteristics often attributed to Pauline exegesis are just as easily seen in almost any exegesis.[62] However, he also notes that Paul's employment of fragmentary quotations, the implied continuance of a quotation, the insertion of ethical instruction, and some of Hillel's rules are found in rabbinic practice.[63]

Ellis, like Doeve, notes the use of midrash in Romans 9–11 and Galatians 3, though he seems to regard Paul's method as superior to the usual rabbinic practice.[64] Ellis shows that Paul also parallels contemporary methodology in occasional reference in order to the law, prophets, and the writings, and in reliance on *qal va-homer* (*a fortiori*), *gezerah shevah* (analogy based on verbal similarity), and rabbinic introductory formulas. Paul also makes use of the *Stichwort* "keyword" (or as it is sometimes called, the hook-word) to connect passages, wherein a word in common between passages allows for their mutual interpretation. Ellis points out that the connections are usually deeper than merely verbal, and may at times be the result of coincident subject matter.[65] Ellis makes the distinction between rabbinic methods and those in the DSS, and characterizes Pauline methodology as

---

[62]Note Doeve's NT examples of *qal va-homer* in argumentation in the gospels (*Jewish Hermeneutics*, 105). Such *a fortiori* arguments are common in almost any rhetoric or exegesis. However, similarity of content may point to dependence on a Jewish model in many NT cases. It is likely that where Jewish writers educated in any of the varied methods of Jewish exegesis employ such arguments they have learned them in their particular Jewish context. In any case, identifying the use of argumentative devices is usually more important than precisely identifying the methodological source.

[63]Ellis, *Paul's Use of the Old Testament*, 45–46.

[64]This may reflect a theological predisposition.

[65]Ibid. 45–50. See also the summaries on Paul's use of these methods by Stephen Pattee ("Stumbling Stone or Cornerstone? The Structure and Meaning of Paul's Argument in Rom 9:30–10:13" [Ph.D. diss. Marquette Univ. 1991] 5–12) and Martin ("The Righteousness of God," 25–26).

nearer to that of Qumran. He demonstrates Paul's employment of elements of both contemporary exegetical systems.

Birger Gerhardsson, in *Memory and Manuscript*, attempted an analysis of the transmission of the oral Torah.[66] He then turned that analysis toward the transmission of the gospel tradition. He attempted to support theories of gospel transmission which grant a high degree of accurate preservation to the oral stage of transmission, consistent with the "preservative" function of the oral Torah. Gerhardsson has been strongly criticized by Morton Smith and Jacob Neusner because of evidentiary weakness regarding such preservative oral transmission prior to 70 C.E.[67] A discussion of the oral transmission of gospel traditions is outside the purview of this study. However, in the process of debate Gerhardsson and his critics provided additional support concerning NT writers' use of the variety of related contemporary Jewish methods of interpretation.

Another work by Gerhardsson, *The Testing of God's Son*, centers on the use of midrash in Matthew's temptation narrative.[68] Gerhardsson describes the systematic exegesis of OT material. Matthew has placed the quotations from Deuteron-

---

[66]*Memory and Manuscript: Oral Tradition and Written Transmission in Rabbinic Judaism and Early Christianity* (ASNU 22; Uppsala: Almquist and Wiksells, 1961).

[67]Smith, "A Comparison of Early Christian and Early Rabbinic Tradition," *JBL* 82 (1963) 169–76; Neusner, "The Rabbinic Traditions About the Pharisees," 57–70. For his part, Gerhardsson buttresses his argument and evidence in response (*Tradition and Transmission in Early Christianity* [ConNT 20; Lund: Gleerup, 1964]), but the evidence for the methodology of oral transmission of traditional material prior to 70 CE remains mixed.

[68]*The Testing of God's Son (Matt 4:1–11 & Par): An Analysis of Early Christian Midrash* (ConBNT 2; Lund: Gleerup, 1966). Following the path taken by Gerhardsson is William Stegner (*Narrative Theology in Early Jewish Christianity* [Louisville: Westminster/John Knox, 1989]). Stegner applied Gerhardsson's method in re-examining the use of the OT and subsequent traditional interpretations of it in the Temptation and several other gospel narratives, most notably the Transfiguration and the Feeding of the Five Thousand. Stegner provides further examples of NT use of Jewish exegetical methods and traditions, and the usefulness of intertextual methodology.

omy 6–8 on the lips of Jesus not simply as apt phrases from antiquity in response to the temptation. Gerhardsson shows that the context of Deuteronomy 6–8 provides the basis for the entire temptation narrative. While one may certainly disagree with some points of Gerhardsson's exegesis, he illustrates how Jewish exegetical methods were applied to the OT in the formation of Christian texts.[69]

The work of Barnabas Lindars concentrates on content rather than method in the use of the OT in the NT.[70] Lindars, like Ellis, relies on the ambiguous term *midrash pesher* to describe much of the early church's exegesis. He applies this term to "any interpretive text-form" as a matter of convenience, recognizing it is "not strictly correct."[71] He follows Ellis's assessment of Pauline exegesis as not rabbinic but "the church's own version of the *midrash pesher*," which Paul has expanded in his own way.[72] Lindars then shows the apologetic use of OT quotations in the development of NT doctrine. Like others, Lindars has restricted his study to clearly quoted material and its modification—a continuing deficiency in many intertextual studies.

Richard Longenecker provides a summary of work on intertextual exegesis up until 1975.[73] He compares the various types of Jewish exegesis and their use in the NT. He gives examples of Paul's exegesis and use of contemporary methods,

---

[69]Comparable to Gerhardsson's study on Matthew as well is Peder Borgen's analysis of haggadic method in the Gospel of John and in Philo, describing their use of the manna tradition (*Bread From Heaven* [NovTSup 10; Leiden: Brill, 1965]). Borgen showed John's use not only of haggadic method but of content as well, finding evidence of parallels between Jesus and Moses in the NT.

[70]Especially *New Testament Apologetic: The Doctrinal Significance of the Old Testament Quotations* (Philadelphia: Westminster, 1961). In this respect his work is like that of Daube, W. D. Davies, and Dodd.

[71]Ibid., 15.

[72]Ibid., 16.

[73]*Biblical Exegesis in the Apostolic Period* (Grand Rapids: Eerdmans, 1975). Longenecker gives four common points of Jewish hermeneutics of all varieties, which are similar to Bloch's characteristics of midrash (ibid., 19–20).

including hook-words, or *gezerah shevah*.[74] His work on Paul's exegesis is limited for the most part to obviously cited material. Giving clear examples in summary fashion in order to prove the use of Jewish methodology in the NT, as Longenecker does, ignores more subtle Pauline exegesis. Longenecker's greatest contribution is in compiling and systematizing previous work.

These defining works represent an era in which scholars were finding a common descriptive vocabulary for the conventions of Jewish midrash and exegesis, and for those conventions at work in the NT. The work of this era provided evidence that an understanding of Jewish exegetical tradition provides rich results in NT studies.

METHODOLOGICAL EVOLUTION

Continuing work has been a process of filling in methodological gaps in the study of NT use of scripture and filling in the gaps in the application of intertextual studies to specific biblical texts and themes.

Establishing Methodological Validity:

Nils Dahl's essay, "Contradictions in Scripture," fills one of those gaps concerning rabbinic harmonization of contradictory scriptures, and Paul's use of that method in Galatians to harmonize the law's place in the light of the gospel.[75] It would have been profitable for Dahl to give more attention to Romans, but the study is very useful nonetheless.

---

[74]Ibid., 116–20.

[75]"Contradictions in Scripture," in *Studies in Paul* (Minneapolis: Augsburg, 1977) 159–77. Segal points out, "Resolving contradictions is one of the basic methods of rabbinic exegesis...Though Paul could not have learned the rule in the form in which it is preserved in rabbinic literature, the method of argumentation has come from Paul's Jewish past. Hence, Paul gives evidence of the antiquity of the technique" (*Paul the Convert*, 122). This is an important point concerning the relationship between Paul and rabbinic use of many exegetical techniques, not only the resolution of scriptural inconsistencies.

Foundational for this study is Carol Stockhausen's dissertation on 2 Corinthians 3.[76] Here, Paul's use of midrashic methodology is described and illustrated. Through analysis of Paul's use of hook-word links between pentateuchal narrative and the prophetic texts used to interpret those narratives, Stockhausen traces out Paul's exegetical path. She demonstrates that the presence of key words and phrases in the Pauline text of 2 Corinthians 3 derives from OT passages not necessarily directly quoted, but out of which exegesis has been done in the service of his developing argument. That exegesis is performed according to the conventions of contemporary Jewish exegesis.

Stockhausen has further summarized her findings concerning Pauline exegetical methodology in her article, "2 Corinthians 3 and The Principles of Pauline Exegesis."[77] Characteristics of Pauline exegesis are identified in 2 Corinthians 3 and Galatians in an effort to demonstrate that the exegesis of 2 Corinthians 3 is typical of Paul's exegesis, and is not a unique or non-Pauline case.[78] In this demonstration she counters the assertions of Hays that Paul has "no systematic exegetical procedures at work in his reading of scripture."[79]

Stockhausen identifies five characteristic Pauline exegetical procedures, the first three of which are primary:

1. Torah is the basis for interpretation. Pentateuchal narrative is central to his arguments. Paul is concerned with the plot, character, and especially with unusual characters or actions in the narrative.

2. Paul usually applies prophetic and/or sapiential texts to the Pentateuchal narrative in application to contemporary situations. The narrative and prophetic texts are verbally linked to one another "forming a

---

[76]*Moses' Veil.*

[77]*Paul and the Scriptures of Israel*, 143–64.

[78]Ibid., 143.

[79]Hays, *Echoes*, 160. Stockhausen, "Principles of Pauline Exegesis," 143 n. 1.

network of mutually-interpreting texts which creates a new synthetic meaning at once scriptural and Pauline."

3. As Dahl has shown, Paul attempts to reconcile contradictions in scripture. Difficult passages are often interpreted as scriptural expressions of the discontinuity between the old way of the law and the new way of the spirit.

4. Paul gives "consistent attention to the context of cited passages" as an "extension of his narrative interest described earlier."

5. Paul employs "*pesher*-like contemporization." That is, Paul will sometimes identify the scriptural reference with the contemporary situation in a "this is that" format.[80]

Stockhausen shows that Paul does use Jewish exegetical procedures. She is careful to point out that those procedures are usually not evident on the surface of the text, and are not described by Paul.[81] But it is possible to construct hypotheses of the course of his exegesis which clarify previously obscure passages.

Donald Juel no longer feels it necessary to prove the NT writers' use of Jewish exegetical methods. In *Messianic Exegesis* he assumes that this has already been done, and sets about the task of describing its impact in the NT.[82] He turns

---

[80]Stockhausen, "Principles of Pauline Exegesis," 144–46.

[81]Ibid., 145. "This is admittedly an abstraction of Paul's exegetical procedure from evidence encountered in his argument and later articulations of specific exegetical rules" (ibid., 156–57). We know that exegetical procedures like these were codified after Paul and used by Jews contemporary with Paul. We see evidence that Paul also used these procedures. Paul's use is actually evidence of their use before their codification.

[82]*Messianic Exegesis: Christological Interpretation of the Old Testament in Early Christianity* (Philadelphia: Fortress, 1988). The as-

to Jewish exegesis and tradition as an explanation for messianic interpretations of OT texts used in the NT, particularly in the gospels. Juel believes the early church turned to midrash to understand the significance and meaning of Christ, rather than attempting to prove Jesus as Christ.[83] He has shown how verbal links found in foundational kingship-messianic texts led NT writers through other texts to find the themes of suffering, servanthood, and exaltation of the messiah; themes which are not well developed in pre-Christian Jewish tradition. Juel's contention that NT use of Jewish exegetical methods is an established fact represents an important shift in emphasis.

Introduction of Cross-Disciplinary Methodology:
Another significant shift comes with Richard B. Hays's already mentioned *Echoes of Scripture in the Letters of Paul*.[84] Dependent upon John Hollander's description of intertextual echo in the field of literary criticism,[85] and in dialogue with intertextual theory, Hays sets aside the idea of Pauline use of midrash and an emphasis on Pauline method. He exchanges these foci for one on Paul's interpretation of the OT as a free-flowing, spirit-led, interaction of text and interpreter bringing new meaning out of the text. The language, imagery, and themes of scripture resonate through Paul's own writing not only in citations and obvious allusions, but in less obvious "echoes," which bring their own meaning to Paul's text.

---

sumption that Jewish exegetical methods are used in the NT without requiring further proof is a new step which represents a maturation in this field. Source, form, and redaction criticism also went through a period in which the validity of their assumptions needed repeated defense, until those assumptions were sufficiently established.

[83]Contra the approach of Dodd and Lindars. I am skeptical that much of a division exists between the two approaches. It seems very likely that the church's use of scripture on the one hand to understand the significance of Jesus as Messiah and on the other to prove that Jesus was Messiah is one enterprise occurring at the same time and in the same way.

[84]Hays has sparked an enormous amount of discussion, e.g., Evans and Sanders, *Paul and the Scriptures of Israel*.

[85]*The Figure of Echo: A Mode of Allusion in Milton and After* (Berkeley: University of California Press, 1981).

As mentioned earlier, Hays does not believe Paul has "systematic exegetical procedures."[86] While Hays affirms the pervasive influence of the OT on Pauline thought, he claims that Paul uses scripture intertextually not with a midrashic methodology but uses openly revisionary readings of scripture to awaken the newly spirit-illumined metaphorical meanings hidden in the OT context. Paul does so in ways ranging from cited quotations, to uncited allusions, to subliminal "echoes." The degree of Paul's intentionality will also vary along a similar spectrum, as will our awareness of these echoes.

> As we move farther away from overt citation, the source recedes into the discursive distance, the intertextual relations become less determinate, and the demand placed on the reader's listening powers grows greater. As we near the vanishing point of the echo, it inevitably becomes difficult to decide whether we are really hearing an echo at all, or whether we are only conjuring things out of the murmurings of our own imaginations.[87]

Hays describes five possible sources of echo: in the author; in the original readers; in the text; in the interpreter; and in the community.[88] Hays also outlines seven tests for hearing echoes.

1. Availability: Was the source of the perceived echo available to the author or readers?

2. Volume: How explicit is the echo in terms of use of vocabulary, and how important is the source?

3. Recurrence: Does Paul cite the same passage elsewhere?

4. Thematic Coherence: How well does the perceived echo fit in with Paul's argument?

---

[86]"Paul...offers helter-skelter intuitive readings, unpredictable, ungeneralizable" (Hays, *Echoes*, 160).

[87]Ibid., 23.

[88]Ibid., 26–27.

5. Historical Plausibility: Could Paul have intended this meaning?[89]

6. History of Interpretation: Has anyone else ever heard this echo?

7. Satisfaction: Does it make sense and illuminate the text?[90]

Hays shows how an understanding of the entire context of a scriptural allusion in Paul is often necessary to fully understand the course of Paul's argument. While admitting the probability that Paul often was not cognizant of all of the contextual details of his citations, Hays feels free to press those details for their maximum effect, and in practice seems unwilling to admit that Paul ever overlooked any of them. However, Hays is not concerned to discover only those echoes intended by Paul.[91]

In the final chapter Hays summarizes his findings about Paul's hermeneutics under five headings:

---

[89]This is an important consideration for Hays. He does not adopt ahistorical intertextual theory as a whole, which in many instances has no regard for authorial intent. Unlike some branches of intertextual theory he does not abandon historical considerations in favor of reader-centered interpretations, but is interested in Paul's historical context and rhetorical situation.

[90]Ibid., 29–33.

[91]Hays receives criticism on this point. See Green, "Doing the Text's Work for It, 58–63). "This book cannot help but display the thoroughgoing extent to which intertextuality is really the reader's work, not the writer's" (ibid., 61). Green seems to think Hays has, perhaps unintentionally, succumbed to a subjectively speculative exegesis which presents Hays's readings of the OT rather than Paul's. While I believe Hays sometimes mixes his readings of the OT with Paul's, he has provided no method for discriminating between the two; nor does he believe that to be an important exercise, because Paul's use of echo "invites the reader to participate in an imaginative act" (*Echoes*, 23). That is not to say that Hays is not concerned with Paul's historical intentionality. He is. But he also understands the reader to be an active participant in the effectiveness of intertextual echo.

1. Hermeneutical freedom. Freedom to reinterpret the scriptures is enabled by the spirit.

2. Revision and continuity. Paul revises the scriptures as trope yet retains the continuity of the overall message.

3. Hermeneutical methods and constraints. There is actually a lack of identifiable method, yet interpretation is constrained by theological concerns in the text.

4. The immediacy of the word. The Word of God is believed to be living and active to the current reader.

5. Eschatological hermeneutics. Paul reads scripture "at the end of the ages."[92]

Hays's proposal rests on certain assumptions about the nature of meaning and texts, and thus provides an example of a particular branch of intertextual studies. This literary branch of studies on intertextuality centers on the fluidity of meaning as earlier texts are appropriated by later texts, with a minimal emphasis upon the method by which those earlier texts are appropriated and incorporated.[93] A brief summary of some of the trends in biblical intertextuality is desirable since

---

[92]Hays, *Echoes*, 155–73.

[93]Hays does not accept all of the philosophical presuppositions which sometimes accompany the word "intertextuality." "I fail to see why my interest in intertextual echo should compel me to accept their ideological framework" ("On the Rebound: A Response to Critiques of *Echoes of Scripture in the Letters of Paul*," *Paul and the Scriptures of Israel*, 80). Hays affirms the fluidity of texts, but within certain constraints. He affirms some stability in texts and a limited concern for authorial intent, unlike others in the field of intertextuality. He goes so far as to say he will give up use of the word "intertextuality" if it is required (ibid., 81).

studies of intertextual exegesis and literary intertextuality cross paths in many instances.[94]

It is in specifically Jewish and OT studies, outside of Hays, that modern literary theory on the indeterminacy of meaning meets the phenomenon of intertextual exegesis and claims to find an ancestor. The collection edited by Hartman and Budick, *Midrash and Literature*, attempts to show that haggadic midrash in effect embodies the application of this philosophy of meaning and the relationship between readers and texts. Fishbane contends that the interpretive freedom characteristic of midrash is also seen in inner-biblical exegesis. The line of demarcation between text and interpretation becomes at once blurred and more distinct. Where inner-biblical interpretation forms new text it blurs, but where the text is distinct from its interpretation and interpreter, even in an inner-biblical context, the demarcation is distinct.[95]

Daniel Boyarin, in *Intertextuality and the Reading of Midrash*, applies a broad definition of intertextuality to a theory of midrash.[96] In this definition all texts and discourses are intertextual, embodying fragments, concepts, and ideology of preceding discourse as well as the conventions of the surrounding culture.[97] Midrash, then, is a re-living and entering into, not just an interpretation of, the biblical text.[98]

---

[94]For a bibliography of literary intertextuality see Udo J. Hebel (*Intertextuality, Allusion, and Quotation: An International Bibliography of Critical Studies* [New York: Greenwood, 1989]).

[95]Michael Fishbane, "Inner Biblical Exegesis: Types and Strategies of Interpretation in Ancient Israel," *Midrash and Literature*, 19–37.

[96](Bloomington: Indiana University Press, 1990).

[97]Ibid., 14–15. For three definitions of intertextuality embracing text, culture, and audience, see Penchansky, "Staying the Night, 77–88. For an application of this definition of intertextuality to the NT using Hays's criteria see Robert L. Brawley, "An Absent Complement and Intertextuality in John 19:28–29," *JBL* 112 (1993) 427–43. For a collection of articles on OT intertextuality, see Fewell, *Reading Between Texts*.

[98]Boyarin, *Intertextuality*, 17–19. In a different context and with somewhat different terminology Boyarin confirms the characteristics of Jewish exegetical methodology given by Bowker: explanation or exploitation of significant, difficult or odd words or phrases; interpretive paraphrase based upon other passages with verbal similarity; resolution

As Boyarin says, midrash in fact does perform the cultural function of propounding the new while at the same time preserving the old: filling the narrative/cultural gaps through a dual meaning founded both in indeterminacy which liberates (the Torah has many meanings which all must be brought out), and in adherence to cultural conventions of acceptability (the breaking of which results in expulsion from the community). In this way, in Boyarin's view, midrash functions intertextually as do all other texts: using, changing, and renewing previous discourse without a necessary tie to the author's intent, yet restrained by the limits of its culture.[99] Meaning is then not authorially determined, but historiographically and culturally determined as past and present are merged.

Certainly the interpretive application of OT texts to the contemporary situation implies this type of interpretive freedom to a great extent in ancient Jewish midrash. Yet to equate the Jewish exegetical and NT attitudes toward meaning with modern conceptions, at least in scripture, is to overstate the case.[100] While Paul cannot at all be thought of as a proponent of strictly authorially intended meaning, his statement that "this was written for us" (1 Cor 9:10; 10:11; Rom 15:4) implies intent guiding meaning, since as a Jewish interpreter Paul considers scripture to have a divine origin.

For Paul and other Jewish interpreters of scripture the source and legitimacy of any fluidity of meaning is believed to rest in the intent of God, and perhaps in the spirit, who participates in both the writing and the reading of the text,

---

and/or exploitation of perceived contradiction or inconsistency; filling narrative gaps (ibid., 39–92).

[99] N. T. Wright makes similar points in his discussion concerning the place of "story" in the establishment and development of a culture's "worldview" (*The New Testament and the People of God*, vol. 1 of *Christian Origins and the Question of God* [Minneapolis: Fortress, 1992] 38–44).

[100] For a discussion of the uniqueness of ancient Jewish attitudes toward scripture in the Greco-Roman world see W. D. Davies, "Canon and Christology in Paul," *Paul and the Scriptures of Israel*, 18–39.

rather than in the interpretive right of the reader.[101] In this way, by attempting to determine God's intent in scripture, Paul's use of the OT may be called exegesis.

METHODOLOGICAL CONCLUSIONS

The foregoing survey lays a foundation concerning current methodology in intertextual exegesis. In the following material I hope to bring the previous findings to bear on the task at hand. Three areas require definition. First, I wish to clarify where this study of Paul's intertextual exegesis fits in the broader realm of intertextuality. Second, I will draw conclusions about the relationship of Pauline exegesis to the broader contemporary world of Jewish exegesis from which it springs. Finally, I will suggest some refinements to previous proposals concerning principles of Pauline exegesis and the method by which that exegesis will be examined in the ensuing study of Romans 2.

INTERTEXTUAL REFERENCES

An issue to be addressed is the relationship of this study to the field of intertextuality. In the context of what is called intertextuality, how does this task differ from others? Many scholars of intertextuality adopt a reader-centered understanding of meaning in texts.[102] They apply it in their own interpretations, as well as exploring those phenomena in the writers they study.[103] Such an approach differs from traditional historical-critical approaches in that it is ahistorical. Ellen J. van Wolde criticizes biblical scholars who only

---

[101]This much may be affirmed without entering into a broader discussion of theories of inspiration, etc.

[102] E.g., Robert M. Fowler, "The Rhetoric of Direction and Indirection in the Gospel of Mark," *Semeia* 48 (1989) 115–134; Ellen J. van Wolde, *A Semiotic Analysis of Genesis 2–3. A Semiotic Theory and Method of Analysis Applied to the Story of the Garden of Eden* (SSN 25; Assen:Van Gorcum, 1989).

[103]These readings are often consciously deconstructive. They attempt to produce "a fresh reading....this new reading is often aimed at displacing the text's dominant interpretation according to critical consensus" (Krause, "A Blessing Cursed, 191).

"stretch their legs at the station of intertextuality," proposing the adoption of reader-centered exegeses dependent upon a wholesale incorporation of intertextual theory.[104]

Minimalist Intertextuality:

Hays takes an approach at odds with this position. He chooses to distance himself from the usual theoretical conclusions and opts for what has been called a "minimalist notion of intertextuality."[105] Historical concerns and authorial intent remain central in such exegesis, unlike that proposed by van Wolde. This study follows Hays's lead in this regard, and centers more on the methodology whereby Paul appropriates OT texts for his own application in his own historical circumstance, and how that methodology results in his conclusions. It has a historical basis.

While there are many points of conjunction, the difference between this approach and even that of Hays is clear. I am concerned with Paul's exegetical conclusions and what he means by their presentation—uncovering in what manner previous texts to which Paul makes reference influence Paul's thought, theology, and argumentation. Hays is also interested in what meanings the reader may infer from the text, and in

---

[104]"[The use of intertextuality in biblical exegesis] becomes significant only when it causes a change in our understanding of texts. With the help of theories about intertextuality it is possible to challenge the idea of causality between texts, which is the basis of the comparative study of texts. It can also become clear that it is not the chronology of texts that should occupy the centre of attention, but the logical and analogical reasoning of the reader in interaction with the text" ("Trendy Intertextuality," *Intertextuality in Biblical Writings*, 43). This study does not seek to "challenge the idea of causality between texts." It does not propose what "should occupy the centre of attention" in intertextual studies of scripture, but simply chooses a center of attention I find most interesting and which offers significant results, van Wolde's objections notwithstanding.

[105]Green, "Doing the Text's Work For It," 59. See Hays for his own description ("On the Rebound," 79–81; *Echoes*, 14–21, 227 n. 60). Timothy K. Beal discusses this tension between the *theoretical* roots of the term "intertextuality" in post-structuralism and the *methodological* appropriation of the term in historical-critical biblical studies ("Ideology and Intertextuality: Surplus of Meaning and Controlling the Means of Production," *Reading Between Texts*, 27–39).

what echoes of OT language and culture may incidentally occur in Paul's language. I consider these tasks as subsequent steps useful for extracting a broader range of meaning for application to a contemporary situation, but not the task of the present study. Therefore, this study deals only with the first of Hays's five possible sources of echo.[106] In that respect, this study is even more "minimalist" in the appropriation of intertextual theory than that of Hays. For this reason I have chosen to refer to Paul's "intertextual exegesis" and forego the term "intertextuality" since that term more and more often suggests an interest in the larger literary and epistemological theories.

The Category of Reference:

It seems to me exegetically legitimate to attempt to uncover what the author has intended to say, insofar as possible. There are many who consider this a fruitless and even naive endeavor. We differ in our presuppositions, and I see little hope of reconciliation on this point. Not all who are interested in echoes of meaning have jettisoned any desire to uncover an author's intent. Hays, for instance, offers his principles for recognizing echo with the assumption that Paul's cognizance and purposefulness in the appearance of echoes in his letters may be more or less measured by the employment of those principles.

However, recognizing the appearance of echo is insufficient for the task I propose to undertake. Echo includes those instances where familiar or appropriate language from the scriptures flows into Paul's writing in a sort of mental word association process. I am interested in uncovering and describing those instances where Paul has engaged in intertextual exegesis, defined as the attempt to understand and explain the meaning of scripture for application to a contemporary situation or to make sense of human experience. It is the purposeful interpretation of scripture which has shaped his conclusions and the course of his developing argument.

---

[106]I am interested in the author as the source of references: "where it can be credibly demonstrated that Paul intended such effects" (Hays, *Echoes*, 26).

My interest is not only in "intended" echoes, wherein language and vocabulary from OT texts resonate with the reader, but those which are derived from exegesis. I propose a distinction between what Hays describes as echo and what I describe as *reference*.

Reference in this definition means not that Paul refers his readers to a particular passage from scripture, though it may function in this fashion on some occasions. Reference here means that Paul himself has referred to scripture in his own thought and study. That "reference work," which may have been done at a time other than that at which the current document was being penned, not only provides convenient or appropriate language or turns of phrase, but has shaped the content and presentation of Paul's theology and therefore his written argumentation. By *reference* I mean to identify not only those places where Paul clearly quotes scripture, but those places where Paul has engaged in what may be called exegesis even without clear quotation.

While this study falls into the realm of intertextuality, I have attempted to narrow the focus for the purpose of uncovering both the method and application of Pauline exegesis in Romans 2. This description of that narrowing process defines where this study fits in the broader category of intertextuality. Criteria for the identification of scriptural references in distinction from scriptural echoes, insofar as they may be determined, will be presented after the discussion of the relationship of Paul's exegesis to Jewish exegesis in general.

PAUL IN THE JEWISH EXEGETICAL MILIEU

The preceding historical survey has shown that the question has been raised as to whether or not Paul's writing is part of the larger Jewish exegetical tradition and entails systematic exegesis. In response to Hays's suggestions that Paul's exegesis ought not to be called midrash, and is not systematic, there are several points to mention.

Systematic exegesis:

A fluid and dynamic conception of scripture and its interpretation is characteristic of Pauline exegesis, but this is true of midrash and of Jewish exegesis in general. There is no reason to divorce one from the other on this basis. Hays's understanding of the characteristics of Pauline use of the OT has many similarities to those already mentioned by other scholars. He makes the important point that investigation of Paul's use of the OT cannot be restricted to places where he specifically quotes scripture; a point many scholars overlook.[107] The greatest difficulty with Hays's proposal is his denial of any systematic exegesis on the part of Paul. While there certainly are allusive non-exegetical echoes in Paul's writings—and Hays's method is useful in their analysis—there is also ample evidence of systematic exegesis.

Craig Evans remarks, "Hays's point [concerning loose use of the label midrash] is well taken. Nevertheless, there are studies where the recognition of the presence of midrash in Paul has aided and advanced the interpretive process."[108] Evans also notes that what Hays regards as Paul's "scandalous inversions" of stories in scripture is patterned on the method of "deconstruction" of earlier scripture practiced by the OT prophets. "Paul's hermeneutic is in fact a biblical hermeneutic."[109] There is structure and method to much of Paul's use of the OT, which ought to be regarded as exegesis as should the nomological and inspirational exegesis of the scribal/rabbinic and non-scribal traditions described by In-

---

[107]See esp. "On the Rebound," 88–89. Hays responds quite decisively to J. C. Beker's erroneous statement that scriptural references are almost absent in Romans 5–8 (Beker, "Echoes and Intertextuality: On the Role of Scripture in Paul's Theology," *Paul and the Scriptures of Israel*, 66).

[108]Evans, "Listening for Echoes of Interpreted Scripture," *Paul and the Scriptures of Israel*, 50.

[109]Evans, "Listening for Echoes," 51, referring to Hays, *Echoes*, 67. Hays responds that this is precisely his point ("On the Rebound," 73–75). He believes Paul is interpreting scripture with the same emphases as the prophets, though Hays concedes nothing about method. Stephen G. Brown, in his demonstration of systematic exegesis in 2 Thessalonians 2, also believes Hays has "overstated his case against Paul's ever using any formal or systematic exegetical method" ("The Intertextuality of Isaiah 66.17 and 2 Thessalonians 2.7: A Solution for the 'Restrainer' Problem," *Paul and the Scriptures of Israel*, 273–74).

stone Brewer. For that reason Hays's sources of echo and his tests for hearing echo will prove inadequate, or rather, too inclusive, for a study such as this which seeks to identify systematic Pauline exegesis.

Jewish exegesis and Paul:

Paul's exegesis has variously been described as rabbinic, targumic, midrashic, haggadic, and pesher-like. Each of those categorizations is correct at some place in Paul's epistles. Likewise, each of them is incorrect at many points. It will be useful to describe Paul's place in the family of Jewish exegesis, while recognizing that his exegesis does not always and only correspond to any one particular type, consistent with a tradition of non-scribal exegesis described by Instone Brewer.[110]

Paul employs some of the methods later described and evident in scribal/rabbinic—primarily halakic—material of the Mishnah and Talmud. Bonsirven at an early date described several elements as characteristic of both rabbinic and Pauline exegesis. Later studies confirmed those findings, and added others. Both Pauline and rabbinic exegesis use fragmentary quotations, at times with the implied continuance of the quotation, with similar introductory formulae. Both rely on the use of hook-words to link passages that may be used to interpret one another, by the rabbis called *gezerah shevah* in a somewhat stricter form. The rabbis occasionally make reference to the law, the prophets, and the writings, in order, as appears to be characteristic of Paul. Both types of exegesis may be turned toward ethical instruction.[111] Daube and W. D. Davies showed Pauline use of Jewish exegetical types, forms, and concepts, later seen in rabbinic material.

But comparison to rabbinic exegesis of the Mishnah and Talmud produces the most difficulties. The problem of anachronism is greatest here. Though many codified rabbinic meth-

---

[110]"However, the general population might not be expected to remain firmly in either camp..." (Instone Brewer, *Techniques and Assumptions*, 221).

[111]See the larger discussions above of Bonsirven, Doeve, and Ellis.

ods are attributed to pre-70 CE rabbis, the authenticity of those attributions is not universally reliable. Other evidence of the pre-70 CE use of methods parallel to those of Paul would be preferable. Also, Pauline and other NT exegesis tends to be contextually aware, as C. H. Dodd and others have demonstrated, while halakic rabbinic exegesis is most often atomistic.[112]

There are other notable differences. Most mishnaic material is halakic, which is not the case for NT or Pauline exegesis. So the purposes and intent of exegesis are divergent. Most of Hillel's and Ishmael's rules do not find a place in Pauline exegesis, though there are some common elements. The use of hook-words in the NT, as Doeve has demonstrated, is similar to *gezerah shevah* in rabbinic material, but in my estimation it is not exactly the same. The rabbinic rule involves a formal halakic relationship between two passages of scripture where a common word or phrase shared between two passages makes both passages applicable to a given case in an argument from analogy.[113] Halakic rabbinic exegesis does not function in the free fashion seen in the NT and in the

---

[112]This thesis of contextual cognizance has often been criticized, recently at the 1993 Annual Meeting of the SBL in a panel review of Joel Marcus's work in which he posits this sort of contextually cognizant exegesis (*The Way of the Lord*). It was noted in supposed rebuttal of Marcus that rabbinic exegesis of the Mishnah and Talmud is characteristically atomistic rather than contextual. Marcus responded correctly that NT and rabbinic exegesis ought not to be thought of as identical, but as similar. Nor is the statement about rabbinic exegesis true of the broader spectrum of Jewish exegesis. As has already been noted, usually "rabbinic exegesis" refers to halakic rather than haggadic material. Haggadic material in the midrashim and targumic paraphrases often displays the contextual cognizance seen in NT and Pauline exegesis. In the same panel review skepticism was expressed about NT writers using large portions of scripture as the background of their exegesis. However, as will be examined below, vocabulary links can adequately establish the exegetical use of such larger well-defined units of scripture.

[113]"Strictly speaking this is only to be used if two given Torah statements make use of identical (and possibly unique) expressions" (Strack and Stemberger, *Introduction to the Talmud*, 21). See also the description of Hillel's rules in Bowker (*The Targums and Rabbinic Literature*, 315).

midrashim, and this includes the less rigid use of hook-words. While there are many similarities that make a familial relationship obvious, there are clear differences between Pauline and halakic rabbinic exegesis.

Many of the methods seen in the Targums are also evident in Pauline exegesis. Both engage in "rewritings" of narrative material from the Torah to clarify its meaning and significance.[114] Both engage in the explanation or exploitation of significant, difficult or odd words or phrases, or perceived inconsistencies or contradictions. Narrative rewritings in the Targums are often based upon other passages with verbal similarity, which corresponds to the use of hook-words to interpret one passage in the light of another. The Targums, like Paul, often interpret the Torah through the prophets.[115]

But the Targums are concerned primarily with retelling the biblical story for the purpose of clarification during the process of translation, not with applying it to a specific historical context or discovering its underlying meaning. Exegesis in the Targums is done only on a limited basis. Recognition of exegesis in the Targums serves primarily to establish the antiquity of methodological practices seen in later Jewish exegesis, including that of Paul.

Ellis and others have focused on the pesher-like quality of Paul's exegesis.[116] Even then Paul's exegesis can only be called "pesher-like." It is not pesher itself. It is not exclusively concerned with the identification of OT events with current referents. It displays none of the formulaic quality of progressive interpretation through an OT text in commentary fashion. Pauline exegesis often involves no "quotation" at all of the passage being interpreted. While Paul's exegesis is often pesher-like, it is also often midrash-like, so to categorize Paul's exegesis as pesher is inadequate.

Like other NT exegesis, notably that of Matthew, Paul's exegesis is perhaps most methodologically parallel with hag-

---

[114]Bowker, *The Targums and Rabbinic Literature*, 13.

[115]See the works of Bowker and Le Déaut and the earlier discussion.

[116]Ellis, *Paul's Use of the Old Testament*, 149.

gadic midrash as typified by the Midrash Rabbah. Certainly there is a concurrence of practices and principles.[117] Pauline exegesis fits Bloch's description of midrash well, though the description is somewhat broad and includes halakic exegesis as well. As with haggadic midrash, Pauline exegesis displays a liberty that halakic exegesis does not. The presence of a hook-word between two passages enabled the interpreter to employ one of the passages in the interpretation of the other. Haggadic and NT writers regularly go to the prophets and the writings for material interpreting the Torah when verbal links between passages exist.[118] They are more interested in narrative, event, and history than in legal technicality.[119]

Yet Paul's exegesis is unlike that in the Midrash Rabbah, and in Matthew, in that they regularly engage in a narrative retelling of the biblical story as a part of their exegesis, which Paul does only occasionally.[120] A further objection to referring to Pauline exegesis as midrash stems from the indeterminate definition of midrash. Pauline exegesis sometimes corresponds to types of Jewish exegesis other than that of the Midrash Rabbah.

Pauline Exegesis:

Jewish exegesis does share some common principles and methods. Paul's exegesis belongs in this broader family of Jewish exegesis. I have preferred to speak of Paul's intertextual exegesis, rather than midrash. This is done simply to avoid the implication that Pauline exegesis can be equated with the exegesis of the midrashim. However, I believe Paul's exegesis is one branch of the family of Jewish exegesis, any

---

[117]1. Its point of departure is scripture. 2. It is homiletical. 3. It is attentive to the text. 4. It adapts the text to the present. Its concern is practical, not purely theoretical. 5. The nature of the text determines whether the midrash is halakic or haggadic (Bloch, "Midrash," 31–34).

[118]Again, see Bloch and Doeve and the earlier discussion of their work.

[119]As in the "inspirational" exegesis described by Instone Brewer, *Techniques and Assumptions*, 165–71, 212–15.

[120]Paul does, however, have a primary interest in narrative as the basis for his understanding of God's relationship with and definition of the people of God.

part of which may be designated as midrash. Therefore, practices and material from each of these branches of the family of ancient Jewish exegesis will prove instructive in a reconstruction of Pauline practices and results.

From earlier studies I find the following primary characteristics and principles of Pauline exegesis, recognizing that those characteristics vary in presence and use in different places in Paul's epistles.[121]

1. The Torah is the basis for interpretation. Like all Jewish interpreters, the source-text for interpretation is scripture, and like all Jewish interpreters, for Paul the Torah is the center of scripture. Pentateuchal narrative is central to his exegetical arguments.[122] Paul is concerned with the plot, character, and especially with unusual characters, features, or actions in the narrative.

2. Paul usually applies prophetic and/or sapiential texts to the Pentateuchal narrative in application to contemporary situations. The great preponderance of these uses come from the prophetic books, most often Jeremiah, Isaiah, and Ezekiel.[123]

3. The narrative and prophetic texts are verbally linked to one another "forming a network of mutually-interpreting

---

[121]For this summary I am most indebted to Hays, Ellis, W. D. Davies, and particularly Stockhausen ("Principles of Pauline Exegesis," 144–46). This proposal of characteristics is simply a synthesis of the work of others, with some slight modifications.

[122]E.g.: Genesis 16, 17, 21 in Galatians 4; the exodus narratives of Exodus 13–14, 16–17, 32 and Numbers 9, 20 in 1 Corinthians 10; Exodus 34 in 2 Corinthians 3; the Abraham narrative of Genesis 12–22 in Romans 3–4, 9; Deuteronomy 28–32 in Romans 2, 10. In fact, the presupposition for Paul's understanding of God's relationship with Israel (and thus the church) is what James M. Scott calls the "deuteronomic view of Israel's history" ("Paul's Use of Deuteronomic Tradition," *JBL* 122 [1993] 645–65). It has as its foundation the blessings and curses of the law in Deuteronomy 27–32 and prophetic parallels. It is the presupposition for most of Second Temple Judaism. For Paul I would add as preliminary to that tradition the presupposition of the promises of the Abraham narrative in Genesis 12–22.

[123]I have learned from Carol Stockhausen that she now believes that when Paul refers to Wisdom traditions he usually opposes them.

texts which creates a new synthetic meaning at once scriptural and Pauline."[124] A few remarks on the use of verbal links, or hook-words, are in order here. One might ask whether it is really hook-words that have provided the link between narrative and prophetic material, or whether those passages might not simply be thematically related, with verbal similarities and parallels being coincidental.

In response several things might be said. First, if thematic links were primary, one would expect to find Paul sometimes reading narrative through prophetic texts where verbal links are missing. Instead, one tends to find clusters of linking vocabulary between the narrative, prophetic, and Pauline texts beyond those one would expect as coincidental for thematically related texts. Second, Paul often passes up what we might consider thematically related passages which would be appropriate to his argument, but which do not have the verbal links found in the passages to which he does refer.[125] Third, it is often specific words which happen to be the links between passages to which Paul draws particular attention. Fourth, the evidence of other Jewish and NT midrash and targumic paraphrase confirm that it is specifically vocabulary that provides the links between passages. Finally, the very processes by which passages come to mind, or "echo" as Hays would put it, are by verbal association. That these verbal associations came to be consciously drawn, and later codified as a methodological principle by the rabbis should come as no surprise or be the subject of skepticism. The frequency of this type of link in midrash, targum, and NT exegesis makes it unlikely that such verbal associations are unconsciously made, but rather that it has become an intentional, if almost automatic, practice.

---

[124]Stockhausen, "Principles of Pauline Exegesis," 144. For another detailed example of the way in which such verbal links may be identified, see Pattee, "Stumbling Stone or Cornerstone?," 108–28.

[125]The following chapter will provide evidence of this when candidate passages are examined which are judged not to serve as Pauline references.

4. Paul attempts to reconcile perceived inconsistencies or problems in scripture.[126] Difficult passages are often interpreted as scriptural expressions of the discontinuity between the old way of the law and the new way of the spirit. Through the prophetic passages Paul reads the new way of the spirit as already present in the old way of the law.

5. Paul usually has the larger context of reference passages in mind, especially narratives. For example, the Abraham and Exodus narratives, the blessings and curses of the law, and defined units of prophetic oracles—not just individual verses or phrases—underlie certain passages. Attention to the wider context of an OT passage, especially with an eye to related vocabulary, will often reveal material that has shaped Paul's conclusions.[127]

6. Paul occasionally makes pesher-like applications of scriptural referents. That is, Paul will sometimes identify the scriptural reference with the contemporary situation in a "this is that" format.

7. Paul's exegetical work is not restricted to those passages he has formally cited or obviously alluded to. In fact, it appears that the greater exegetical work and conclusions stem from passages that have not been presented as a quotation. Repeated studies have demonstrated consistent application of these methodological principles in Pauline exegesis.

A question which might be raised is, in what way can what Paul is doing properly be called exegesis?[128] All of the

---

[126]Dahl, "Contradictions in Scripture." See also, Stockhausen, "Principles of Pauline Exegesis," 144, 158–60.

[127]"Professor Dodd has shown that the primary meaning must be ascertained by reference to the whole passage. Generally quotations in the New Testament have not been selected with complete disregard of the original context. Their meaning has been already fixed by the process of working over whole passages which seem most relevant to the Church's fundamental doctrines" (Lindars, *New Testament Apologetic*, 16–17).

[128]It must be recognized at the outset that to speak of any ancient exegesis at all requires a definition broader than modern conceptions of exegesis concerned primarily with grammar, philology, historical context, etc.

other types of Jewish exegesis approach the biblical text with the primary purpose of interpreting the text for its own sake, with varying degrees of importance being attached to the application of that interpretation to a contemporary situation. NT writers on the other hand, including Paul, produce no interpretive translations of biblical books. Nor do they produce sequential explications of the minutiae of the Torah, or midrashim on Genesis, or commentaries on Habakkuk. They do, however, engage in exegesis. They attempt to understand and explain the meaning of scripture for application to a contemporary situation or to make sense of human experience, including the experience of Christ.[129]

The occasional character of Paul's writings presents modern interpreters with an application of Jewish exegesis to a Pauline epistolary context. Paul writes letters to specific groups of people, addressing their particular circumstances. This is not the case for most other examples of Jewish exegesis. The family of Jewish interpretive methods has many elements in common with those of Paul, and they are certainly close relatives. However, in light of their different rhetorical settings attempts to place Pauline exegesis in any one of those categories of Jewish exegesis are destined to frustration.

While we may not be able to categorize Paul's exegesis as specifically rabbinic, midrashic, pesher, nomological, or inspirational, it has been important that we be able to identify methodological parallels to Paul's interpretive method. The fact that elements of his methodology conform to the patterns found in several kinds of Jewish exegesis is merely supporting evidence for the fact that his references to the OT are in fact exegetical rather than merely allusive. Paul is certainly a product of Jewish exegetical training.[130] The greatest differ-

---

[129]Segal makes a strong case that it is Paul's own conversion experience which determines the course of his exegesis. It does not alter the fact that what he engages in is still exegesis. Although Segal is referring specifically to Paul's exegesis in Galatians, his statement is more broadly applicable. "So Paul's conversion experience turns scripture on its head and makes it come true in an ironic, unexpected way" (*Paul the Convert*, 123). See esp, ibid., 118–25.

[130]This may be said even without recourse to Gal 1:14, Phil 3:5,

ence between most Jewish exegesis and that of Paul is not in the exegetical method itself but the genre in which the results of his exegesis appear.

Paul attempts to understand and explain the meaning of scripture for application to a contemporary situation or to make sense of human experience. He believes scripture to originate with God. He attempts to determine what God intends, and to integrate that understanding into his experience. There is no better word to describe his work with scripture in the pursuit of meaning for his faith than "exegesis."

IDENTIFYING PAULINE REFERENCES TO SCRIPTURE

The preceding discussion has outlined the main characteristics of Pauline exegesis. What remains is to propose a method for the analysis of that intertextual exegesis. This method must be able to identify the presence and describe the use of the OT in a given passage. It also must provide analysis of Paul's own exegetical method in that passage. At the same time the method of this study must provide constraints and limits which will lead toward the identification of intended Pauline references rather than intertextual echoes or "the murmurings of our own imaginations."[131]

Methodological Criteria:

I propose several criteria for identifying those passages from the OT that may be a source of Pauline exegesis: first a group of primary criteria, then a group of confirmatory criteria.[132] An OT passage which meets the primary criteria may be considered a source in a Pauline text, but the certainty of that identification grows as confirmatory criteria are added. Primary criteria are presented first.

1. Common Vocabulary. The first evidence that an OT passage may serve as a reference for Pauline exegesis is

---

and the secondary allusion to Paul's training in Acts 22:3.

[131]Hays, *Echoes*, 23.

[132]These criteria are largely modifications dependent upon the work of Stockhausen, Hays, and Fishbane. They are also applicable to extra-canonical material.

common vocabulary between the OT passage and the Pauline text. This will be especially true of any rare or technical vocabulary. It is not necessary that the specific grammatical form from the OT text appear in the Pauline text, since Paul, like other Jewish exegetes, freely modifies forms to conform to the grammar and purpose of his own writing, and occasionally refers to the Hebrew rather than the LXX text.[133] However, the presence of specific grammatical forms from the OT heightens the likelihood that an OT reference has been made. More often, vocabulary may appear which is not so rare or technical. Where language that is widely present in the OT is found in a Pauline text, one cannot use this criterion alone to identify passages which have served as a source for exegesis. The second criterion, which is a proposed modification to previous studies, offers a means to limit the OT passages which may be considered references.

2. Vocabulary clusters. The likelihood that an OT passage serves as a Pauline exegetical reference is heightened when several significant vocabulary correspondences can be drawn between the Pauline text and an OT context. The vocabulary correspondences need not be found in one verse, or paragraph, since Paul is contextually cognizant. Where clusters of vocabulary correspondence can be identified in a thematically coherent limited passage, it is more likely that a passage is a reference. In larger narrative contexts this clustering means that the vocabulary may appear as *groups* of words in close proximity to one another scattered over that context.

In the largest contexts such as the blessing and curses of the covenant or the Abraham narrative this effect may be described as follows. One may find four significant links from a Pauline text in three sequential OT verses, and two more in one verse somewhat later. There then may be one or two more similar groups of words clustered within the next chapter. If that entire OT section is a logical or thematic unit, this would

---

[133]How well Paul could read Hebrew is disputed, but he is able to exploit translational ambiguities, as will be seen.

be strong evidence that Paul has referred to this context in his exegesis. He may not make use of the entire context, but may focus on those portions nearest to the vocabulary clusters. The more clustered correspondences in a unit, and the greater the relative significance of the vocabulary represented, the greater the likelihood that Paul has referred to that passage. In prophetic references the contexts are more limited.

This corresponds in some degree to Hays's test of Volume of an echo, but is more precise. It corresponds more closely to the density of occurrence which Fishbane describes as "the dense occurrence in one text of terms, often thoroughly reorganized and transposed, found elsewhere in a natural, uncomplicated form."[134] Where Paul overtly cites from an OT context in which these vocabulary correspondences are also found, even if the citation is not in the immediate Pauline context in which the correspondences are perceived, the evidence of exegesis is even stronger. It might also be noted that identifiable exegesis is often lacking from passages which Paul quotes. Quoted texts often provide none of these criteria beyond the obvious vocabulary correspondence of the particular verse. Their rhetorical function, whether as proof-text, doxology, summation, or simply the appropriation of an apt phrase, is different from that of exegetical references.

3. Links with other Texts. The presence of vocabulary links with other OT passages which also meet the criteria of exegetical use, especially if those links are multiple or clustered, is good evidence of Paul's exegetical reference to an OT passage. Since it is characteristic of Pauline exegesis to link texts together by the use of hook-words in the formation of a complex of mutually interpreting texts,[135] the discovery of such links supports the initial evidence of vocabulary correspondence that an OT passage serves as an exegetical refer-

---

[134]Fishbane, *Biblical Interpretation*, 291. See also O'Day's use of this criterion ("Jeremiah 9:22–23 and 1 Corinthians 1:26–31, 267) and Beker's support ("Echoes and Intertextuality," 64).

[135]Stockhausen, "Principles of Pauline Exegesis," 144.

ence. Of course, such links may be questioned should the supposedly linked texts show no evidence of contributing to Paul's thought. This caveat introduces the final primary criterion.

4. Explication. An OT text which meets the preceding criteria will be judged more likely to have served as an exegetical reference if it helps to explain Paul's argument or the presuppositions underlying his argument. This criterion cannot stand independently. Likewise, it is the necessary corollary to the preceding criteria. This corresponds to Hays's tests of Thematic Coherence and Satisfaction, but goes farther in attempting to determine not only if an OT passage "fits" into Paul's line of argument, but if it has helped shape Paul's argument.[136]

Obviously even in these initial criteria some are primary (1 and 2) and others secondary (3 and 4). But they all serve as the fundamental criteria for the identification of OT passages serving as sources for Pauline exegesis. These initial criteria may be supported by what I refer to as confirmatory criteria.

5. Recurrence. I borrow this test from Hays. Whether by allusion or citation, often there is evidence that Paul has referred to the same passage more than once, not necessarily in the same epistle. This may be true of larger OT contexts (e.g., again, Deuteronomy 28–32, Isaiah 50–54, and the Abraham narrative), as well as of specific verses. "Where such evidence exists that Paul considered a passage of particular importance, proposed echoes from the same context should be given additional credence."[137] This is true for references as well as echoes. Where a passage is evident in other epistles, the importance of that passage in Pauline thought is doubly confirmed.

6. Common Themes. Where Paul picks up or treats the same themes as those found in a perceived OT reference, this will serve as confirmation. This differs from the criteria of vocabulary and clusters, in that vocabulary from an OT context

---

[136]Hays, *Echoes*, 30, 31.
[137]Ibid., 30.

may confirm exegetical reference to a passage without appropriation of some of the major themes from that passage, though this is uncommon. On the other hand, the presence of themes from an OT passage in a Pauline text without supporting vocabulary correspondence is not deemed sufficient evidence to indicate exegetical reference to that passage.

7. Common Linear Development. Pauline reference to an OT passage is confirmed when the Pauline text parallels the linear development of the OT text: that is, when vocabulary correspondences and/or themes develop in the Pauline text in the order in which they appear in the OT text. While this criterion would offer supporting evidence, it is often lacking. Its absence should not be thought of as evidence against a candidate passage.

These criteria offer a methodology for the identification of OT passages which have been the subject of Pauline intertextual exegesis. They provide reasonable constraints to limit the passages identified to those most likely to have actually been in use by Paul.

Applying the Methodology:

Another word might be said about constraints. It is important to limit the range of a search for clusters of vocabulary to logical and thematic units, though at times the discovery of clusters may lead one on further into an OT context. As a general guideline, except for the primary narrative material of the Abraham story and portions of Deuteronomy, Paul most often seems to limit the size of the passages to which he refers to several verses. Even in the case of the narrative material, where the immediate context from which Paul draws may comprise a chapter or two, with multiple references from one narrative, the exegetical impact of each individual reference is usually restricted to a more limited context, again of several verses. The broader the range of text in which clusters of vocabulary are found, and the greater the distance between them, the less certain are the conclusions that may be drawn about Paul's reference to intervening material. Still, should one find one or two clusters of vocabulary per chapter in an OT book for a sequence of three chapters, when that vocabulary is not evident elsewhere in this density, nor common in the rest of the book, it is likely that the entire sequence serves as a Pauline reference if sufficient other criteria are met.

Hays mentions three other tests which I do not consider important to this study. The test of Availability is obviously not in question when we are dealing with OT references, though translational, targumic, or rabbinic connections might raise the question. The test of Historical Plausibility does have some bearing. But at times interpreters' conceptions about what is historically plausible are dependent upon their own incomplete understanding of Paul's situation and thought. The test of History of Interpretation, or the question of whether others have perceived the supposed connections, is often excluded, since this study attempts to show that OT connections exist in Paul which may have been overlooked. Previous identification of references would be confirmatory evidence when it does exist.

Having identified OT passages to which Paul refers, the next task will be to examine the surrounding context of those OT passages to determine if they contain material or themes which have informed Paul's argument. The primary source text will the LXX, since Paul regularly draws his OT references from that translation, but attention to the Hebrew text will be given when it is seen to have an impact upon Pauline exegesis and his alteration or modification of his references.

The study of the identified OT references and their contexts will then be specifically applied to the Pauline passage under investigation. The task is to work through the Pauline text itself in dialogue with the literature on the passage to determine how, where, and by what process those OT texts have informed his conclusions. This approach is historical-critical in nature. Attention will be given to Paul's intent in Romans and the effect of his references in the course of his argument. Considerations of the context of Romans, its purposes, audience, and occasion will both inform and be informed by the analysis of references in Rom 2:17-29. Where they are relevant to the analysis, grammatical and rhetorical issues will be addressed.

In attempting to identify OT sources of Pauline material there will be similarities to source criticism. The analysis of Paul's editing and reshaping of the biblical material as it is woven into his own argument has elements in common with redaction criticism. However, those disciplines are not identical with the task undertaken here. In what may better be called "reference integration criticism" Paul's OT references in Rom 2:17–29 will be examined as they integrate Paul's theological conclusions from scripture into the argument and as they pertain to the historical and epistolary context of Romans. It is in this step that one may form hypotheses about the exegetical steps Paul has taken and about the impact of that exegesis on the development of his theology and argumentation.

2

Identification of Intertextual References in Rom 2:17–29

The previous chapter defined a method by which intertextual references will be analyzed. The initial step in that
method is to identify those texts which meet the criteria and
are determined to be intertextual references. A concurrent
task is to conduct an analysis of the context of those references in order to ascertain themes which may inform Paul's
argument. A proposal for the manner in which those references and themes are integrated into Rom 2:17–29 will be
provided in the following chapter. First, however, some discussion is appropriate regarding the limitation of the passage
to be examined to Rom 2:17–29.

DELIMITING THE PASSAGE

For the purposes of commentary, Rom 2:17–29 is usually recognized as a well-defined unit.[1] It is part of a pro-

---

[1]See, e.g., Dunn, *Romans 1–8*, 108–9; Barrett, *Epistle to the Romans*, 51–52; Murray, *Epistle to the Romans*, 80–81; Rudolf Pesch,
Römerbrief (Die Neue Echter Bibel, Kommentar zum Neuen Testament
mit der Einheitsübersetzung 6; Würzburg: Echter, 1983) 34–35.

Lietzmann does not treat vv. 17–29 as a separate unit, since there
are few breaks in the entire commentary, but the passage has a different page heading (*An die Römer*, 43). Fitzmyer divides the passage into
vv. 17–24 and vv. 25–29 (*Romans*, 314–15, 319–20).

John Paul Heil treats 2:17–3:8 as a single unit (*Romans–Paul's
Letter of Hope* [AnBib 112; Rome: Pontifical Biblical Institute, 1987] 21).

gressing logical argument: an extension of points made and developed in 1:18–32 and 2:1–16.[2] While 2:1–16 and 2:17–29 are closely connected, in the second half of the chapter Paul has moved on to another point beyond that made in the preceding passage.[3] It is at 2:17 that the specific indictment of Paul's Jewish interlocutor begins. The break between chaps. 2 and 3 is more pronounced. Chap. 3 takes up the interlocutor's supposed objections to Paul's conclusions in chap. 2. The argument has taken a definite turn, but the flow of the argument remains logically progressive.

From an intertextual standpoint the definition of 2:17–29 as an individual unit is not as easily made. Rom 2:17–29 is not unique in this regard. It is true for almost any passage in Romans, since much of Romans is bound together by a web of interconnected intertextual references. For instance, possible references to Deuteronomy 28–30 are in evidence in 2:1–16, 2:17–29, and chap. 10, while the Abraham narrative taken up in chap. 4 recurs in chap. 9. The presence of the same intertextual references throughout two connected passages opens the question of whether or not they may be regarded as independent units. If the two passages are found to be intertextually interdependent to a significant extent, they would have to be analyzed together as a unit. There are possible references which might seem to bind 2:1–16 to 2:17–29, notably Deut 10:16–17 and Deut 28:53–29:29.

The preliminary vocabulary research which forms the basis for the following analysis reveals that Deut 28:53–29:29 is a narrative reference context upon which the two halves of

---

While 3:1–8 does continue the discussion of Jewish advantage, Heil ignores the significant shift in the argument.

[2]1:18–32 describes the judgment of God upon wicked humanity. 2:1–16 extends that judgment to those who would judge those in the first group. 2:17–29 specifies the address to Jews, and provides reasoning. See, e.g., Dunn, *Romans 1–8*, 76–77.

[3]Later discussion on the place of 2:17–29 in the context of the entire epistle will point out some of the interesting structural and thematic parallels between vv. 1–16 and vv. 17–29.

Romans 2 are both developmentally dependent.[4] This reveals a common narrative basis for Paul's larger argument throughout the chapter, indicating that the entire chapter may be conceived of as a single unit to some extent. Deut 10:16–17, on the other hand, does not appear to meet the criteria as a reference in both halves of the chapter, nor does any other OT passage.

Aside from the larger narrative of Deuteronomy 28–29, Rom 2:17–29 appears also dependent upon a distinct group of linked OT references separate from 2:1–16.[5] 2:17–29 has its own complex of references which are joined by hook-word associations mutually interpreted by Paul, and which do not appear in 2:1–16.

There is the one broad reference context the two halves of the chapter have in common (Deut 28:53–29:29), and for that reason they could be intertextually analyzed together as a unit. However, that appears to be the only referent they share. It functions more as a referential bridge than as part of a group of texts binding the chapter together. For this reason and because of the rhetorical and logical divisions recognized

---

[4]Vocabulary correspondences with Rom 2:1–16 include: θλῖψις and στενοχωρία ("trouble and distress," Rom 2:9) in Deut 28:53, 55, 57; forms of ὀργή ("anger") and θυμός ("wrath") and their combination (Rom 2:5, 8) in Deut 29:20, 24, 28; τὰ κρυπτά ("the hidden/secret things," Rom 2:16) in Deut 29:29; and a parallel to τὰ τοῦ νόμου ποιῶσιν ("doing the things of the law," Rom 2:14) in Deut 29:29: ποιεῖν πάντα τὰ ῥήματα τοῦ νόμου τούτου ("to do all the words of this law"). A common pair in the OT is θλῖψις καὶ στενοχωρία ("trouble and distress"), which Paul picks up fairly often. See n. 7 below for other common words. See also Victor Paul Furnish, *II Corinthians* (AB 32A, New York: Doubleday, 1984) 343.

Deuteronomy 27–30, at least, provide quite a broad foundation for many Pauline passages. James Scott finds several supposed correspondences in Romans 2 ("For as Many," 194, 213–14). He makes the case, along with Hays (*Echoes*, 163–64), for Paul's heavy dependence upon this section of Deuteronomy, though they differ upon the limits of what Paul reads as a unit.

[5]This conclusion is based on a preliminary analysis of the chapter as a whole.

by most commentators, Rom 2:17–29 will be treated as an individual unit.

NARROWING THE FIELD

The process of identifying possible intertextual references, beginning with common vocabulary, initially provides an abundance of possibilities from the OT. The application of the criteria previously described immediately eliminates most of them as obviously coincidental correspondences. A more careful examination is required to determine which passages provide the best evidence for being references in Rom 2:17–29, while setting aside others which, while remaining possibilities, must be judged to be too uncertain for the purposes of this proposal. Only those passages which provide the strongest evidence for being Pauline references will be used in the intertextual analysis of the following chapter.[6]

There are, of course, a great number of OT passages which share some minimal common vocabulary with Rom 2:17–29. In most cases shared vocabulary includes merely very common words in isolation, with no vocabulary clusters, links with other texts, or common themes.[7] These passages are quickly eliminated from consideration. In a few instances the shared vocabulary is comprised of uncommon or specialized words, but again there are no other words to support those passages as references by forming vocabulary clusters, or no evidence of thematic significance or explication.[8] Those

---

[6]In order to clarify what criteria are being considered at a given point, they will be placed in italics when necessary.

[7]For instance, θέλημα ("will"), δοκιμάζω ("test"), δόξαν καὶ τιμήν ("glory and honor"), ἡμέρα ὀργῆς ("day of wrath"), and of course νόμος ("law") are very common and do not indicate referential use of a passage without further confirmation. See n. 4 above concerning θλῖψις καὶ στενοχωρία ("trouble and distress"). A listing of the vocabulary correspondences based on such common words would make up a small concordance of its own.

[8]The criterion of explication will receive only cursory attention in this chapter. It is in the next chapter, which will demonstrate the way in which these references inform Paul's argument, that explication will be examined in more detail.

passages for which the evidence is stronger, but not sufficient for identification as Pauline references, will be addressed briefly in order to demonstrate the selection process.

THE PSALMS

There are several passages from the Psalms which draw attention as possible references.

Psalm 19:

Ps 19:7–11 (LXX 18:7–11) has several possible *vocabulary links* with Romans 2, but perhaps its most striking correspondence is with Rom 2:2 rather than 2:17–29. The parallel is strong between "the judgments of the Lord are true" (τὰ κρίματα Κυρίου ἀληθινά) in Ps 19:9 and "the judgment of God is according to the truth" (τὸ κρίμα τοῦ θεοῦ ἐστιν κατὰ ἀλήθειαν) in Rom 2:2. The concept of the truth of the law or of God's word is not uncommon in the OT.[9] In the psalm the goodness of the law is being extolled, along with a promise of reward for keeping the law. The *theme* of reward for obedience recurs in Romans 2, but with more specific language. In Rom 2:2 the statements are more judgmental against those who do wrong than the tone of praise for the law in the psalm.

The idea of "instructing infants/the simple" is paralleled between Ps 19:7 σοφίζουσα νήπια and Rom 2:20 διδάσκαλον νηπίων, though the *vocabulary* is not identical. In the psalm it is "the testimony of the Lord" doing the instructing, while in Romans Paul uses this language of his interlocutor's supposed self-image. Ps 19:8 speaks of the rightness of "the precepts" or "requirements" of the Lord (τὰ δικαιώματα), and v. 11 speaks of the reward for the servant who keeps them (φυλάσσει/ἐν τῷ φυλάσσειν). Rom 2:26 says the uncircumcised person who keeps the precepts of the law (τὰ δικαιώματα τοῦ νόμου φυλάσσῃ) will be regarded as circumcised. Also, of course, the very common νόμος appears in the psalm extolling the law, as does καρδία, but with no other discernible tie to Rom 2:17–29.

---

[9]E.g., Neh 9:13; Ps 119:142, 151, 160.

While there is some support for a referential use of this psalm by Paul because of the *cluster of vocabulary*, and especially because of the possible echo of the image of "instructing infants" (if Paul has a Hebrew text in mind), the supposed links are common enough ideas to require a high degree of *explication and thematic parallel* in order for Ps 19:7–11 to be identified as a Pauline reference in Rom 2:29. There may be a stronger case for the presence of this psalm in Rom 2:1–16. Since *explication and thematic parallels* are not apparent, Ps 19:7–11 does not satisfy the criteria for identification as a Pauline reference in Rom 2:17–29.[10]

Psalm 51:

Psalm 51 (LXX 50) is a difficult passage about which to make a determination because it meets more of the criteria for being a Pauline reference than the passage already discussed. It has important, if somewhat common, *clustered vocabulary*. Some of these same words provide *links* with Deuteronomy 29 and Ezekiel 36, which will be important passages later in this study.[11] Paul quotes Ps 51:4 in Rom 3:4 fulfilling *the criteria of recurrence*, and there appear to be at least some *themes* common to Pauline thought.

The psalm is introduced as pertaining to David's repentance upon being confronted by the prophet Nathan concerning his adultery with Bathsheba. The *vocabulary links* with Rom 2:17–29 bear little relation to the theme of the Psalm. The psalmist in v. 3 says "I know my iniquity" (γινώσκω), while the Jew of Rom 2:18 "knows" the will (γινώσκεις). The

---

[10]The process of accepting and rejecting possible references has not always proceeded in the form in which those decisions are presented here. Instead, all of the candidate references selected on the basis of vocabulary correspondence were subjected to the tests for meeting other criteria during the analysis of Rom 2:17–29 itself. Some candidate passages, such as Psalm 19 and Hosea 4, were not eliminated until late in the process as it became clear that other passages provided stronger explication and thematic parallels to Rom 2:17–29. To present the process in writing as it occurred in practice would be unnecessarily confusing and cumbersome, carrying into the analysis of Rom 2:17–29 in the following chapter candidate references which were finally rejected.

[11]E.g.. τὰ κρύφια, καρδία, πνεῦμα.

"hidden things" (τὰ κρύφια) of God's wisdom are made known in Ps 51:6, while it is the one who is a Jew "inwardly" (ἐν τῷ κρυπτῷ) who is the true Jew in Rom 2:29. The psalmist "will teach" (διδάξω) transgressors (v. 13), while the Jew of Rom 2:20, 21 is a "teacher of infants" (διδάσκαλον νηπίων) and "teaches another" (διδάσκων ἕτερον). The psalmist in v. 10 requests a "clean heart" (καρδίαν καθαράν) and a "right spirit" (πνεῦμα εὐθές), while v. 18 speaks of a broken spirit and broken and humbled heart. All of these concepts echo in Ezekiel 36, which informs the use of καρδία and πνεῦμα in Rom 2:29.

Themes from Psalm 51 which might be said to be found in Paul's thought, though not necessarily in Romans 2, include the humility and self-effacement evident in this penitential psalm. Paul's descriptions of his own pre-Christian life and reliance on grace could be construed as a thematic parallel. But this has nothing to do specifically with Rom 2:17–29. The recognition of guilt in the Psalm is, however, the direct antithesis of the attitude of Paul's interlocutor, whom Paul describes as assuming innocence. But nothing in Romans 2 indicates that an antithetical comparison is to be drawn between the interlocutor and the psalmist.

Though the *vocabulary correspondence* and *links with other OT texts* are somewhat significant on the surface, the *links directly to Rom 2:17–29* are not as strong as other references in that they do not inform the argument. It is certainly possible that something of the prayer for a clean heart and a right spirit might "echo" through Ezekiel 36 to Paul's text, and one could speculate that a glimmer of the psalm is alive in Paul's mind as he writes this passage since he will quote from it shortly. But such "echoes" do not imply the referential exegetical use of a passage by Paul with which this study is concerned.

Psalm 51 offers no *explication* of its own. It is only through Ezekiel 36 that Psalm 51 might be thought to help explain Paul's argument. Verbal links between OT texts are only criteria pointing toward identification of Pauline references when each of the OT texts meet the criteria of explication independently, as well as in combination. Nothing in Psalm 51 stands out as a basis for Paul's discussion. It has probably not served as an exegetical reference in Rom 2:17–29.

THE PROPHETS

A special difficulty arises when one begins to examine the OT prophets for possible Pauline references. The themes of judgment and restoration stemming from the blessings and curses of the covenant in Deuteronomy 27–30 will be seen to be important in Rom 2:17–29. However, the themes of judgment and restoration, with accompanying generic vocabulary, are common in most prophetic texts. While it may be true that the entire corpus of judgment and restoration oracles forms a background for Pauline thought on God's relationship to the Jews, the aim of this study is to identify only those passages which give evidence of being specific referents in Rom 2:17–29. The methodology for discriminating between prophetic passages to which Romans 2 is merely allusive and those to which Paul refers exegetically is especially important in these texts.

Isaiah 42:

A passage often noted in connection with Rom 2:19 is Isa 42:6b–7.[12] It certainly has *vocabulary* which "echoes" in Romans 2. There God says his servant Israel will be given as "a light to the nations, to open the eyes that are blind, to bring out the prisoners from the dungeon, from the prison those who sit in darkness" (εἰς φῶς ἐθνῶν ἀνοῖξαι ὀφθαλμοὺς τυφλῶν, ἐξαγαγεῖν ἐκ δεσμῶν δεδεμένους καὶ ἐξ οἴκου φυλακῆς καθημένους ἐν σκότει).[13] Similar language occurs at v. 16: "I will lead the blind by a road they did not know,…I will

---

[12]Lietzmann not only recognizes a parallel but maintains that Rom 2:19 is dependent upon Isa 42:6–7 (*An die Römer*, 43). Stowers (*Rereading*, 152) says Romans "echoes" Isaiah. Also mentioning a possible connection are Fitzmyer (*Romans*, 317), Barrett (*Epistle to the Romans*, 53), Cranfield (*The Epistle to the Romans*, 1.166), and many others.

[13]The LXX version of Isaiah 42, unlike the Hebrew text, specifies "Jacob" as the servant of the Lord, and "Israel" as the chosen one.

turn the darkness into light for them"(καὶ ἄξω τυφλοὺς ἐν ὁδῷ, ἧ οὐκ ἔγνωσαν... ποιήσω αὐτοῖς τὸ σκότος εἰς φῶς). The blind, or the idea of being blind, show up again in vv. 18, 19.

Though the metaphors are slightly different, the import is the same and the *vocabulary is in common* with Rom 2:19. Paul characterizes the self-description of his interlocutor as "a guide to the blind, a light to those in darkness" (ὁδηγὸν εἶναι τυφλῶν, φῶς τῶν ἐν σκότει). This *cluster of vocabulary* of "blind...darkness...light" is stronger because the only occurrence in the OT of the combination "blind...darkness...light" is Isaiah 42. The only places where "blind" and "darkness" are found together is Deuteronomy 28 (part of the blessings and curses which will be seen to be a Pauline reference), Isa 29:18, and in Isaiah 42. There are a few other vocabulary links. The common ἔθνη occurs at Isa 42:4, 6, and πνεῦμα occurs at vv. 1, 5.

There are some *links with other texts* which will prove to be referent passages; Jeremiah 7, 9 and Ezekiel 36. A concern for the name of God which will be noted in the passages from Jeremiah and Ezekiel is found in Isa 42:8, again with vocabulary in common with Rom 2:24. God makes the declaration, "I am the Lord God, that is my name" (ἐγὼ κύριος ὁ θεός, τοῦτό μού ἐστιν τὸ ὄνομα). Both Isaiah 42 and Ezekiel 36 speak of the new things God will do. Isa 42:9 says, "and new things I now declare" (καὶ καινὰ ἃ ἐγὼ ἀναγγέλω). Ezek 36:26 promises a new heart and spirit (καρδίαν καινὴν καὶ πνεῦμα καινόν).

There are *themes* which resonate in Romans 2 as well. Isa 42:2 says Israel will bring justice "to the nations" (τοῖς ἔθνεσιν). The antithesis is stark with the quotation of Isa 52:5 quoted in Rom 2:24. There, in Paul's modification of the text, God's name is blasphemed "among the nations" (ἐν τοῖς ἔθνεσιν) because of Israel.

In harmony with a *theme* being developed in Romans, and consistent with the belief of Paul's interlocutor about the Jews, Isa 42:4 states that the nations (ἔθνη) will also find hope in Israel. The LXX texts offer variants. The majority text reads καὶ ἐπὶ τῷ νόμῳ αὐτοῦ ἔθνη ἐλπιοῦσιν, while the

Greek codices read καὶ ἐπὶ τῷ ὀνόματι αὐτοῦ ἔθνη ἐλπιοῦσιν.[14] Both LXX variants state that the nations or Gentiles
will find hope in Israel, a point consistent with Paul's mission
to the Gentiles.[15] It also, however, is characteristic of Jewish
self-understanding as a "light to those in darkness," a point
with which Paul's interlocutor would concur.

Another *theme in common* with Romans 2 comes from
the irony of Isa 42:19–25, in parallel with Paul's ironic, or
even sarcastic characterization of his Jewish interlocutor. In
these verses, after extolling the virtues of God's servant Israel, the Lord says, "Who is blind but my servant, or deaf like
my messenger whom I send? Who is blind like my dedicated
one, or blind like the servant of the Lord?" This makes the
same point Paul is making in Rom 2:17–29. Though his Jewish interlocutor claims to be a guide to the blind, it is his interlocutor who is in fact blind, not obeying the Lord's law
(οὐδὲ ἀκούειν τοῦ νόμου αὐτου, Isa 42:24). The teacher does
not teach him or herself, and the guide does not see.

While *vocabulary and themes* from Isaiah 42 "echo" in
Romans 2, meeting some of the criteria for identification as a
referent, the question remains as to whether Isaiah 42 functions as an exegetical referent in Romans 2. There are reasons to question that identification. First, there is no
recurrence of Isaiah 42 obvious in Paul. Finally, and more
conclusively, the criterion of *explication* is important. Not only
must themes appearing in an OT passage appear in Romans
2, where one might conclude that Paul appropriated an idea,
but the OT passage must help explain the exegetical path
Paul has traveled to reach his conclusions.

As will be demonstrated, Jeremiah 7, 9 and Ezekiel 36
do give strong evidence of being used by Paul exegetically to

---

[14]Joseph Ziegler, ed., *Isaiah*, vol. 14 of *Septuaginta: Vetus Testamentum Graecum* (Göttingen: Vandenhoeck & Ruprecht) 277. This is
not immediately obvious in the Hebrew text, where the phrase may be
variously translated as "and the coastlands wait for his teaching"
(NRSV, NEB) or "in his law the islands put their hope" (NIV).

[15]Either of the LXX variants would provide another vocabulary
link with ὄνομα or νόμος.

interpret Deuteronomy 28–30, which itself is used to interpret the Abraham narrative of Genesis 17. This is entirely in accord with what one would expect in contemporary Jewish exegesis. This type of exegesis interprets texts by one another, usually narrative texts through the prophets. Unlike Paul's use of Jeremiah and Ezekiel to interpret Deuteronomy, Isaiah 42 gives no evidence of being used exegetically to interpret another text, nor does it give evidence of being interpreted itself. It makes a few points in common with Paul, and those points resonate in Romans 2, but Isaiah 42 does not appear to provide *explication* as an exegetical reference such as those with which this study is concerned. That is not to exclude the possibility that any "echo" of Isaiah 42 in Romans 2 might be intentional. Paul may consciously allude to or echo a passage without having employed it as an exegetical reference.

Ezekiel 11:

Ezek 11:18–21 is in the context of a judgment pronouncement upon Jerusalem. In a note of restoration, those people who are already in exile will return to inhabit the land and undergo spiritual renewal with attentiveness to the law. The passage shares some *vocabulary* with Rom 2:17–29.[16] More importantly, the passage refers to Israel receiving a "new spirit" and another heart, replacing the "heart of stone" with a "heart of flesh" (v. 19). This language possibly informs Paul's rhetoric in Rom 2:29.[17] But this vocabulary more likely stems from Ezekiel 36, which gives more evidence of referential use by Paul, and includes the same phrases. Like many prophetic passages, Ezekiel 11 speaks of the *themes* of judg-

---

[16]βδέλυγμα "abomination," Ezek 11:18, 21/βδελύσσομαι "abhor," Rom 2:22.

σάρξ "flesh," Ezek 11:19/Rom 2:28.

πνεῦμα "spirit," Ezek 11:20/Rom 2:29.

καρδία "heart," Ezek 11:19, 21/Rom 2:29.

τὰ δικαιώματά μου φυλάσσωνται "keeping my requirements," Ezek 11:20/ τὰ δικαιώματα τοῦ νόμου φυλάσσῃ " if [those who are uncircumcised] keep the requirements of the law," Rom 2:26.

[17]Pesch (*Römerbrief*, 36) notes Ezekiel 11 at this point, but specifies "v. 9 ff." There does not seem to be any possible connection before v. 18.

ment and restoration, as do other passages which will be
identified as references, but beyond that offers little by way of
explication to Rom 2:17–29.[18] The *vocabulary links and common themes* which do exist are duplicated and expanded in
Ezekiel 36. If Ezekiel 11 has served as a Pauline reference, its
influence has been subsumed by the use of Ezekiel 36.

Hosea 4:

A similar case is Hos 4:1–2, wherein sins and charges
against Israel are recounted immediately following the promise of the nation's repentance "in the last days" (3:5). There is
some *vocabulary correspondence* between Rom 2:17–29 and
Hosea 4:2. Along with cursing, lying, and murder, Israel is
charged with theft (κλοπή) and adultery (μοιχεία). Rom
2:21–22 as much as accuses the interlocutor of stealing
(κλέπτειν) and committing adultery (μοιχεύειν) along with
temple robbery. In antithesis with the interlocutor of Rom
2:18–20 of whom it is said "you know the will" (γινώσκεις τὸ
θέλημα), "having the embodiment of knowledge and truth in
the Law" (ἔχοντα τὴν μόρφωσιν τῆς γνώσεως καὶ τῆς
ἀληθείας ἐν τῷ νόμῳ), Hos 4:1 says that in Israel "there is no
truth...nor knowledge of God" (οὐκ ἔστιν ἀλήθεια...οὐδὲ
ἐπίγνωσις θεοῦ).[19] There is, then, some vocabulary which
forms at least a minimal cluster.

As to *the criterion of common themes*, the antithesis
mentioned above is not sustained, but the passages actually
become parallel. Paul will charge that "the Jew" he addresses
is guilty, as Hosea charges Israel's priesthood. If Paul assumes that the covenant regulations have been broken—resulting in judgment upon Israel which continues into
his own day, as will be discussed—then the recitation of Is-

---

[18]Schweizer mentions Ezek 11:19 as a passage which joins the
concept of a new heart to eschatological spiritual restoration, along with
Ezek 39:29 and Joel 3:1 ("'Der Jude im Verborgenen,'" 119). These concepts are even more closely connected in Ezekiel 36.

[19]It may be thought that this is not an antithesis, because Paul's
statements are ironic. However, Paul does believe the Jews "know the
will" and "have the embodiment of the law" without irony. At the same
time, the passages are parallel in the sense that Paul will shortly point
out Jewish disobedience, as does Hosea.

rael's unfaithfulness in Hosea 4 could provide some degree of *explication* for Paul's conclusion on that point.

The *criterion of recurrence* is of some importance here as well, since Hos 2:23 is quoted in Rom 9:25, and is only six verses from Hos 4:1. However, the two passages, while spatially proximate, are thematically disparate. The import of Paul's contextual cognizance begins to weaken when the contextual material differs from the referent passage itself. It does not, of course, rule out the possibility that the context could have been in mind.

Like Ezekiel 11, however, there are reasons not to consider Hos 4:1–2 a reference. The statement of the absence of truth and knowledge of God in Israel does have some thematic and verbal parallel with Romans 2, but the *verbal parallels* are indefinite. Most importantly, to find stealing and adultery together in a list of Israel's sins is not uncommon. The presence of the entire Pauline triad of charges (stealing, committing adultery, and robbery in the temple) in Jeremiah 7 points to that text as a more likely reference for those words in Rom 2:21–22.[20] Jeremiah 7 also accounts for other vocabulary and themes better than does Hosea 4.

Even without Jeremiah 7, the case for Hos 4:1–2 would remain tentative. As it is, it is unlikely that this passage is a reference source for Rom 2:17–29. The passage does illustrate the need to examine not just the presence but the strength of the methodological criteria for identifying references in each individual case.

Daniel 9:

One passage which is not presented here as a possible referent for Rom 2:17–29 but which deserves some special comment is Daniel 9. James Scott makes the case that Daniel 9 shows strong links to Deuteronomy 27–32, which gives evidence of being a Pauline referent in Rom 2:17–29.[21] Scott finds numerous vocabulary links between Daniel 9 and Deuteronomy, and demonstrates their importance in Paul's ar-

---

[20]This triad will be discussed further when Jeremiah 7 is examined.

[21]"For as Many," 198–99.

gument in Galatians.[22] But the evidence is lacking for significant links of Daniel 9 with Rom 2:17–29.

However, Scott's analysis of Daniel 9 does provide support for an important point of this study: that there is a strand of Jewish tradition wherein the curses of Deuteronomy 27–32 are understood as enduring. Scott sees Daniel 9 as evidence of a theme, before Paul and along with other Jewish literature, that Israel remained under the curse for an extended period (490 years in Daniel).[23] These texts "envision a prolonged disruption in the covenantal relationship...before the inauguration of the restoration."[24] While Scott believes the basis of this tradition to be found in Daniel 9, and Rom 2:17–29 gives no evidence of dependence upon Daniel 9, such a tradition is consistent with the Pauline conclusion that because of disobedience the covenant relationship of the Jews no longer guarantees covenantal blessing.[25]

These are only a few of the examples of passages considered and rejected as Pauline OT references in Rom 2:17–29. The examples could of course be multiplied if minor vocabulary correspondences or common themes with Romans 2 were given undue weight without a strong combination of methodological criteria.[26] These examples demonstrate how the

---

[22]James Scott cites keywords "transgressed," "turned aside," "refusing to obey," "oath," "poured out," "sinned," "wrath," "temple," "people" as those which link Daniel 9 and Deuteronomy 27–32.

[23]Ibid., 201. "There is a widespread penitential prayer tradition based on Daniel 9 which recognizes that the curse of exile warned about in Deuteronomy 27–32 for violating the covenant has indeed come upon Israel as of 587 BCE, and that the condition of exile would persist until God, in accordance with his own mercy and timetable, would listen to Israel's confession of sin and bring in the restoration as Deuteronomy 27–32 had promised."

[24]Ibid., 205–6.

[25]The question of whether or not this is in fact Paul's conclusion is yet to be addressed. Stowers does not believe Paul is making any such statement about the covenantal relationship of the Jews to God, but that Paul attacks only a hypothetical competitor (*Rereading*, 128–29).

[26]Initial vocabulary analysis provided over fifty candidate passages to be considered. Most were immediately eliminated from consideration.

evidence has been weighed in identifying Pauline references. Some of the examples used could indeed be references, but the evidence available for investigation is insufficient to make that determination with the degree of certainty desired in this study. The next task is to present those passages for which the evidence is strong enough to support the thesis of their referential use in Rom 2:17–29.

REFERENCES IDENTIFIED

Those OT passages which do give evidence of being Pauline references in Rom 2:17–29 center in prophetic parallels to the blessings and curses of the law in Deuteronomy 28–30, which itself is a reaffirmation of the Abrahamic covenant of Genesis 17.[27] These prophetic passages take up the theme of judgment for Israel's breaking of the covenant and the ensuing restoration of Israel. Of course, judgment and restoration are themes in most prophetic texts, as has already been mentioned, and this fact must be taken into account when attempting to determine if Paul is coincidentally echoing language, merely alluding to a text, or if he is utilizing a passage exegetically.

Only when other criteria for identifying Pauline references are met can a passage containing the *vocabulary and themes* of judgment and restoration be understood as informing Paul's argument in Rom 2:17–29. Not only *vocabulary correspondence*, but *links with other texts* and *the criterion of explication* will be of particular importance. The task here is

---

[27]The Deuteronomy narrative actually extends from Deuteronomy 27 to 32, but it is chaps. 28–30 which appear to parallel the prophetic passages to which Paul refers, and it is a smaller section of chaps. 29–30 to which Paul refers directly.

Deuteronomy also does more than simply reaffirm the Abrahamic covenant. It introduces new elements such as the curses themselves, and extensions of the blessings. Paul's use of the plural "covenants" at 9:4 illustrates his cognizance of a distinction. On multiple covenants, both conditional and unconditional, see Sanders, *Paul and Palestinian Judaism*, 94–95. Although there is strong support for a singular variant at Rom 9:4, the plural is the more difficult reading and is to be preferred (Bruce M. Metzger, *TCGNT*, 519).

simply to identify that exegetically interconnected group of texts which meets the criteria for being Pauline intertextual references. An examination of the way those passages are interpreted together to inform the argument of Rom 2:17–29 will be taken up in detail in the analysis of the next chapter.

THE PROPHETS

The most obvious instances of common vocabulary with Rom 2:17–29 are in Jeremiah 7 and 9. These texts include not just shared vocabulary but a clustering of vocabulary correspondences. Jer 7:2–11 shares common vocabulary with Rom 2:19–22. Jer 9:23–26 does so with Rom 2:17–18, 25–29. The context of these two passages runs together and extends through a lengthy indictment against Judah. The indictment includes an assumtion of the curses against Israel for breaking the covenant paralleled in Deuteronomy 27–30.

Jeremiah 7:

Common vocabulary with Rom 2:19 is first found in Jer 7:4. Paul characterizes the self-image of his interlocutor and includes the statement "if you are sure (πέποιθάς τε σεαυτὸν) that you are a guide to the blind."

Jer 7:4 addresses Jewish assurance of their special status with the warning, "Do not trust in yourselves (πεποίθατε ἐφ᾽ ἑαυτοῖς) with lying words, for they will not profit you at all, saying, 'It is the temple of the Lord, the temple of the Lord.'" The address continues in v. 8: "But since (or if) you have trusted (εἰ δὲ ὑμεῖς πεποίθατε) in lying words." These two verses in Jeremiah share with Romans 2 the *vocabulary* and the *common theme* of misplaced trust or confidence. It is possible that εἰ δὲ ὑμεῖς of v. 8 also informs Rom 2:17, Εἰ δὲ σύ.

Indictments follow in Jer 7:9–12. The result of disobedience is announced beginning with v. 13, repeating the *vocabulary and theme* of misplaced trust. Because Judah has done all these things, God will do to the temple "in which you trust" (ἐφ᾽ ᾧ ὑμεῖς πεποίθατε) what he did to Shiloh (v. 14).

The most important *vocabulary correspondence* has to do with the triad of charges against the Jew in Rom 2:21–22 of stealing (κλέπτειν), committing adultery (μοιχεύειν), and temple robbery (ἱεροσυλεῖν). They are paralleled in the list of indictments in Jer 7:8–11.[28] As was clear in Hosea, vice lists including especially adultery and stealing are fairly common within and without the OT.[29] Only a few examples closely parallel the indictment in Romans.

Pss. Sol. 8:8–11 speaks of lawbreaking in general, and specifically of adultery and stealing from the sanctuary, among numerous other sins. Likewise *T. Levi* 14:4–8 speaks of plundering and stealing from offerings and of adultery, in a list of charges. Neither of these pseudepigraphic texts, even if dated early enough, gives evidence of being a Pauline reference. Philo has a very close verbal parallel to Rom 2:21–22 in *Conf. Ling.* 163, including stealing, adultery, murder, and temple robbery or sacrilege (ἱεροσυλεῖν).[30] Philo is of course

---

[28]The presence of "temple-robbery" in Jeremiah will be discussed shortly.

[29]Scholars often note similar vice lists. Dunn suggests several comparable lists in addition to Jer 7:8–11 (*Romans 1–8*, 113). Most include one or two elements of Paul's charges in a much longer list. The most notable parallel with the vocabulary of Romans is Ps 50:18–19 (LXX 49), which alleges consorting with thieves and adulterers, and deceit. It has nothing corresponding to temple-robbery. Although the indictment against the wicked in the psalm has thematic parallels with Rom 2:17–24, Jer 7:8–11 contains stronger evidence of its presence in Romans 2 as a reference.

Mal 3:5–9 initially looks like a very attractive candidate as a Pauline reference with, among many other things, a judgment against adulteresses (μοιχαλίδας) and the charge of robbing God (MT; LXX, however, changes this to "insulting" God, which would be the type of translational ambiguity leading Jewish exegetes to this text). However, it has no parallel with κλέπτειν at all, a regular feature of such lists. While the passage resonates with themes in common with Paul in Romans 9–11 (esp. Mal 3:6–7, again, specifically the MT), and it is tempting to include it as a reference for that reason, the vocabulary evidence is insufficient to establish it as a reference in Rom 2:17–29.

Fitzmyer believes the origin of Paul's list is in the Decalogue of Exod 20:14–15 (*Romans*, 318). That tradition, if not the text itself, is ultimately where the prohibitions originate, but that is not the source of the vice list.

[30]See Dunn, *Romans 1–8*, 114; Fitzmyer, *Romans*, 318; Barrett, *Epistle to the Romans*, 54 n. 1. One may well ask if Philo is also depend-

not available as a Pauline reference, nor is the context comparable to Rom 2:17–29.

The specific triad of stealing, adultery, and temple robbery or sacrilege does not appear to be a widely used traditional or formulaic expression. Jer 7:8–11, though, contains these three elements and meets the other methodological criteria for identification as a Pauline reference, to be discussed shortly.

In both Jeremiah 7 and Rom 2:19–23 those who were sure or trusting (πέποιθάς/πείθω) in their special relationship to God are charged with sin. The list of sins is longer in Jer 7:9 than in Rom 2:21–22. "You murder, commit adultery (μοι-χᾶσθε), steal (κλέπετε), swear falsely, make offerings to Baal, and go after other gods that you have not known." Paul's rhetorical questions in Rom 2:21–22 repeat those charges: "do you steal (κλέπτεις)?...do you commit adultery (μοιχευ-εις)?...do you rob temples (or commit sacrilege; ἱεροσυλεῖς)?" When Paul makes an uncited or unattributed exegetical reference his text is laced with the language of the originating text. The list is not repeated verbatim as in a quotation.

However, no *verbal correspondence* is found to ἱερο-συλεῖς. It is not to be expected in this text, since the word is found nowhere in Jewish literature until 2 Macc 9:2.[31] We cannot expect the actual word ἱεροσυλεῖς to show up in Jeremiah 7, since it was not in current use. However, a reference to robbery being perpetrated in the temple does occur in v. 11. In Jer 7:10–11, Judah is protesting that they have "refrained from doing all of these abominations" (βδελύγματα).[32] God makes the charge, "Is not my house a den of robbers (σπήλαιον λῃστῶν)...in your eyes?" This provides a striking

---

ent upon Jeremiah, but there is no evidence to indicate that this might be the case as there is in Romans. On the widespread use of similar vice lists in Greek and later rabbinic literature, although not in this particular combination, see also Gottlob Schrenk ("ἱεροσυλέω," *TDNT* 3.256) and Str-B (3.107–15).

[31]The word appears in Greek literature c. 400 BCE (Schrenk, "ἱεροσυλέω," 255–57).

[32]βδελύγματα provides another verbal link with Rom 2:22 βδε-λυσσόμενος.

parallel to the mention of temple robbery or sacrilege in Rom 2:22, especially in conjunction with the other verbal links.

The question to be raised is why Paul has not charged the Jew of Rom 2:22 with making the temple "a den of robbers" (σπήλαιον λῃστῶν) in a direct quotation of Jer 7:11, as do the Synoptics.[33] First, as was discussed in the previous chapter and also applies to Paul's failure to quote the entire list of sins from Jer 7:9, Jewish exegetes often do not quote directly from passages which are used exegetically, but reflect their vocabulary more indirectly. Often that vocabulary is changed or manipulated to accommodate a particular situation or to make an exegetical point or application.[34] Such changes, rather than being misquotations or incidental changes, are sometimes made in order to make the reference fit grammatically into the sentence, and sometimes are intended to draw the readers' attention to the change and its import.

In this instance there is some evidence of the currency in Paul's day of the term ἱεροσυλεῖν and related forms as a charge against Jews of temple robbery or sacrilege, whatever that might have entailed.[35] It would be fully in accord with contemporary exegetical practice for Paul to pick up a word perhaps at that time carrying a specific connotation in substitution for a word in the text to which he refers in order to make a point or catch the attention of his audience. The charge of idolatry in Jer 7:9 connects Paul's question concerning idolatry to his contemporary term ἱεροσυλεῖν. In Jeremiah it is because of idolatry that the charge is made that the temple has become a den of robbers.[36] In this way, what to

---

[33]Mark 11:17; Matt 21:13; Luke 19:46.

[34]See Renée Bloch, "Midrasch," 34–44.

[35]Philo, *Conf. Ling.*, 163, Josephus, *Ant.*, 4.207, 17.163; *Ap.*, 1.310, 318. See Schrenk, "ἱεροσυλέω," 255–57. See Str-B, 3.113–15 for examples, almost always in connection with stealing gold and silver from heathen temples. This question will be further addressed in the next chapter.

[36]This interpretation also brings the two halves of the question, "you who abhor idols, do you rob temples?" into conformity with the rhetorical model of the two previous questions (steal/steal; commit adul-

Paul and his readers is an "ancient" text is made contemporary by the insertion of modern terminology. The outdated situational vocabulary concerning Baal and Shiloh is discarded and replaced. Far from detracting from his reference to Jeremiah, the use of ἱεροσυλεῖν brings the prophet's message into the world with which his readers are familiar.

A further *verbal link* with Jeremiah 7 exists with Rom 2:24: the quotation from Isa 52:5/Ezek 36:22. There it is "the name of God" (τὸ...ὄνομα τοῦ θεοῦ) that has been dishonored and blasphemed. Paul has adjusted the grammar of the quotation to make himself, and not God, the speaker. Both Isa 52:5 and Ezek 36:22 make this a first person statement by God, "my name" (τὸ ὄνομά μου). The phrase τὸ ὄνομά μου is quite common, appearing over 75 times in the OT in connection with the name of God. However, the most concentrated use of the phrase in the OT occurs in Jer 7:10–12, 14.[37] There the mark of the special relationship of Judah to God mentioned in v. 4 is "the temple of the Lord," thereafter referred to as "my house...called by my name," the destruction of which is foretold (v. 14). In this passage the concepts of sacrilege and the dishonoring of the name of God associated with the temple are expressed. They are *themes in common* with Rom 2:21–24. Given the other links with this passage, it is possible that the vocabulary of Jer 7:10–14 has also provided a link to Isa 52:5.

The context of chap. 7 is a warning for Judah not to trust in the outward manifestations of religion, in this case specifically the temple. Instead the nation is urged to do the

---

tery/commit adultery; abhor idols/rob temples). The difficulty of the illogical sequence of this third question for interpreters and an answer in a discussion of idolatry in Jeremiah 7 will be further discussed in the following chapter.

[37]This concentration is equaled only by Ezek 36:20–23, to be examined below, the dedication of the temple by Solomon in 1 Kings 8:16–19/2 Chron 6:5–9, and Mal 1:11–14 where the name of God is extolled before the charge is made that the priests have profaned the name by bringing polluted food to the table. A great many of the remaining occurrences are parallels in Kings and Chronicles, in connection with "the house that bears my name."

good works that God desires lest they suffer the fate of Israel: the accomplishment of the curses for breaking the covenant also found in Deuteronomy 28. The language of the curses is recounted in the list of consequences Jeremiah warns will be the result of continued disobedience.[38] This warning is apparently rhetorical. It appears that it is too late for Judah; the covenant is broken, judgment approaches, and Jeremiah is instructed: "So do not pray for this people... for I will not listen to you" (7:16).

Chaps. 7–9 continue to warn of the terrible destruction to be visited upon the nation, with striking parallels to Deuteronomy 28. Though the passage is broken up by Jeremiah's "fountain of tears" (9:1), the Lord is unrelenting: "Because they have forsaken my law that I set before them, and have not obeyed my voice" (v. 13). The tirade is completed with another passage linked to Rom 2:17–29: Jer 9:23–26.

Jeremiah 9:

Common vocabulary between Rom 2:17 and Jer 9:23–24 has long been noted by others.[39] In Romans 2 the one accepting the designation of "Jew" is said to "boast in God" (καυ-χᾶσαι ἐν θεῷ, v. 17), to "know the will" (γινώσκεις τὸ θέλημα, presumably of God, v. 18), and to "boast in the Law" (ἐν νόμῳ καυχᾶσαι, v. 23). Jeremiah 9 instructs the wise, the strong, and the wealthy not to boast in those attributes (9:23). Rather, "let those who boast boast in this (καυχάσθω ὁ καυχώμενος), to understand and to know (γινώσκειν), that I am the Lord, exercising mercy and judgment and righteous-

---

[38]These links between Jeremiah and Deuteronomy will specifically dealt with when those passages from Deuteronomy 28–30 are taken up.

[39]William Sanday and Arthur C. Headlam, *A Critical and Exegetical Commentary on the Epistle to the Romans* (ICC; Edinburgh: T. & T. Clark, 1958) 64; Dunn, *Romans 1–8*, 110; Black, *Romans*, 59; Pesch, *Römerbrief*, 35; J.–M. Cambier, "Le jugement de tous les hommes par Dieu seul, selon la vérité, dans Rom 2:1–3:20," *ZNW* 67 (1976) 206. "Moreover, the allusion to Jer 9:25–26 in Rom 2:29 shows that the passage was important to Paul" (Furnish, *II Corinthians*, 474).

ness upon the earth, for in these things is my will (τὸ θέλημά μου), says the Lord" (v. 24).[40]

Paul's list of items in which one might boast is not so general, but specifically applies to those who boast in their relationship with God and their knowledge of God. But the indictment of his interlocutor in reference to Jer 9:24 indicates that this boasting is inappropriate because the interlocutor's behavior gives the lie to his or her knowledge of God's will.

In both the passage from Romans and that of Jeremiah there then follows the contrast between external and internal marks of God's people. Jer 9:25 warns that days are coming when God "will visit upon all the circumcised their uncircumcision" (περιτετμημένους ἀκροβυστίας αὐτῶν). The clear implication, to be confirmed in the next verse, is that though physically circumcised unlike the gentile nations who are "uncircumcised in flesh" (ἀπερίτμητα σαρκί, Jer 9:26/Rom 2:28) Israel is considered to be like "the uncircumcision" (ἀκροβυστία).[41] Paul likewise indicates that the circumcision of those who break the law will become uncircumcision (ἡ περιτομή σου ἀκροβυστία γέγονεν, Rom 2:25).

The reason that those who are physically circumcised are considered uncircumcised in Jer 9:26 is that they are not circumcised inwardly or spiritually: "all the house of Israel is uncircumcised in their hearts" (ἀπερίτμητοι καρδίας αὐτῶν).[42] This is also the case implied in Rom 2:25, where the circumcision of those who break the law becomes uncircumcision. Likewise, what is explicitly called for in Rom 2:28–29,

---

[40]This passage fulfills the *criterion of recurrence*. Paul elsewhere refers to Jer 9:24 in 1 Cor 1:31 and 2 Cor 10:17: "Let the one who boasts, boast in the Lord."

[41]In these verses it appears that the surrounding nations are both circumcised and uncircumcised. Richard C. Steiner suggests that these nations practiced "partial circumcision," and that Israel's lack of heart circumcision is likewise considered incomplete ("Incomplete Circumcision in Egypt and Edom: Jeremiah 9:24–25 in the Light of Josephus and Jonckheere," *JBL* 118 [1999] 497–505.

[42]Schweizer discusses OT and Jewish statements about one's state of heart before God ("'Der Jude im Verborgenen,'" 118–19).

rather than an outward circumcision in the flesh (ἐν τῷ φανερῷ ἐν σαρκὶ περιτομή), is a circumcision of the heart (περιτομὴ καρδίας). Paul appropriates the dichotomy between
inward and outward spirituality as applied to Israel in
Jeremiah and applies it to his Jewish interlocutor.[43]

These two passages from Jeremiah 7   and 9 meet all of
the possible criteria for identification as Pauline intertextual
references. As to *primary criteria*, they share *common vocabulary* with Rom 2:17–29, and that *vocabulary is clustered* in
two short passages. There are solid *verbal links* with other OT
texts. They include Deuteronomy 28–30 and Ezekiel 36, both
of which are texts which will shortly be shown to inform Rom
2:17–29.[44]

Though a detailed analysis will be taken up in the next
chapter, the preliminary work of identifying the passage as a
reference has already shown several ways in which these passages provide *explication* for Paul's argument. They inform
Paul's conclusions about Jewish misplaced confidence, disobedience to the covenant, and the consequences of disobedience. They bring up a concern for the honor of God's name.
They also address the issue of internal vs. physical circumcision, and circumcision of the heart.

These passages also meet the *confirmatory criteria*.
Paul's *recurrent use* of Jeremiah 9 has already been mentioned. These passages deal with *themes in common* with Rom

---

[43]The concept of heart circumcision occurs in a few other OT passages, but in the LXX it reads "circumcise your hard-heartedness"
(περιτέμεσθε τὴν σκληροκαρδίαν) as in Jer 4:4. However, in that passage the Hebrew reads הסרו ערלות לבבכם "remove the foreskin of your
hearts." In Deut 30:6 the Hebrew reads ומלתם את ערלת לבבכם "circumcise
the foreskin of your hearts." Jer 4:4, while part of the overall condemnation of Judah which includes Jeremiah 7 and 9, gives no other evidence
of being a Pauline reference. Deut 30:6, however, does so. This is the
type of translational ambiguity that Paul would be expected to exploit,
as will be discussed further. Stanislas Lyonnet notes on the subject of
circumcision of the heart that Jeremiah "appears to have borrowed from
Deuteronomy" (*Etudes sur l'Epître aux Romains* [AnBib 120; Rome:
Pontifical Biblical Institute, 1989] 77).

[44]Specific verbal links will be pointed out as each of those passages is discussed.

2:17–29. In both Jeremiah and Romans there are charges of lawbreaking against God's people, and there is a contrast between the internal and external identifying characteristics of God's people. Those who trust in their supposed relationship with God on the basis of external criteria, whether it be identification with the temple or circumcision, are warned that those external criteria do not provide certainty of a privileged position before God.

Finally, there is a *common linear development* between these passages from Jeremiah and Rom 2:17–29.[45] Jeremiah 7:8 begins εἰ δὲ ὑμεῖς πεποίθατε ("but if you trust") while Rom 2:17 begins with the parallel, Εἰ δὲ σύ, and goes on in v. 19 to speak of trusting or considering (πέποιθάς) oneself to be a guide to the blind, etc. The triad of charges of stealing, adultery, and temple robbery or sacrilege follow in Jer 7:9–11, and Rom 2:21–22. The language of abomination and abhorrence (βδελύγματα/βδελυσσόμενος) is found at Jer 7:10 and Rom 2:22. The concern for the name of God enters at Jer 7:10–11, and Rom 2:24.

A similar *linear development* occurs in Jer 9:23–26. Jer 9:23–24 and Rom 2:17–18 both begin with language concerning boasting about (καυχάσθω/καυχᾶσαι) knowing God (γινώσκειν) and his will (θέλημα). Jer 9:25 and Rom 2:25 introduce the concept of circumcision (περιτομή) becoming uncircumcision (ἀκροβυστία). The contrast between circumcision of the flesh and circumcision of the heart is drawn in Jer 9:26 and Rom 2:28–29. On the basis of both primary and confirmatory criteria, Jer 7:2–11 and Jer 9:23–26 give clear evidence of serving as exegetical references to Paul's argument in Rom 2:17–29.

Ezekiel 36:

Another prophetic passage linked to Rom 2:17–29, as well as to Jeremiah 7 and 9, is Ezek 36:16–27. Several *links with other texts* include Jer 7:2–11 and Jer 9:23–26. The concentrated repetition of the phrase "my name" (τὸ ὄνομά μου)

---

[45]This is similar to the concept of "order" in synoptic source criticism.

noted in Jer 7:10–14 is nearly equaled in Ezek 36:20–22. The very common phrase "house of Israel" (οἶκος Ἰσραήλ) occurs at Jer 9:26 and Ezek 36:17, 21, 22. It is so common that it is of no great consequence, but it is another verbal link. Another common phrase appearing in both passages is "the nations/gentiles" (τὰ ἔθνη) at Jer 9:26 and throughout the passage from Ezekiel.

Jer 9:25 urges that one boast to understand "and to know that I am the Lord" (καὶ γινώσκειν ὅτι ἐγώ εἰμι κύριος). Ezek 36:23 advises that God's name, which has been profaned among the nations, will be sanctified "and the nations will know that I am the Lord" (καὶ γνώσονται τὰ ἔθνη ὅτι ἐγώ εἰμι κύριος).[46] Since this phrase is fairly uncommon outside of Exodus and Ezekiel, this link is more weighty than it at first appears. Also linking the passages is the combination of "flesh" (σάρξ) and "heart" (καρδία, Ezek 36:26/Jer 9:26). These links of Ezek 36:16–27 with Jeremiah meet the *criterion of verbal links with other texts*, and of *clustered vocabulary linking texts*. Links with Deuteronomy will be noted shortly.

Of primary importance, however, is the fact that there is *vocabulary* from Ezek 36:16–27 *in common* with Rom 2:17–29. The most obvious link is the parallel of Ezek 36:21, 22 to Paul's modified quotation of Isa 52:5: "for the name of God is blasphemed among the Gentiles because of you" (τὸ γὰρ ὄνομα τοῦ θεοῦ δι' ὑμᾶς βλασφημεῖται ἐν τοῖς ἔθνεσιν, Rom 2:24).[47]

---

[46]Nearly three quarters of the over 75 occurrences of the phrase "to know that I am the Lord" appear in Ezekiel. Most of the rest are from Exodus. The only other occurrence in Jeremiah is at 24:6.

[47]Cf. Isa 52:5b, δι' ὑμᾶς διὰ παντὸς τὸ ὄνομά μου βλασφημεῖται ἐν τοῖς ἔθνεσι.

It is important to note that this is simply the most obvious link, and therefore the one which first gains attention. However, it may not be the initial link Paul noticed. The greater argumentative and theological import comes from the reference to Ezekiel. It is possible, or even likely, that the other linking vocabulary between Rom 2:17–29 and Ezekiel 36, to be examined in a moment, initially informs Paul's argument without dependence on Isaiah. Paul then brings Isa 52:5 into his argu-

The parallels are found in the high concentration of allusions to the name of God shared with Jeremiah 7. In Ezek 36:21–23 God has concern "for my holy name, which the house of Israel had profaned among the nations" (διὰ τὸ ὄνομά μου τὸ ἅγιον, ὃ ἐβεβήλωσαν οἶκος Ἰσραήλ ἐν τοῖς ἔθνεσιν). God is about to act on behalf of Israel, not for the sake of Israel, "but for the sake of my holy name, which you have profaned among the nations" (ἀλλ᾽ ἢ διὰ τὸ ὄνομά μου τὸ ἅγιον, ὃ ἐβεβηλώσατε ἐν τοῖς ἔθνεσιν). God will sanctify "my great name, which has been profaned among the nations, and which you have profaned among them" (τὸ ὄνομά μου τὸ μέγα τὸ βεβηλωθὲν ἐν τοῖς ἔθνεσιν, ὃ ἐβεβηλώσατε ἐν μέσῳ αὐτῶν).[48] The *verbal links* with Rom 2:24 of "the nations/gentiles" and "the name" are important, but they are part of an oft-noted refrain more apparent in the *thematic parallel* of the charge itself.[49] It is the passage from Ezekiel, even more so than Isaiah, which makes the same point Paul makes.[50]

There are, however, several other significant *verbal links* not dependent upon the parallel with Isaiah, some of which are also shared with the passages from Jeremiah. The combination of "flesh" (σάρξ) and "heart" (καρδία, Ezek 36:26/Jer 9:26), and the addition to the *cluster* of "spirit" (πνεῦμα) links this passage with Rom 2:28–29: "nor is true circumcision something external and physical (ἐν σαρκί). Rather, a person is a Jew who is one inwardly, and real circumcision is a matter of the heart (καρδίας) —it is spiritual (ἐν πνεύματι)."

---

ment as a supporting authoritative quotation based on verbal links to his Ezekiel reference.

[48]At this point I am primarily interested in establishing the verbal links between Ezekiel 36 and Romans 2:17–29. The function of Isa 52:5 and its parallel in Ezekiel 36:21–22 in the argument of Romans 2 will be taken up in more detail in the next chapter.

[49] Dodd (*Epistle*, 39), Fitzmyer (*Romans*, 318), and Barrett (*Epistle to the Romans*, 54) merely note Ezek 36:20 in comparison with Isa 52:5 without significant comment. Dunn, however, says the quotation is also a "probable allusion to Ezek 36:20–23" (*Romans 1–8*, 118).

[50]See the discussion of Rom 2:24 in chap. 3.

In Ezek 36:26 Israel is promised, "A new heart (καρδίαν καινήν) I will give you, and a new spirit (πνεῦμα καινόν) I will put within you; and I will remove from your flesh (ἐκ τῆς σαρκός) the heart of stone (τὴν καρδίαν τὴν λιθίνην) and give you a heart of flesh (καρδίαν σαρκίνην)." The *theme* of interior spirituality links the passages.

Another *verbal connection* is found between "by their idols" (ἐν τοῖς εἰδώλοις αὐτῶν) in Ezek 36:17 and "your idols" (τῶν εἰδώλων ὑμῶν) in v. 25 and τὰ εἴδωλα of Rom 2:22. There is also a link between Rom 2:26: "if (the uncircumcised) keep the righteous requirements of the law" (τὰ δικαιώματα τοῦ νόμου φυλάσσῃ) and Ezek 36:27 "and I will make you walk in my statutes (ἐν τοῖς δικαιώμασί) and keep (φυλάξησθε) my ordinances."

Ezek 36:23 promises, "and the nations shall know that I am the Lord" (καὶ γνώσονται τὰ ἔθνη ὅτι ἐγώ εἰμι κύριος). This provides a link through γινώσκω, as does Jer 9:25, with Rom 2:18, "and you know the will" (καὶ γινώσκεις τὸ θέλημα). This is a *theme in common* with Paul: that gentiles, though physically uncircumcised, can know the Lord or have an inward circumcision, that is "a circumcision of the heart" (Rom 2:26–29).

There is, then, considerable *vocabulary correspondence* between Ezek 36:16–27 and Rom 2:17–29, with most of that *vocabulary occurring in clusters*. We have already seen the evidence of *links with other texts*. The concepts in Ezek 36:16–29 of Israel's sinfulness, the requirement for an inward change "in heart," and the shift away from external and formal adherence to the law to a spiritual adherence are all ideas that provide *explication* for the development of Paul's argument in Rom 2:17–29.

Ezekiel 36 shows not only *common themes* with the Pauline passage, but a *common linear development*. Ezek 36:16–27 also fulfills *the criterion of recurrence*, since Paul makes another intertextual reference to the passage in 2 Cor 3:3.[51] Though the intertextual connections of Ezek 36:16–27

---

[51]See Stockhausen, *Moses' Veil*, 48–49, 56, 68–71.

with Rom 2:17–29 are not as strong as those of Jeremiah 7 and 9, Ezekiel fulfills all of the criteria for identification as an intertextual reference.

The passage fills an important niche in the developing argument of Romans. In addition to the contributions this passage makes to Rom 2:17–29 in particular, the note of restoration for Israel found in the deuteronomic blessings and curses and reflected in Romans 11 is central in Ezekiel 36.[52] The renewal of the covenant blessings of restoration to the land, renewed fruitfulness, and rebuilt cities accompany the spiritual restoration, which includes cleansing, a new heart, and a new spirit (36:24–36). This theme is not reflected in the Jeremiah passages, but is dealt with later in Romans. The unstated presupposition of Israel's restoration already exists through Paul's reference to Ezekiel 36.

This restoration may be understood eschatologically (at least by readers such as Paul) on the basis of the immediately following vision of the valley of dry bones and promise of the reunited eternal Davidic kingdom of chap. 37: "I will make a covenant of peace with them; it will be an everlasting covenant" (v. 26). While these themes of restoration do not appear directly in Rom 2:17–29, they form part of the intertextual web underlying the entire epistle, and are dealt with explicitly in Romans 9–11. This is the strongest possible example of *recurrence*.

---

[52]James Scott finds a protracted exile in Ezekiel 4, which places Ezekiel in connection with that strand of tradition ("For as Many," 208). Schweizer notes that Ezek 36:25–27 still has the expectation of restoration in the future; it is not a present reality ("Der Jude im Verborgenen," 119). Paul appropriates this tradition in his assumption that the covenant has been broken, and that Israel remains under the curses of the covenant because of their disobedience. Don B. Garlington notes Paul's reliance upon this tradition in Galatians as well, stating "that the divine judgment begun in 587 continues on Israel and that the Jewish people remain in exile until the present day. In this regard, the tack of Gal. 3.10 resembles the employment of Isa. 52:5 [Ezek 36:21–23] in Rom. 2:24" ("Role Reversal and Paul's Use of Scripture in Galatians 3.10–13," *JSNT* 65 [1997] 109). See also Hafemann, "The Spirit of the New Covenant," *Evangelium-Schriftauslegung-Kirche*, 174.

THE LAW

A characteristic of Jewish exegesis contemporary with Paul, as seen in the last chapter, is the interpretation of narrative texts through the prophets. In Rom 2:17–29 Paul relies upon two pentateuchal narratives as exegetical references, using Deuteronomy 29–30 as a bridge from Genesis 17 to his prophetic references. The narratives are primary texts for Paul, being the source of event or story, with which the "inspirational" branch of Jewish exegesis is concerned.[53]

Genesis 17:

The foundational narrative reference in Rom 2:17–29 is the reaffirmation of the covenant in the Abraham narrative, along with the promise of Isaac's birth and the circumcision of Ishmael, specifically Gen 17:9–27.[54] In keeping with another characteristic of Jewish exegesis, this passage serves as the text which requires explanation.[55] It specifies physical circumcision "in the flesh" as the mark identifying the people of God, with no mention of heart circumcision. For Paul, it requires re-interpretation through the prophets and Deuteronomy because of his experience with gentile Christianity.

Paul's concern to deal with difficult passages has been recently reaffirmed by Carol Stockhausen. The third of what she calls the primary characteristics of Pauline exegesis is

---

[53]See again Instone Brewer, *Techniques and Assumptions*, 165–71, 212–15.

[54]I am indebted to Carol Stockhausen for encouraging me to reexamine the importance of Genesis 17 when I had initially given it insufficient attention.

[55]See the description of Jewish exegesis by Bloch, particularly her third point, that "it is attentive to the text, in order to understand it and to illuminate any obscurities found there. Scripture interprets Scripture whenever possible by recourse to parallel passages" ("Midrasch," 31–34). Paul's exegesis in Romans 2 is haggadic as Bloch defines the term: "attempting to discover the true meaning of events in the narrative passages" (ibid.). In this case the parallel passages are interpretive representations of the Abrahamic covenant in Deuteronomy and the prophets. Le Déaut lists similar characteristics of targumic exegesis including "the explanation of perceived inconsistencies" (*The Message of the New Testament*, 8–15). Nils Dahl points out Paul's concern for just that in Galatians ("Contradictions in Scripture," 159–77).

that "Paul attempts to reconcile contradictions in Scripture. Those difficult passages are often interpreted as scriptural expressions of the discontinuity between the old way of the Law and the new way of the Spirit."[56] This is precisely what Paul is doing with the Abraham narrative of Genesis 17 in Romans 2, 4, and 9. In terms of meeting *methodological criteria* for identification as a reference in Rom 2:17–29, Gen 17:9–27 shares rare or *specialized vocabulary* with Rom 2:17–29, *clustered vocabulary, links with other referent texts, explication, recurrence,* and a *common theme.*

Although they are not numerous, the *vocabulary links* are strong because they involve *specialized vocabulary.* Surprisingly rare in the OT are forms of ἀκροβυστία ("foreskin"), or as it is used in Romans 2 "uncircumcision/uncircumcised person" (2:25–27).[57] Most often in the OT ἀπερίτμητος is preferred. In Genesis 17, as in most other OT occurrences, ἀκροβυστία specifically denotes "foreskin." It appears in its greatest OT concentration in Genesis 17, where it occurs four times in conjunction with verbal forms of περιτομή (περιτέμνω, "circumcise"), often along with σάρξ ("flesh") in constructions such as "circumcise the flesh of the foreskin." Another verbal link is apparent where Sarah is given a new ὄνομα ("name") in the passage (Gen 17:15). This is *clustered vocabulary,* with some specialized vocabulary as well.[58]

Links with other reference texts are numerous. Forms of περιτέμνω and the rare ἀκροβυστία appear in Jer 9:25. Forms of σάρξ occur in Jer 9:26 and Ezek 36:26. There is a repeated use of δώσω (δωρέομαι, "I will give") in Gen 17:16, 20 and five times in Ezek 36:26–29. Also evident is ὄικος in Gen 17:13,

---

[56]"Principles of Pauline Exegesis," 144–46.

[57]It appears in only 14 passages in the OT. Four of those are in Genesis 17, two others in Genesis 34, and one in another referent passage, Jeremiah 9. Of the 18 occurrences in the NT, 9 are in Romans 2–4.

[58]Note Stockhausen's emphasis on specialized or "unusual vocabulary" as a pointer to links between texts (*Moses' Veil,* 42; "Principles of Pauline Exegesis," 155). Where such vocabulary exists, the evidence of linkage is stronger. However, clusters of more common vocabulary in combination with other criteria may also demonstrate Pauline reference.

Jer 7:10–14, and Ezek 36:22. Forms of ἀλλότριος ("foreigner") occur in Gen 17:12 and Jer 7:6, 9. The more common ὄνομα and ἔθνη occur numerous times in Gen 17:9–27 and the referent passages from Jeremiah and Ezekiel. The effect of these *links with other texts* is that not only are there individual words, but there are *clusters of vocabulary linking* the various OT references.[59]

With regard to *the criterion of recurrence* , the Abraham narrative recurs significantly in Paul; in Galatians 3, 4 and Romans 4, 9 to name only the most obvious instances.[60] The reaffirmation of the covenant and the promise concerning Ishmael from Gen 17:11–27 in particular inform Rom 9:6–10. Paul's heavy reliance upon the Abraham narrative in Romans in itself leads one to suspect its referential use whenever significant vocabulary is found in common between a passage in Romans and the Abraham narrative. But there must be more evidence to confirm referential use of a passage.

Thematically Genesis 17 speaks of the giving of the covenant, while Rom 2:17–29 will be shown to speak to the status of the covenant. However, the covenant in Genesis 17 is linked to physical circumcision, while Paul de-emphasizes physical circumcision in preference to circumcision of the heart. The *common vocabulary* in Genesis 17 is found almost exclusively in specific reference to the physical act of "circumcision of the flesh of the foreskin." In Rom 2:17–29 the emphasis of this *vocabulary* is upon the circumcised or uncircumcised state of a person as it signifies (or does not signify) one's identification as a Jew.

In this instance *explication* is found in Paul's reading and reinterpreting of the Abraham narrative through Deuteronomy and the prophets. In effect, Paul is arguing against

---

[59]This is separate from the clusters of vocabulary linking each passage to Rom 2:17–29, although some individual and clustered words do link numerous references to Romans.

[60]Bruce L. Fields acknowledges Paul's reference to Genesis 17 in Philippians 3 as well ("Paul as Model: The Rhetoric and Old Testament Background of Philippians 3:1–4:1" [Ph.D. diss. Marquette University, 1995] 323).

Genesis 17 as evidence for the primacy of physical circumcision as an identifying mark of the people of God. From Deuteronomy and the prophets he concludes that through disobedience physical circumcision becomes uncircumcision, and true circumcision was always a circumcision of the heart. He then explicitly introduces the Abraham narrative in Romans 4 and 9 as the proof of the primacy of heart circumcision and faith as the basis for identification of the people of God, both Jew and gentile. The manner in which Gen 17:9–27 provides explication and is applied and reinterpreted will be examined in more detail in the following chapter.

Deuteronomy 29–30:

The final reference to be identified provides a precedent and foundation for Paul to reach the conclusions he does on the basis of Jeremiah 7, 9, and Ezekiel 36.[61] The prophetic references do not stand alone in their characterization of Israel. A part of the blessings and curses of the covenant in Deuteronomy 29–30 forms an interpretive bridge between Genesis 17 and the prophetic reference texts by reinterpreting the Abrahamic covenant of circumcision as heart circumcision. It also introduces the prophecy of covenant breaking disobedience and the promise of restoration.[62]

The narrative of the blessings and curses of the covenant begins in Deuteronomy 27 with a description of a Levitical recitation of the law and congregational response. The blessings and curses for obedience and disobedience follow in chap. 28. Some of the language of this section is paralleled in the contexts of Pauline reference passages from Jeremiah and Ezekiel. Deuteronomy 29–30, where verbal connections with

---

[61]Paul, of course, is unaware that the common deuteronomic view of Israel's history "founded" in Deuteronomy and "recurring" in the prophets derives from their shared period of development.

[62]As was mentioned earlier, Paul's references to this passage are recognized by others. See James Scott, "For as Many," 194, 213–14. Hays points out the importance of this entire section of Deuteronomy in Paul's epistles (*Echoes*, 163–64).

Rom 2:17–29 occur, is Moses' summary restatement, establishment, and expansion of the covenant with the people.[63]

Moses recounts the events of the exodus (29:2–8), admonishes the nation to follow the terms of the covenant (vv. 9–15), and gives warning of the curses to come for disobedience (vv. 16–28). The curses and disobedience are regarded not as potential but as apparently inevitable (30:1; reaffirmed in 31:16–17, 27–29). This will come about because of "all who hear the words of this oath and bless themselves, thinking in their hearts, 'We are safe even though we go our own stubborn ways'" (29:19). This is precisely the attitude Paul characterizes as that of his interlocutor in Rom 2:17–24.[64]

Verbal connections with Rom 2:17–29 are more significant than usual because they involve *unusual or specialized vocabulary*. The first is found at the end of Moses' recitation of the curses, and before he moves on to speak of restoration in Deut 29:29. Deut 29:29 makes the statement that "The secret things (τὰ κρυπτά) belong to the Lord our God, but the revealed things (τὰ δὲ φανερά) belong to us and to our children forever."

This is the only instance of a combination of any form of τὰ κρυπτά and τὰ φανερά in the entire OT. This *unique vocabulary combination* is *linked* to Rom 2:28–29: the contrast between being a Jew, or being circumcised, outwardly (ἐν τῷ φανερῷ) and being a Jew inwardly (ἐν τῷ κρυπτῷ). Paul appropriates this language to show that the hidden or inward

---

[63]"Deut. 27.1–30.20 is devoted to the renewal of the covenant" (Garlington, "Role Reversal," 96). Beyond renewal, Deuteronomy adds the curses and other elements. In describing Paul's application of this material to his contemporary situation N. T. Wright observes that "Deuteronomy 27–30 is all about exile and restoration, understood as covenant judgment and covenant renewal" (*The Climax of the Covenant: Christ and the Law in Pauline Theology* [Edinburgh: T. & T. Clark, 1991] 140).

[64]Cf. "We are safe!" at Jer 7:10, in the middle of a passage already identified. There Judah commits adultery, murder, etc., yet because of reliance upon the temple fears no consequence. However, no vocabulary link was described between these two passages, because different words are used in both Hebrew and Greek. The import is obviously the same, however, and can hardly have escaped Paul.

things of the heart, rather than the external marks of the written law, are what identify the people of God. The possibility of gentile inclusion in the people of God was always "hidden" with God.

Deuteronomy 30 continues to assume that Israel will be disobedient. After the blessings and curses of the covenant have been accomplished, Israel will be restored to favor (vv. 1–5). A link with more *specialized vocabulary*, "circumcision of the heart" (περιτομὴ καρδίας) in Rom 2:29, occurs as part of the restoration of which Moses speaks.[65] Moses says in Deut 30:6, "Moreover, the Lord your God will circumcise your heart and the heart of your descendants."[66]

The idea of circumcision of the heart is not common, occurring only here, at Jer 4:4, and at Deut 10:16, where Israel is called to fear the Lord.[67] Its antithesis, uncircumcision of the heart, occurs in Jeremiah 9 as seen above, and Lev 26:41, where it is said that Israel will be restored if they humble

---

[65]This link is widely recognized. See, e.g., Pesch, *Römerbrief*, 36; Dodd, *Epistle*, 42; Lietzmann, *An die Römer*, 44; Cranfield, *The Epistle to the Romans*, 1.127.

[66]The LXX reads περικαθαριεῖ ("purify") rather than περιτέμνω or περιτομή. However, the Hebrew reads מול ("circumcise"). It is not uncommon in contemporary Jewish exegesis to utilize a variety of readings and translations, and in fact to be attracted to translational ambiguities as interpretively significant. This instance of the concept of heart circumcision, because of the translational difference, may be the pivotal consideration in Paul's use of Deuteronomy to re-interpret the Abraham narrative in Romans 2. It is evidence that Paul can use both the LXX and Hebrew text since this is one of only three appearances of the idea of heart circumcision in the entire OT (as opposed to instances of "uncircumcised hearts"), and the only appearance in a text which gives evidence of being a Pauline reference.

[67]Deuteronomy 10–11 is a thematic parallel to chapters 28–30 with a re-giving of the law in new tablets (10:1), a call for obedience and reaffirmation of the Abrahamic covenant (10:12–22), recitation of the events of the exodus (11:1–7), and promise of blessings and curses (11:8–28). Ties with Jeremiah and Ezekiel, and the vocabulary correspondences with Romans 2 mentioned here, make it more likely that Deuteronomy 29–30 is Paul's referent. Stowers, however, emphasizes parallels with Deuteronomy 10 (*Rereading*, 155). Schweizer mentions Deut 10:16 and Jer 4:4 as well as Deuteronomy 30 when discussing heart circumcision ("'Der Jude im Verborgenen," 118).

their "uncircumcised hearts."[68] Ezek 44:7, 9, in a call for a purified Zadokite priesthood, condemns Israel, claiming that the covenant has been broken because they allowed foreigners "uncircumcised in heart" to minister in the temple. Of these few instances of the concept of heart circumcision in the OT, the context of Deut 30:6 gives the best evidence of being a Pauline referent.

Other less specialized *vocabulary links* exist as well. At 29:17 Moses reminds the nation of the gods of the Egyptians, "their abominations and their idols" (τὰ βδελύγματα αὐτῶν καὶ τὰ εἴδωλα αὐτῶν). The root βδελυ– is part of the phrase in Rom 2:22 ὁ βδελυσσόμενος τὰ εἴδωλα ("the one abhorring idols)."[69] Moses promises blessing in Deut 30:10 and 16 if Israel "observes the requirements" (φυλάσσεσθαι τὰ δικαιώματα, v. 16). In Rom 2:26 the uncircumcision of the uncircumcised will be considered circumcision if that person

---

[68]This passage, too, is a recitation of blessings and curses for obedience and disobedience (Lev 26:1–39), with a call for repentance and restoration (vv. 40–41), and ensuing reaffirmation of the Abrahamic covenant (v. 43). Here the Lord promises never to break his covenant with the nation (v. 44). It is possible that by the use of the idea of heart circumcision Paul intends a reference to the entire body of material on blessings and curses of the covenant which embody the concept, including Leviticus 26, Deuteronomy 10–11, and 28–30. However, for the purposes of this study, it is only the version attached to Deuteronomy 29–30 which is gives sufficient verbal evidence of being a Pauline referent.

[69]The LXX sometimes substitutes βδελύγματα/βδελυγμάτων for Hebrew phrases translated along the lines of "detestable idols," using "abominations" as an equation for "idols." E.g., 1 Kings 11:7, where idols of several countries are mentioned, then Astarte is mentioned by name, καὶ τῇ Ἀστάρτῃ Βδελύγματι Σιδωνίων ("and to Astarte, the abomination of the Sidonians"). Cf. 2 Kings 21:11. There is a clear OT association between idols and nominal uses of βδελυ–. Deut 7:25–6 uses a verbal form in reference to images and gods but not the word εἴδωλ–. Deut 29:17 puts βδελυ– and εἴδωλ– in very close proximity but there it is not a verbal form, and in fact the passage speaks of two different items, τὰ βδελύγματα, and τὰ εἴδωλα: "And you saw their abominations, and their idols" (καὶ ἴδετε τὰ βδελύγματα αὐτῶν, καὶ τὰ εἴδωλα αὐτῶν). See also Str-B, 3.111–12. This language combining the root βδελυ– with εἴδωλ– in Rom 2:22 emphasizes the "idol" context of the question (see chapter 3), and supports the interpretation of that question as dependent upon Jeremiah 7.

"keeps the requirements of the law" (τὰ δικαιώματα τοῦ νόμου φυλάσσῃ).[70] Numerous other *verbal links* are found throughout the passage in forms of θέλω, ἔθνος, γράφω, ὄνομα, and νόμος. The size of the passage and the common nature of the words themselves lessen the significance of this number of vocabulary correspondences. They may be viewed as supporting evidence of the referential use of the passage.

Another methodological criterion met by Deuteronomy 29–30 is *vocabulary links with the previously identified referents*, Jeremiah 7, 9, and Ezekiel 36. The links of Jeremiah and Ezekiel to the narrative of the covenant blessings and curses show that they parallel that narrative and represent the larger deuteronomic view of Israel's history.[71] The *links* connecting the Deuteronomy, Jeremiah, and Ezekiel references provide this tradition as an underlying substructure with which Paul interacts as he interprets the application of the covenant through the prophets.[72] This extensive *vocabulary in common* in the deuteronomic tradition not only confirms Deuteronomy 29–30 as a Pauline reference, it illustrates how strongly interconnected are Paul's intertextual references with one another.

---

[70]Fitzmyer notes that Deut 30:16 supports Paul's contention in Rom 2:25 that "[circumcision] means little without the observance of the law" (*Romans*, 321).

[71]The deuteronomic tradition is more readily apparent when the larger context of the blessings and curses surrounding the actual reference passage is taken into account.

Parallel statements are made concerning the dispersion of the Israelites in Deut 28:64 and Ezek 36:19. Deuteronomy warns, "and the Lord your God will scatter you among all the nations" (καὶ διασπερεῖ σε κύριος ὁ θεός σου εἰς πάντα τὰ ἔθνη). Ezek 36:19 uses the same language to describe the accomplishment of that scattering, "and I scattered them among the nations" (καὶ διέσπειρα αὐτοὺς εἰς τὰ ἔθνη).

[72]See esp. James Scott, "Deuteronomic Tradition," 645–65. Also, N. T. Wright ("The Messiah and the People of God: A Study in Pauline Theology with Particular Reference to the Argument of the Epistle to the Romans" [D. Phil. thesis, University of Oxford, 1980] 218), and Peter Stuhlmacher (*Paul's Letter to the Romans: A Commentary* [Louisville: Westminster/John Knox, 1994] 48). Paul's interaction with the deuteronomic tradition receive more extensive treatment in chap. 3.

Deuteronomy 29–30 and Ezekiel 36:

Ezekiel 36 is a prophecy to the mountains of Israel about the restoration of Israel. The basis for that prophecy lies in the tradition of blessings and promises of restoration also reflected in Deuteronomy 29–30 which are part of the view of Israel's history which Paul accepts. These parallels are not simply *linked vocabulary*, or even *clustered vocabulary*, but often whole phrases and *parallel themes*.

In Deut 30:5 Moses promises, "the Lord your God will lead you into the land which your fathers possessed, and you will possess it" (καὶ εἰσάξει σε κύριος ὁ θεός σου εἰς τὴν γῆν, ἣν ἐκληρονόμησαν οἱ πατέρες σου, καὶ κληρονομήσεις αὐτήν). In speaking to the land itself—the mountains of Israel—Ezek 36:12 makes a similar promise to possess the land: "I will lead people upon you —my people Israel —and they shall possess you, and you shall be their possession" (καὶ γεννήσω ἐφ᾽ ὑμᾶς ἀνθρώπους τὸν λαόν μου Ισραηλ, καὶ κληρονομήσουσιν ὑμᾶς, καὶ ἔσεσθε αὐτοῖς εἰς κατάσχεσιν).[73]

Verbal and thematic links concerning the restoration also occur at Deut 30:4b–5 and Ezek 36:24. In this case Moses gives a promise in Deut 30:4b–5: "and from there the Lord your God will bring you back, and will bring you to the land" (καὶ ἐκεῖθεν λήμψεταί σε κύριος ὁ θεός σου· καὶ εἰσάξει σε κύριος ὁ θεός σου εἰς τὴν γῆν). The statement remains an unfulfilled promise in Ezek 36:24: "I will take you from the nations...and bring you into your own land" (καὶ λήμψομαι ὑμᾶς ἐκ τῶν ἐθνῶν καὶ...εἰσάξω ὑμᾶς εἰς τὴν γῆν ὑμῶν).[74]

---

[73]Paul understands these promises concerning the land eschatologically, as discussed earlier. He must also depend upon a translation also reflected in Sir 44:21, in which "land" is transformed to "earth" (γῆ in both cases). There the promise to Abraham is reinterpreted to say, "and give them an inheritance from sea to sea and from the Euphrates to the ends of the earth." I thank Carol Stockhausen for bringing this to my attention.

[74]The idea that the results of the curse are still in effect and that the restoration has not yet occurred carries through to Pauline teaching, in that the restoration of Israel he portrays in Romans 9–11 is a future occurrence.

Again in reference to restoration to the land Deut 30:20 says the restoration will occur "so that you may live in the land that the Lord swore to give to your ancestors, to Abraham, to Isaac, and to Jacob" (κατοικεῖν σε ἐπὶ τῆς γῆς, ἧς ὤμοσεν κύριος τοῖς πατράσιν σου Αβρααμ καὶ Ισαακ καὶ Ιακωβ δοῦναι αὐτοῖς). Ezek 36:28 makes the promise, "Then you shall live in the land that I gave to your ancestors" (καὶ κατοικήσετε ἐπὶ τῆς γῆς, ἧς ἔδωκα τοῖς πατράσιν ὑμῶν).

Finally, the summary statement of the covenant relationship between God and Israel is made in both passages, as it is in Jeremiah. Deut 29:13 says, "in order that he may establish you as his people, and he will be your God" (ἵνα στήσῃ σε αὐτῷ εἰς λαόν, καὶ αὐτὸς ἔσται σου θεός). Ezek 36:28 has only slightly different wording, "and you shall be my people, and I will be your God" (καὶ ἔσεσθέ μοι εἰς λαόν, κἀγὼ ἔσομαι ὑμῖν εἰς θεόν).[75]

In addition to *sharing common vocabulary and themes* with the passage from Deuteronomy, when the surrounding context is taken into account Ezekiel 36 also has a *linear development in common* with Deuteronomy 28–30.[76] Deuteronomy 29–30 shares with Ezekiel 36 not only *linking vocabulary* and *common themes* but a deuteronomic view of Israel's history which Paul appropriates from both references in Rom 2:17–29.

It might be noted that verbal and thematic links between passages are not dependent upon changes in grammatical number. While it is possible, there is insufficient evidence to conclude that Paul viewed the change of address in Deuteronomy and Ezekiel as an expansion of the promise of restoration in the same way he exploits the expansion of the Abrahamic promise in Gen 17:3–4.

[75]Schweizer discusses the fact that the promise is eschatological, and so yet to be fulfilled in Ezekiel ("Der Jude im Verborgenen," 119).

[76]Deut 30:5 and 29:13 disturb the common linear development. They form a sort of inclusio concerning the inheritance of the land and relationship of the covenant. These will be seen to correspond to similar exceptions to common linear development between Deuteronomy 28–30 and Jeremiah 7.

Deuteronomy 29–30 and Jeremiah 7:

The *verbal and thematic links* between Deuteronomy 27–30 and Jeremiah 7 again meet the *criterion of links with other texts*, and establish the common deuteronomic view of Israel's history.[77]

Deut 30:20 says, "So that you may live in the land that the Lord swore to give to your ancestors, to Abraham, to Isaac, and to Jacob" (κατοικεῖν σε ἐπὶ τῆς γῆς, ἧς ὤμοσεν κύ- ριος τοῖς πατράσιν σου Αβρααμ καὶ Ισαακ καὶ Ιακωβ δοῦναι αὐτοῖς). This statement is paralleled in Jer 7:7: "then I will cause you to dwell in this place, in the land that I gave to your

---

[77]As with Ezekiel, the deuteronomic tradition is more readily apparent when the larger context of the blessings and curses surrounding the actual reference passage is taken into account.

Deut 27:17, 19 pronounces a curse: "Cursed be anyone who moves a neighbor's boundary marker....Cursed be anyone who deprives the alien, the orphan, and the widow of justice" (ὁ μετατιθεὶς ὅρια τοῦ πλησίον... Ἐπικατάρατος ὃς ἂν ἐκκλίνῃ κρίσιν προσηλύτου καὶ ὀρ- φανοῦ καὶ χήρας). Jer 7: 5–6 parallels this language in saying that God will dwell with the people of Judah if "[you] do justice between a person and their neighbor, and do not oppress the alien and orphan and widow" (ποιήσητε κρίσιν ἀνὰ μέσον ἀνδρὸς καὶ ἀνὰ μέσον τοῦ πλησίον αὐτοῦ καὶ προσήλυτον καὶ ὀρφανὸν καὶ χήραν μὴ καταδυναστεύσητε).

The blessing in Jer 7:6 is also significant: "[if you do not] shed innocent blood in this place" (αἷμα ἀθῷον μὴ ἐκχέητε ἐν τῷ τόπῳ τούτῳ). This resonates with the language of Deut 27:25: "Cursed be anyone who takes a bribe to slay a person of innocent blood" (Ἐπικατάρατος ὃς ἂν λάβῃ δῶρα πατάξαι ψυχὴν αἵματος ἀθῷου). Another condition of the blessing in Jer 7:6 is "if you do not go after other gods" (ὀπίσω θεῶν ἀλ- λοτρίων μὴ πορεύησθε). This language occurs in Deut 28:14: "[not] following other gods to serve them" (πορεύεσθαι ὀπίσω θεῶν ἑτέρων λατρεύειν αὐτοῖς). While this sentence in Jeremiah speaks of potential blessing for obedience, it comes in the context of condemnation for the disobedience which has actually occurred.

Jeremiah includes a vivid image of the curses also found in Deut 28:26: "Your corpses shall be food for every bird of the air and animal of the earth, and there shall be no one to frighten them away" (καὶ ἔσονται οἱ νεκροὶ ὑμῶν κατάβρωμα τοῖς πετεινοῖς τοῦ οὐρανοῦ καὶ τοῖς θηρίοις τῆς γῆς, καὶ οὐκ ἔσται ὁ ἀποσοβῶν). The same language is used in Jer 7:33: "The corpses of this people will be food for the birds of the air, and for the animals of the earth; and no one will frighten them away" (καὶ ἔσονται οἱ νεκροὶ τοῦ λαοῦ τούτου εἰς βρῶσιν τοῖς πετει- νοῖς τοῦ οὐρανοῦ καὶ τοῖς θηρίοις τῆς γῆς, καὶ οὐκ ἔσται ὁ ἀποσοβῶν).

ancestors" (καὶ κατοικιῶ ὑμᾶς ἐν τῷ τόπῳ τούτῳ ἐν γῇ, ᾗ ἔδωκα τοῖς πατράσιν ὑμῶν).

Also like Ezekiel 36, Jeremiah presents the summary statement of the covenant relationship between God and Israel also found in Deut 29:12: "in order that he may establish you as his people, and that he may be your God" (ἵνα στήσῃ σε αὐτῷ εἰς λαόν, καὶ αὐτὸς ἔσται σου θεός). The phrase is inverted in Jer 7:23: "I will be your God, and you will be my people" (ἔσομαι ὑμῖν εἰς θεόν, καὶ ὑμεῖς ἔσεσθέ μοι εἰς λαόν).

When the surrounding context of Deuteronomy is taken into account, Jeremiah shows a *common linear development* with the covenant blessings and curses. It is striking that there are two exceptions which are the same as those of Ezekiel 36. The first is the promise to dwell in the land. The second is the summary statement of the covenant relationship found in Deut 29:12, "you will be my people and I will be your God." As in the case of Ezekiel 36, they interrupt the otherwise *common linear development*. Deuteronomy 29–30 shares with Jeremiah 7 as well as Ezekiel 36 not only *linking vocabulary* and *common themes* but the deuteronomic tradition upon which Paul is dependent.

Deuteronomy 29–30 meets the methodological criteria as a Pauline intertextual reference in Rom 2:17–29. There is *specialized common vocabulary* between Deuteronomy 29–30 and Rom 2:17–29. The combination of "secret things and hidden things" (Deut 29:29) and the phrase "circumcise your hearts" (Deut 30:6, MT) are near one another in the text. Though this cannot be characterized as *clustered vocabulary*, it is more than the appearance of isolated words.

The *criterion of links with other texts* is more than met as Deuteronomy 29–30 is linked to Jeremiah 7–11 and Ezekiel 36. The warnings that Israel will break the terms of the covenant and the call for an inward obedience and spiritual restoration provide *explication* for Paul's argument in Rom 2:17–29. The *criterion of recurrence* is met as well, not only in the Pauline corpus but specifically in Romans.[78] Paul quotes Deut 29:4 at Rom 11:8, and Deut 30:12, 14 at Rom 10:6, 8. From these quotations and from referents in Rom 2:1–16 it is clear that Paul has engaged in intertextual exegesis of Deuteronomy 29–30.

Several texts, then, meet the primary methodological criteria for identification as exegetical referents in Rom 2:17–29. Deuteronomy 29–30, Jer 7:2–11, 9:23–26, and Ezek 36:16–27 provide a deuteronomic view of Israel's history which in turn helps reinterpret Genesis 17. All of these texts have *vocabulary in common* with Rom 2:17–29, usually in *clusters*. These texts are *linked to one another* by vocabulary and *theme*. All provide *explication* of Paul's conclusions in Rom 2:17–29, both individually and as mutually interpretive texts. These texts also meet the confirmatory criteria. They *recur* in Pauline literature, have *themes in common* with Paul's argument, and in some cases even have a *common linear development* with Rom 2:17–29. The next task will be to examine how those identified intertextual references are integrated into Paul's argument in Rom 2:17–29.

---

[78]James Scott affirms that Paul reads Deuteronomy 27–32 as a unit in his passage from Galatians. "In fact, the formulaic expression γεγραμμένα ἐν τῷ βιβλίῳ τοῦ νόμου τούτου which Paul cites in Gal. 3.10 runs through Deuteronomy 27–32 like a leitmotif (cf. Deut. 28.58, 61; 29.19, 20, 26; 30.10). Paul is citing from Deuteronomy 27–32 (33), the section on Blessings and Curses which comes after the exposition of 'the statutes and the ordinances' in Deuteronomy 12–26" ("For as Many," 194). Hays sees the unit as more restricted, but also says, "Paul thinks of Deuteronomy 27 and 28 as a unit, setting forth the conditional blessings and curses of the Law" (*Echoes*, 43).

3

An Intertextual Analysis of Rom 2:17–29

After defining a methodology for the identification of intertextual references, that methodology has been applied to Rom 2:17–29. The analysis provides the result that four sources: Jer 7:2–11, 9:23–26, Ezek 36:16–27, Gen 17:11–27, and Deuteronomy 29–30, are identified as intertextual references in Rom 2:17–29. The identification of passages which serve as intertextual references in Rom 2:17–29 is only the first step necessary to understand Paul's reliance upon and exegesis of those passages.

What remains is to exegete Paul's text to determine how those intertextual references inform and shape the development of his argument in Rom 2:17–29. Sufficient attention will be given to epistolary and rhetorical context at this stage, though a broader contextual analysis will follow in the next chapter. This analysis will proceed progressively through Rom 2:17–29, with summary observations to follow. It will focus upon Paul's intertextual exegesis, but will also engage the historical-critical issues and literature relevant to a study of Rom 2:17–29.

A BRIEF ASSESSMENT OF THE EPISTOLARY SETTING

While further discussion will follow in the next chapter, it is necessary briefly to outline some salient points in Paul's preceding argument and conclusions about his interlocutor which have an impact on the exegesis of Rom 2:17–29. It is almost universally acknowledged that much of Romans is presented in the form of a diatribe with an imaginary Jewish interlocutor. This is particularly the case for chaps. 2–4.[1] In 2:17–29 the imaginary interlocutor with whom Paul interacts is characterized as a Jew who relies on the law and circumcision for deliverance from God's wrath, while engaging in activity not in keeping with the stipulations of the law.[2]

What is less clear is whether the interlocutor of 2:17–29 is the same person addressed in 2:1–16.[3] While 1:18–32 speaks predominantly about gentiles,[4] and though the interlocutor is not called "a Jew" until 2:17, many commentators believe a Jewish interlocutor is addressed throughout, or at least throughout chap. 2—with the argument drawing down

---

[1]See, e.g., Fitzmyer, *Romans*, 91; Dunn, *Romans 1–8*, lxii; Stowers, *Rereading*, 11–15, 100–102. For a full discussion of diatribe in Romans, see Stanley Kent Stowers, *The Diatribe and Paul's Letter to the Romans* (SBLDS 57; Chico, CA: Scholars Press, 1981). See Stowers's discussion of characteristics of diatribe present in 2:17–24 paralleled in Epictetus, *Discourses*, 2.8.11–12, which include: an attack on hypocrisy and inconsistency; the use of quotations and allusions; the use of σύ to address the interlocutor; and the presence of vice lists (*Diatribe*, 95–97, 100–115).

[2]Pesch, *Römerbrief*, 35; Krentz, "The Name of God," 430; Käsemann, *Commentary on Romans*, 168; Schlier, *Der Römerbrief*, 38; Dunn, *Romans 1–8*, 108; Fitzmyer, *Romans*, 315. Opinions vary as to whether a typical Jew representative of the entire nation is meant, or a more limited representation such as Jewish missionaries (Goppelt, "Der Missionar des Gesetzes," 138–39), or a fictitious "pretentious teacher" of gentiles—a missionary in competition with Paul (Stowers, *Rereading*, 143). These questions will be addressed in detail shortly.

[3]While the interlocutor is presumably engaged in the argument from 1:18, such a person is not explicitly brought into dialogue until 2:1.

[4]Although see the important point made by Cranfield that Paul never specifies Greeks or gentiles alone (*The Epistle to the Romans*, 1.105). On the basis of what she believes are "unambiguous" allusions to Jer 2:11 and Ps 106:20 at Rom 1:23, Jouette M. Bassler concludes that "one cannot maintain that in Chapter 1 Paul has *only* gentiles in mind" (*Divine Impartiality: Paul and a Theological Axiom* [SBLDS 59; Chico, CA: Scholars Press, 1982] 122; emphasis hers). See also Morna Hooker, "Adam in Romans 1," *NTS* 6 (1960) 299; reprinted in *From Adam to Christ: Essays on Paul* (Cambridge: Cambridge University Press, 1990) 75.

with "increasing specificity" to the Jew in 2:17–29.[5] Others, however, believe the "judge" of 2:1–16 may be meant to include any judging person with a morally or philosophically superior self-image.[6]

Stowers has recently put forward the argument that through speech-in-character 2:1–16 addresses a "pretentious gentile" in parallel with a "pretentious Jewish teacher" in 2:17–29.[7] Stowers cites apostrophes similar to Rom 2:1–5 in Plutarch and Seneca, and notes that they are not thought to be addressing Jews.[8] However, Plutarch's and Seneca's arguments do not further develop to deal with an explicitly Jewish subject as does Paul's.

To blame the identification of the interlocutor as a Jew on historical anti-Jewish polemic alone, as Stowers does, is to ignore the Jewish interlocutor in the closely connected epistolary context. Stowers's citation of the earliest, pre-Augustinian, interpreters' failure to mention the possibility of a Jewish interlocutor at 2:1 may very well be understood as those interpreters' lack of contextual awareness, especially in light of the imaginative proposals they did make to identify that interlocutor. Still, Stowers is correct that there is nothing in 2:1–11 to indicate that the Jew explicitly addressed in v. 17 is meant to be specifically addressed in v. 1 as well. Stowers presents impressive evidence of a character-type of pretentious gentile represented by a speech-in-character having much in common with the beginning of Romans 2. Is it then decisive for identifying the interlocutor at 2:1 specifically as a gentile?

In keeping with the majority of commentators and the results of the analysis to be presented here, I conclude that the epistle speaks to both Jews and gentiles in a mixed com-

---

[5]Dunn, *Romans 1–8*, 76. See also, e.g., Lietzmann, *An die Römer*, 38; Schlier, *Der Römerbrief*, 38; Cranfield, *The Epistle to the Romans*, 1.163; Dodd, *Epistle*, 30; Black, *Romans*, 54.

[6]Barrett, *Epistle to the Romans*, 41–42; Markus Barth, "Speaking of Sin: Some Interpretive Notes on Romans 1:18–3:20," *SJT* 8 (1955) 293.

[7]Stowers, *Rereading*, 11–13, 100–104, 127–28.

[8]Ibid., 13.

munity, and at least deals with the relationship and expectations of both Jewish and gentile Christians.[9] Without more closely specifying the purpose of the epistle at this point,[10] this study will proceed from the position that 2:1–16 is directed to an imaginary gentile interlocutor, or that it is at least generally applicable. However, the Jew introduced in 2:17 is also presupposed as included in the diatribe against the pretentious judge of vv. 1–16. Paul's argument encompasses the pride of both gentiles and Jews. But it is the pride of the explicitly Jewish interlocutor in reliance on the law which is principally addressed by Paul in Romans 2. His corrective argument forms the basis for the immediately following chapters which argue for the inclusion of both Jews and gentiles among God's people.[11]

---

[9]So, e.g., Dunn (*Romans 1–8*, xliv–liv); Werner Georg Kümmel (*Introduction to the New Testament* [Nashville: Abingdon, 1975] 309–10); Anthony J. Guerra (*Romans and the Apologetic Tradition: The Purpose, Genre, and Audience of Paul's Letter* [SNTSMS 81; Cambridge: Cambridge University Press, 1995] 22–42); and many others. I find Stowers's attempt to refute this conclusion unconvincing, simply discounting a large amount of data (*Rereading*, 21–33). For another argument for a predominantly gentile audience, see Peter Lampe ("The Roman Christians of Romans 16," *The Romans Debate*, 225 n. 38). Lampe, however, does not argue that Romans is written exclusively with gentiles as the intended audience, as does Stowers.

[10]This question will receive extensive discussion in the following chapters in light of the following analysis.

[11]Segal makes a strong case for the fact that Paul's assessment of the inadequacy of Jewish law-keeping for salvation stems not only from his exegesis but also from his own conversion experience. He summarizes: "Those who stress that Paul was merely a Jew whose messiah has come have missed Paul's point. Paul was a Jew who did not have to convert to become a Christian. Theoretically, he could have just slid over as an adherent by claiming Judaism was fulfilled by the messiah's arrival. In that case, he would have insisted that the rules of Jewish life be imposed on all Christians, as did the Jewish Christians. Or he would have insisted that the Gentiles remain God-fearers and not become part of the community. But Paul, though Jewish, and because he had been a believing Pharisee, had to go through a radical reorientation to enter Christianity. Paul then said that everyone needs radically to reorient his or her way of thinking in order to become a Christian" (*Paul the Convert*, 147). In fact, it is Paul's conversion which influences his new

Therefore, interpretations which assume only a Jewish
target as well as those which exclude a Jewish target of the
initial diatribe of 2:1–16 do not adequately take into account
either the audience of the letter as a mixed congregation or
the primary focus of the epistle. The unspecified nature of the
interlocutor at 2:1 may be intentional. Paul may intend to be
inclusive of any judge by not specifying gentile or Jew.[12]
Stowers's argument that a gentile audience would recognize
the speech-in-character as representing a character-type has
merit in establishing the currency of the form. But this is not
to exclude a Jewish audience from also recognizing that character-type in 2:1–16 in a Jewish context and seeing that type
further developed in 2:17–29. Paul's argument addresses both
Jews and gentiles, in keeping with the purpose of the entire
epistle.

To touch briefly on the surrounding context, by the time
he reaches 2:17 Paul is in the midst of demonstrating that all
people, Jews and gentiles alike, stand under God's judgment
and in need of justification.[13] That argument continues in two

---

exegetical conclusions. For discussion of Paul's conversion as also a
commissioning, see James D. G. Dunn, "Paul's Conversion–A Light to
Twentieth Century Disputes," *Evangelium-Schriftauslegung-Kirche*, 91.

[12]So Barth ("Speaking of Sin," 293) and Barrett (*Epistle to the
Romans*, 41–42).

[13]Martin defines 1:18–3:20 as part of the *probatio* rather than the
narratio ("The Righteousness of God," 327–28). The proofs in the argument have already commenced.

On Paul's concept of justification as it relates to Paul's purpose of
stressing equality before God and unity in the church, Segal is again instructive. "Justification becomes the merciful acquittal of all humanity,
equally guilty at first...The implication is that sin is inherent in every
creature whether they practice Torah or not. In effect he removes the
benefit to the convert of complete membership in the Jewish community.
Those who have had the Torah have the advantage of knowing what sin
is, but they are all the more intransigent for having spurned the message that Jesus is Christ...When Paul addresses the issue of justification, he is also attempting to create a single community where all share
a single moral standard. His life as an apostle is thereafter devoted to
solving the practical problems of creating a single community, based on
being in Christ, out of two diverging ones with competing ideas about
what community entailed" (*Paul the Convert*, 183). Throughout his

parts, in Rom 2:17–24 and 25–29.[14] In chap. 1 Paul borrows from Wisdom 13–15 to describe the "godlessness and wickedness" of humanity.[15] In 2:1–16 he levels an indictment against the one who would "pass judgment" on others while doing "the same things." What Paul asserts is that both Jews and gentiles who do evil will receive God's wrath, while those who do right will receive reward. He states that it is doers, not hearers, of the law who will be justified before God, whether Jew or gentile.[16]

AN INTERTEXTUAL SYNOPSIS

As another preliminary step, it will be helpful briefly to review the major themes of those intertextual references which appear in Paul's text. In Genesis 17 the reaffirmation of the Abrahamic covenant with its emphasis upon physical circumcision as the sign of the people of God, including the promise of Isaac's birth and Ishmael's circumcision, serves as the foundational text requiring reinterpretation in order for Paul to make his argument. In Romans 2 Paul seeks to redefine the meaning of circumcision as a mark of God's people.[17]

---

study Segal notes the irony that Paul's attempts to unify were probably instrumental in accentuating the discontinuity between Judaism and Jewish Christianity on the one hand and gentile Christianity on the other.

[14]The turn in the argument at v. 25 is widely recognized. For discussion of the progressive steps in all of Romans 2, see Aletti, "Romains 2," 153–77.

[15]See, e.g., Fitzmyer, *Romans*, 272; Dodd, *Epistle*, 27; Dunn, *Romans 1–8*, 53. As already noted, Cranfield states that 1:18–32 is speaking of all people (*The Epistle to the Romans*, 1.105). In chap. 1 Paul never specifies Greeks or gentiles. If Cranfield is correct, the puzzling "therefore" of 2:1 makes sense, since Paul was speaking of "all people" all along.

[16]For the disputed question as to whether Paul really believes in the efficacy of works, and whether or not he is only speaking hypothetically of gentiles being able to "do the things of the law," see chap. 4.

[17]This exegetical argument concerning the value of circumcision in the Christian community follows experience. God-fearers like Titus had already been accepted into fellowship without circumcision (Gal 2:3). While this simply follows Jewish practice regarding God-fearers, Paul extends the argument by his exegesis to re-evaluate the purpose,

The blessings and curses and the reaffirmation of the covenant given in Deuteronomy 29–30 allow Paul to interpret and re-present true circumcision as heart-circumcision. Additionally, in this passage Israel is given warning of the loss of their covenant blessings should they break the covenant. The assumption is that such disobedience will in fact occur. In Jeremiah 7 and 9 and the surrounding context, the nation of Israel as a whole stands before God as having indeed broken the covenant and having relinquished their special status. The nation is "uncircumcised in heart." This allows Paul to make the unprecedented claim, central to his entire argument in the first chapters of Romans, that Jews and gentiles stand in the same condition requiring justification before God.

Especially from the text of Ezekiel 36, salvation for Israel now no longer is bound up with the requirements of the law of the covenant, but will be brought about through spiritual restoration. This addresses the themes of heart obedience also found in Deuteronomy and Jeremiah. Paul interprets these passages to conclude that since identification with the people of God is not bound to physical circumcision but to circumcision of the heart, gentiles as well as Jews are in need of and are capable of receiving such heart-circumcision "by the spirit."

It is important to remember that the order in which the intertextual references occur in the Romans text does not necessarily bear any relation to the order in which Paul has read those texts or used them as references. For instance, the foundational text to be reinterpreted, Genesis 17, is not evident until Rom 2:25. The larger narrative text from Deuteronomy, while forming the interpretive background to the whole, does not become obvious until at least v. 22 or, more likely, at the end of the passage, vv. 28 and 29. The primary interpretive texts from Jeremiah, which shape Paul's conclu-

---

meaning, and result of circumcision on a much broader scale. See also Segal, *Paul the Convert*, 187–223. For further discussion on gentiles as proselytes or adherents to Judaism with regard to the necessity of circumcision see Terence Donaldson, *Paul and the Gentiles: Remapping Paul's Convictional World* (Minneapolis: Fortress, 1997) 54–69.

sion about Israel's guilt, are evident from v. 17 on. While we will investigate Paul's application of these texts in their "Roman" order, we must remember that the exegesis of OT reference texts must be understood to stand behind the entirety, from beginning to end.

ANALYSIS OF ROM 2:17–29

THE INTERLOCUTOR

Beginning with 2:17 Paul speaks directly to a Jewish interlocutor.[18] Just what type of person this interlocutor is supposed to be remains in dispute. Dunn describes the interlocutor as "the typical Jew...conscious of his Jewishness, of his distinctiveness from the nations."[19] A more specific identification is proposed by Goppelt. Goppelt believes Paul's argument is directed against Jews styling themselves as self-appointed missionaries, in contradistinction to his mission to the gentiles.[20]

Goppelt concludes that the interlocutor is a type of the person who relies on the law, and does not extend to the

---

[18]"Paul...now names his interlocutor directly 'Jew'" (Pesch, *Römerbrief*, 35).

[19]*Romans 1–8*, 109. Dunn avoids the common caricature of a monolithic Judaism characterized by Pharisaic legalism. That caricature is rightly criticized by Stowers: "Neither Paul's audience in Rome nor anyone else in the Roman empire would have or could have recognized 2:17–29 as a depiction of the typical Jew. The caricature did not yet exist" (*Rereading*, 144). This is correct if "typical Jew" means "Pharisaic legalist." Dunn's more limited description of a "typical Jew" is, however, likely to have been widely recognized.

Sanders has dispelled the myth of a legalisitic Jewish religion of works righteousness: "Repentance was considered to be the condition on the basis of which God forgives. God did not force one to maintain an obedient and repentant attitude against his will. What is wrong with the view that repentance in Rabbinic religion is a *work* which earns 'mercy' is that it leaves out of account the fundamental basis of that religion, namely, God's election of Israel. The theme of repentance and forgiveness functions within a larger structure which is founded on the understanding that 'All Israelites have a share in the world to come.' This view, it is clear, is based on an understanding of the grace of God" (*Paul and Palestinian Judaism*, 177). See also, ibid., 233–25.

[20]Goppelt, "Der Missionar des Gesetzes," 138–39.

whole nation. As already mentioned, Stowers takes this missionary hypothesis a step further, proposing a hypothetical competitor to whom Paul can freely attribute the status of "transgressor" as he wishes.[21] Stowers also makes the important point that "the first two chapters of Romans speak of Jews and gentiles as peoples and not in abstract-individual-universal terms."[22]

However, because Stowers believes the interlocutor to be a specific character-type, he, like Goppelt, does not understand the accusations of 2:17–24 to extend to the entire Jewish nation.[23] He argues that Paul nowhere says "the Jews have lost their basic relation to God," which is true in itself.[24] But Stowers wants to read this as a promise to gentiles of equality before God, elevating gentiles rather than leveling Jews. This misses the point of the intertextual references, which show that the relationship of the Jews to God, while not lost, has changed. Stowers is correct that "[Paul] never argues or implies the end of God's covenant with the Jews."[25] However, the curses of the covenant from Deuteronomy have been instituted. Jews can no longer rely on their status as Jews for assurance of the covenant blessings or, in Pauline terms, for salvation.

Even though the caricature of Jewish legalism did not yet exist, the intertextual references used by Paul allow him to address the nation as a people-group (which Stowers himself emphasizes) through the pretentious teacher. Paul is not attempting to gain acceptance with an unbelieving gentile audience against Jewish missionaries.[26] Nor is he addressing

---

[21]Stowers, *Rereading*, 155; "Paul speaks to a Jewish teacher about his work with gentiles" (ibid., 149).

[22]Ibid., 107–8. That is, Paul speaks generally of the guilt of Jews and gentiles as people groups rather than individual guilt.

[23]"Paul does not speak of Judaism in general in 2:17–29, but rather he addresses an imaginary individual Jew" (ibid., 144).

[24]Ibid., 128–29.

[25]Ibid., 129.

[26]Stowers, *Rereading*, 142, 150; "the pretentiousness of the Jewish teacher comes from his thinking that he can transform the gentiles by getting them to do works of the law" (ibid., 151).

only gentile believers to clarify their relationship to Jews and the law.[27] Rather he is speaking to a mixed audience, all of whom are being instructed about the equal standing of Jews and gentiles before God.

The fact that diatribal attacks against pretentious teachers are typical does not mean this is an "attack on a pretentious teacher" only.[28] Because of the intertextual references it has wider application to the Jews as a whole who, as Dunn pointed out, were aware of their distinctive identity and believed themselves to have a special covenantal relationship with God. This judgment is confirmed at the very outset of the following analysis.

THE JEWISH CHARACTERIZATION IN ROM 2:17–20
Calling Oneself a Jew:

The opening phrase of Rom 2:17, Εἰ δὲ σὺ Ἰουδαῖος ἐπονομάζῃ ("but if you call yourself a Jew"), engages as a dialogue partner any Jewish reader/hearer who accepts the prevailing self-understanding of Jewish identity, however general it may be.[29] The use of a diatribal imaginary interlocutor does not negate the fact that a Jewish hearer of the phrase, "but if you call yourself a Jew," will give participatory attention as one being addressed, though perhaps not addressed individually.

In fact, a rhetorical effect of such an interlocutor is to allow the writer to address a group or person indirectly. This point in itself makes it likely that Paul has Jews as well as gentiles in mind as his intended audience. The type of a pretentious teacher allows Paul to level otherwise objectionable

---

[27]Stowers, *Rereading*, 36. In this conclusion Stowers has modified his earlier position, wherein he assumed that the presence of an "influential but small Jewish Christian minority at Rome" helps account for the discussion of "Jewish questions" in Romans (*Diatribe*, 183).

[28]Stowers argues against Jews as part of the intended audience of the epistle (*Rereading*, 29–33). In so doing he ignores his own evidence that diatribe indirectly addresses a real situation although without discussing "their particular problems in any direct way" (*Diatribe*, 180–81).

[29] Or "if you are called a Jew." The self-descriptive nature of the entire section points toward the middle rather than the passive reading.

accusations, which through his intertextual references are
applicable to Jews who trust in their identification as the
people of God.

The address Ἰουδαῖος now takes on a significance it
would not have if the OT texts Paul is drawing from were not
taken into consideration.[30] Paul is addressing not only those
"having the embodiment of knowledge and the truth in the
law" (ἔχοντα τὴν μόρφωσιν τῆς γνώσεως καὶ τῆς ἀληθείας ἐν
τῷ νόμῳ, 2:20). In vv. 17–24 he considers them also to be
those having the necessary corollary derived from his OT references which charge all of Israel with law-breaking. They are
law-breakers under condemnation because of their self-
identification as Jews. In the same way that gentiles as a
whole are condemned in chap. 1, self-identification as a Jew
automatically makes one a participant in the guilt of Israel,
as Paul learns from his reference texts.

In vv. 17–20 many of the positive designations of the
Jew, even those which do not originate in a Pauline reference
text, have either OT antecedents or were common stock in
Jewish sources.[31] The first identifying characteristic of a Jew
in v. 17, "and [if you] rely on the Law" (καὶ ἐπαναπαύῃ νόμῳ),

---

[30]This is not to assume that the original readers were aware of
Paul's references to those texts. But for those who were they give a
greater understanding of how this passage fits into the larger whole of
the epistle. For the development of Ἰουδαῖος, "Jew," see esp. Dunn (*Romans 1–8*, 109) and Käsemann (*Commentary on Romans*, 69).

[31]This is particularly true of vv. 19–20, as will be seen. There is
ample support for Krentz's statement that "In Rom 2:17–20 Paul describes claims made by his fellow Jews about their fidelity to the law"
("The Name of God," 430). Cranfield makes the same point: "In vv.
17–20 Paul appears to be deliberately taking up claims which were actually being made by his fellow Jews, echoing the very language in
which they were being expressed" (*The Epistle to the Romans*, 1.164).
See Str-B, 3.96–105 for a few parallels beyond those that follow. However, it is pride in relationship to God and the law as identifiers of Jews
as people of the covenant rather than pride in their fidelity to the law itself which is the point. It is not simply that they claim to keep the law
but do not. The implications of not keeping the law are larger in the OT
references which inform Paul's argument. It is because of infidelity to
the law that the covenant relationship of the Jews is not what they believe it to be.

continues the establishment of a Jewish self-identification with the interlocutor. The attitude of reliance upon God when such reliance is unwarranted is not unknown.[32]

Being "people of the law," along with being "children of Abraham," is the bedrock of Jewish self-understanding.[33] Relationship to the law as the basis of religious and cultural norms sets apart the Jews as the covenant people who recognize their status as chosen. To "rely (or rest) on the law" implies not relying on the law itself to save but to recognize one's position among the people of the law of the covenant as a position of special relationship with God.[34] This understanding is not uncommon in the OT and Jewish literature, and is well summed up in 2 Apoc. Bar. 48:22–24:

> In you we have put our trust, because, behold, your Law is with
> us, and we know that we do not fall
> as long as we keep your statutes.
> We shall always be blessed; at least, we did not mingle
> with the nations.

---

[32]Cambier ("Le jugement de tous les hommes," 206), Dunn (*Romans 1–8*, 110) and Käsemann (*Commentary on Romans*, 69) mention similar language in Mic 3:11, but I find no evidence of specific intertextual reference. The passage does share a surface similarity in the use of ἐπαναπαύομαι and an attitude of false security. Though the religious leaders are corrupt, "yet they lean upon the Lord and say, 'Surely the Lord is with us! No harm shall come upon us.'"

[33]It is exactly that other stratum of bedrock, "children of Abraham," which Paul will address in chap. 4.

[34]See James D. G. Dunn, *The Theology of Paul the Apostle* (Grand Rapids: Eerdmans, 1998) 137. Dunn points out that the way of life of the law sets apart the Jew as "distinctive" from the gentile, and that Paul attacks reliance on that distinctiveness (*Romans 1–8*, 110). Paul later takes up the question of the law's inability to save. For a description of covenant theology and Jewish identity, see Wright, *The New Testament and the People of God*, 159–79). He describes the function of suffering, forgiveness, and restoration on both the national and individual levels under the covenant. E. P. Sanders extensively addresses the ancient Jewish conception of salvation from distress in this world and as participation in the world to come. In that discussion Sanders shows that Jewish assurance of a place in the world to come derived not from keeping the law, but from membership among the chosen people (*Paul and Palestinian Judaism*, 125–182).

For we are all a people of the Name;
we, who received one Law from the One.
And that Law that is among us will help us,
and that excellent wisdom which is in us will support us.[35]

As is clear from Rom 3:1–2 and 9:4–5, Paul, like his Jewish interlocutor, understands the Jews as people of the law to have a special covenant relationship with God. It is that fact which he establishes in 2:17 and does not dispute. Rather, he seeks to establish this common understanding with his interlocutor. However, the intertextual references of these verses undercut Jewish reliance upon that relationship because of covenant-breaking disobedience. Once the interlocutor, or a Jew identifying with that interlocutor, acknowledges relationship with God and the law as a Jew, Paul then introduces the references which call into question Jewish assurance of covenantal blessing on that basis.[36] Those references are not yet apparent, and the conclusions to which they lead will not be drawn until v. 21.

Implied Consequences of Jewish Identity:

Such references become apparent immediately after establishing an assumed acknowledgment of Jewish identity.[37]

---

[35]*OTP*, 1.48. See also 46:4–6; Bar 3:37–4:4; Dunn, *Romans 1–8*, 110; Fitzmyer, *Romans*, 316.

[36]Even without the impact of the intertextual references the passage is rhetorically effective in calling that assurance into question, though not as logically effective. 2:17–20 are an example of anacoluthon. "[T]he protasis, the conditional form begun in 2:17, has no grammatical apodosis" (Cambier, "Le jugement de tous les hommes," 206). Käsemann describes the effect of the anacoluthon as "materially appropriate. The advantages of the Jew are impressively accumulated, and then when they reach their crest they break to pieces like a wave" (*Commentary on Romans*, 69). He calls vv. 17–23 "a masterpiece of rhetoric." See also Pesch, *Römerbrief*, 35.

[37]Käsemann says, "the attack is yet to come," and, "these claims [of Jewish virtue] lose their credibility only when they no longer coincide with reality" (*Commentary on Romans*, 69). Actually the OT references already underlie v. 17. Käsemann himself says that καυχᾶσθαι of vv. 17, 23 derives from Jer 9:23 and is a "key word." Why, then, does he deny that the attack is already underway? Even on the surface of the text the "if" at the beginning of the description of Jewish identity indicates something to follow. The credibility of the claims of Jewish superi-

In the following phrases in v. 17, "and you boast in God and know the will" (καὶ καυχᾶσαι ἐν θεῷ καὶ γινώσκεις τὸ θέλημα), the words καυχᾶσαι ("you boast"), γινώσκεις ("you know"), and θέλημα ("will"), all derive from Jer 9:23–24.[38] There the one who boasts is enjoined not to boast in wisdom, strength, or wealth, but to boast in the knowledge of God (ἀλλ᾽ ἢ ἐν τούτῳ καυχάσθω ὁ καυχώμενος, συνίειν καὶ γινώσκειν ὅτι ἐγώ εἰμι κύριος), the will of whom (ὅτι ἐν τούτοις τὸ θέλημά μου) is to do mercy, justice, and righteousness upon the earth.

The context is a warning of judgment upon those who are disobedient and who trust in things other than the Lord. Jeremiah goes on to assert that all Israel is uncircumcised in heart. Paul will refer to this shortly, but the assumption already underlies his argument. The verses are actually a warning to those who trust in their security to watch out for the days of judgment to come. Even though a call for a return to God is included, the assumption of the passage is that repentance is not forthcoming and that judgment is impending. Those who are boasting are putting their confidence in the wrong things, and will reap the consequences, including loss of status as God's "circumcised." As already seen, Jeremiah assumes a broken covenant and the institution of the deuteronomic curses. Paul is exegetically dependent upon this context, bringing it to bear in his own argument.

In Rom 2:18, "you test (approve) the things that are important" (δοκιμάζεις τὰ διαφέροντα)[39] has to do with the ability to distinguish between those things that are essential to a life of righteousness and those that are not.[40] It is trans-

---

ority is lost if Paul already refers to Jeremiah 9. The positive statements are not simply ironic, and can be taken as Jewish self-affirmation, but they carry with them the double-edge of the references behind them.

[38]Though this evidence was presented in chap. 2, in order to prevent continuous cross-reference to chap. 2 and to facilitate clarity, some of that evidence is presented again here.

[39]The phrase is difficult to translate: "determine what is best" (NRSV); "approve of what is superior" (NIV).

[40]Walter Grundmann, "δόκιμος," *TDNT* 2.260; Konrad Weiss, "διαφέρω," *TDNT* 9.63–64. Cf. Phil 1:10 εἰς τὸ δοκιμάζειν ὑμᾶς τὰ

lated in a variety of ways, but in any case the point in the end
will be, as in the rest of these descriptions, that the Jew in
fact has misunderstood what is important. Jewish identity
and the external requirements of the law in which the Jew
takes pride in having been instructed (κατηχούμενος, 2:18)
have been substituted for "the obedience of faith" (1:5).[41]

Misplaced assurance is also reflected in Rom 2:19 in the
reference to Jeremiah 7. As noted when references were identified, Jer 7:8 warns against trusting in deceptive words (εἰ δὲ
ὑμεῖς πεποίθατε ἐπὶ λόγοις ψευδέσιν). Judah is trusting in
(πεποίθατε) relationship to God's temple (7:4), yet is guilty of
gross disobedience (v. 9). In Rom 2:17, 19 the Jews are characterized as trusting in statements which identify them as
God's people "but if you...believe yourself... to be" (Εἰ δὲ σὺ
...πέποιθάς τε σεαυτὸν...εἶναι). Yet in 2:21–22 they will be
charged with disobedience in the very language of Jer 7:9.

By identification with the security thought to be com-
mensurate with being a Jew—relying on the law, boasting in
God, and knowing God's will—the interlocutor is in reality
choosing to identify himself or herself as one standing under
condemnation as a law-breaker who is "uncircumcised in
heart," though Paul has yet to bring those exegetical conclusions to the surface.

The language of Isa 42:6–7 echoes in v 19. The Jew considers himself or herself to be "a guide to the blind" (ὁδηγὸν...τυφλῶν), and "a light to those in darkness" (φῶς τῶν ἐν
σκότει).[42] Isaiah does not provide the explication necessary to

---

διαφέροντα ("to help you to determine what is best" [NRSV]; "so that
you may be able to discern what is best" [NIV]). For references to hellenistic use of τὰ διαφέροντα in the sense of "essential" or "important.
things" see Lietzmann, *An die Römer*, 43. See also Cranfield, *The Epistle
to the Romans*, 1.164.

[41]It is probably unnecessary to go so far as Käsemann and assume that Paul uses κατηχούμενος in a technical sense about "the fixed
catechetical traditions of Judaism" (*Commentary on Romans*, 70).
Though clearly "being instructed in the law" and being in relationship
with the law is one of the identifiers of a Jew, it is not clear that there
was a single fixed tradition of catechetical instruction.

[42]And 49:6. Lietzmann may be correct that Paul is dependent

be understood as an exegetical reference. However, the ideas need not be dependent upon Isaiah. They are common, and define Paul's interlocutor in familiar and positive terms.[43] This is also true to a certain extent for the Jewish role of "instructor," although it is not as broadly familiar. Similar language appears in Qumran literature.[44] The descriptions in v. 20, "corrector of the foolish" (παιδευτὴν ἀφρόνων), and "teacher of children" (διδάσκαλον νηπίων), are positive labels.

Another positive designation follows: "having the embodiment/form of knowledge and truth in the Law" (ἔχοντα τὴν μόρφωσιν τῆς γνώσεως καὶ τῆς ἀληθείας ἐν τῷ νόμῳ). Fitzmyer's statement is correct: "Paul does not speak with irony in these verses...he realizes the privileged status of Israel."[45] However, in Paul's view this understanding of the role

___

upon these passages for the language (*An die Römer*, 43), but the phrases and ideas are common enough that this is not necessarily the case.

[43]*1 Enoch* 105:1: "for you are their [the children of the earth] guides; and [you are] a reward upon the whole earth"; *Sib. Or.* 3:194–95: "And then the people of the great God...will be guides in life for all mortals"; Isa 49:6: "I will give you [the servant of the Lord] as a light to the nations"; Wis 18:4: "through whom [God's holy ones] the imperishable light of the law was to be given to the world"; In *T. Levi* 14:4 a warning is given because "you want to destroy the light of the Law which was granted to you for the enlightenment of every person."

[44]1QS 3:13: "that he may inform and teach all the sons of light about the history of all the sons of man"; 1QS 9:12, 18, 20: "These are the regulations for the Instructor...He should lead them with knowledge and in this way teach them...and he will teach them about all that has been discovered." Translation from Florentino García Martínez, *The Dead Sea Scrolls Translated: The Qumran Texts in English* (trans. Wilfred Watson; Leiden: E. J. Brill, 1994). These texts, however, though often cited, do not speak of Israel as instructor of gentiles. Rather, they speak of the Teacher of Righteousness instructing the sons of light. See also Dunn, *Romans 1–8*, 112; Käsemann *Commentary on Romans*, 70. Dunn also mentions Hos 5:2; Sir 37:19; *Pss. Sol.* 8:29; 4 Macc 5:34. However, these last merely use forms of παιδευτής and offer no real parallels to the idea of Jews having a role as instructors.

[45]Fitzmyer, *Romans*, 315. He follows Anders Nygren, *Commentary on Romans* (Philadelphia: Muhlenberg, 1949) 131. Contra Johannes Behm: "This judgment, which is stated with obvious irony by Paul, is not the same as his own estimate of the significance of the Law, in spite

of the law is certainly inadequate.[46] The phrase serves as a climactic over-arching statement under which all of the other positive statements are included.[47] Yet, by identification as a Jew through these phrases the interlocutor bears the condemnation also being appropriated through Paul's intertextual references.[48] Paul intermingles Jewish self-identifying phrases which have an entirely positive connotation with the double-edged identifying phrases of his intertextual references. The conclusions Paul has reached on the basis of those references become explicit beginning in Rom 2:21–24.

THE INDICTMENT OF ROM 2:21–24

The references exist in the exegetical background of Paul's rhetoric, and are not produced as proofs. They are the source rather than the structure of his argument to this point, and have been beneath the surface. With 2:21–24 Paul will bring the recognition of the guilt that his references imply

---

of R. 7:7 ff; 2:13 ff; 3:31; 9:4; 13:8" ("μόρφωσις," *TDNT*, 4.754–55). It appears that a predetermined opinion about a Pauline antithesis between law and grace implying a thoroughgoing antipathy to the law leads Behm to dismiss the significant evidence of Paul's high estimation of the law. Paul certainly shares with his interlocutor the belief in the "embodiment of truth in the law," though he now understands the limitations of the law as well and Jewish misunderstanding of it. For the currency of the concepts see also Sir 24:23 (where the attributes of wisdom are "the covenant-book of God Most High, the law which Moses enacted"), Bar 4:1 ("[Wisdom] is the book of the commandments of God, the law that stands forever") and *2 Apoc. Bar.* 44:14 ("They have preserved the truth of the Law").

[46]Paul's view of the law is Jewish, too. But because of his experience of Christ he understands the role of the law as limited.

[47]Cranfield, *The Epistle to the Romans*, 1.167.

[48]Lietzmann states that vv. 19–20 "give the impression that Paul cites the words of a Jewish writing intended for proselytes" (*An die Römer*, 43). Schlier adopts Lietzmann's view: "Indeed, one may even surmise that behind the expression 'the form of knowledge and truth' stands a title for a piece of Jewish propaganda" (*Der Römerbrief*, 44). Again, the ideas are so common that it is unnecessary to posit a specific document behind Paul's words. In Str-B 3.98 it is stated that most hellenistic-Jewish literature is at its base "Propagandaliteratur."

near to the surface of his argument by direct confrontation.[49] Those who claim to be knowledgeable guides, who blindly and ignorantly identify themselves with Israel and who trust in a superior position based on their possession of the law, cannot rely on possession of the law to be the advantage they have assumed.[50] In Paul's intertextual references the prophets have characterized the people of the law as law-breakers no longer enjoying the benefits of the covenant.

The Propriety of the Indictment:

In v. 21, asking the teachers if they teach themselves calls into question the assumptions behind all of the preceding designations of Jewish identity. But it is the following three questions, which accuse the Jew of stealing, adultery, and temple robbery, that most clearly show the exegetical background of Paul's thought.[51] These accusations in vv. 21–22 comprise the section commentators find most difficult to account for, and the section best explained by Paul's use of intertextual references in his exegesis.[52]

Previous attempts to explain how Paul can legitimately make the kind of charges he does are many and varied.[53]

---

[49]Cambier says that "if the tone of the first part [vv. 17–20] is ironic, the second [vv. 21–24] is polemical: it is a direct attack against the conduct of the Jew" ("Le jugement de tous les hommes," 207).

[50]"In Rom 2:21 Paul's first rhetorical question implies that in reality the law does not do for the Jews what they claim it does" (Krentz, "The Name of God," 430).

[51]"We can read these five equally constructed sentences as questions or as assertions. They have in any case an affirmative sense" (Goppelt, "Der Missionar des Gesetzes," 139).

[52]"The challenges posed here have puzzled many commentators, since the moral caliber of Judaism was one of the features which made it most attractive…It is the rhetorical flourish which constitutes the exaggeration" (Dunn, *Romans 1–8*, 113). When Paul's references are understood the passage is not merely a rhetorical flourish nor is it really an exaggeration.

[53]A unique interpretation is proposed by Neil Elliott, in which nothing in Rom 2:17–3:20 is an indictment at all. Rather, Paul assumes his interlocutor will agree with him regarding Jewish *accountability* for their sin. Elliott presupposes a gentile Christian audience, and argues that Paul presents a Jewish understanding of even Jewish accountability for their sin as evidence of the accountability of all people: "Romans

Some commentators ignore the question of the legitimacy of the charges entirely, simply assuming Paul's indictment as applicable to Jews in general, perhaps viewing its rhetorical effect as sufficient to carry the weight of the argument.[54] The observation of Stowers, followed by Pattee, that the diatribal attack centers on hypocrisy and inconsistency, still requires some basis in reality for the charges, even if the interlocutor is imaginary and the diatribe attacks a position only indirectly.[55] Dunn explains the universal character of the charges

---

2–3 are written not *against* the Jew but *with* the Jew, so to speak" (*The Rhetoric of Romans: Argumentative Constraint and Strategy and Paul's Dialogue with Judaism* [JSNTSup 45; Sheffield: JSOT Press, 1990] 203, 127–46, 191–223). Elliott's attempt to remove the sense of indictment from the passage is ultimately not convincing when one reads the text as it stands. The tone of indictment is definite, even though it is a critique from within the Jewish community. George P. Carras conceives of 2:1–29 as "an interpretation of the Jewish ideals by two Jews who offer differing perspectives" ("Romans 2,1–29: A Dialogue on Jewish Ideals," *Bib* 73 [1992] 206). Carras's conclusion is marred by his starting point. It seems odd to look to Paul's argument in Romans 2 "to determine whether within Paul's critique of the Jewish religion there are common elements of Judaism" (ibid., 188). There probably are some common elements in Second Temple Judaism, and some of them may be evident in Romans 2; but an exegetically and theologically driven portrait like Paul's hardly seems like the most reliable source for identifying those elements.

[54]E.g., Schlier, *Der Römerbrief*, 45; Fitzmyer, *Romans*, 318; Black, *Romans*, 59–60; Brunner, *To the Romans*, 22–23. Stowers (*Rereading*, 155) has no difficulty with the charges and whether or not they are literally true because he believes, as I do not, that the audience is entirely gentile, so rhetorical effect is all that is necessary. It is worth noting in either case that the passage has been understood as rhetorically effective for centuries without attention to the intertextual connections. One of the reasons is the familiarity of both ancient and modern readers with such blanket indictments in the OT. See, e.g., Frank Thielman (*Paul & The Law: A Contextual Approach* [Downers Grove, IL: InterVarsity, 1994] 291 n. 39). However, the question of the universal application of the indictment has continually resurfaced.

[55]On hypocrisy and inconsistency as the center of the diatribal attack, see Stowers (*Diatribe*, 110–15) and Pattee ("Stumbling Stone or Cornerstone?," 88); "but the diatribe makes no sense unless certain students...at least have the tendencies displayed by the interlocutor" (Stowers, *Diatribe*, 181). Stowers offers no evidence in his own assess-

as a warning to those righteous Jews not to put their trust in being people of the law.[56]

C. H. Dodd, on the other hand, attributes Paul's charges to a degrading of Jewish morals which actually resulted in the behavior alleged.[57] He does acknowledge that it is a nation-wide claim that is being made, not a charge to an individual Jew. However, there simply isn't the evidence of a "terrible degradation of Jewish morals." E. P. Sanders contends that the entire section of Romans (1:18–2:29) is a rhetorical exaggeration.[58] If so, for Paul it is hyperbole based *in scripture* and speaks to the status of Jews under the covenant.

Barrett and Cranfield address the legitimacy of the charges.[59] Barrett draws an explicit parallel between Paul's charges in Romans and Matt 5:21–48. "[B]ut the nation was inwardly guilty already. When theft, adultery, and sacrilege

---

ment of his proposed Jewish pretentious teachers that the diatribe has a basis in actual behavior, concluding only that Paul attacks "Jewish teachers who behave like the one in 2:17–29" (*Rereading*, 144–50). The evidence will be found in Paul's intertextual references.

[56]*Romans 1–8*, 114. While Dunn cites numerous OT and extra-canonical parallels, he has not made mention of Paul's exegetical reference to them. Käsemann (*Commentary on Romans*, 69) also notes, "The Jew was summoned to all this by the OT," yet fails to follow up on the ties of OT passages to Paul's argument.

[57]Dodd, *Epistle*, 39.

[58]"Paul's case for universal sinfulness, as it is stated in Rom 1:18–2:29, is not convincing: it is internally inconsistent and rests on gross exaggeration. In Paul's own time this sort of exaggerated statement may have had rhetorical force, but nevertheless, we should recognize that Rom 1:18–2:29 was not written to give an objective, or even a consistent, description of Jews and gentiles. Paul knows the conclusion he wants to draw, and it is the conclusion which is important to him" Sanders, *Paul, the Law*, 125). Paul could not have come to this conclusion if he did not believe the statements he makes to have a basis in fact.

[59]"Paul's argument is lost if he is compelled to rely on comparatively unusual events, and it is simply not true that the average Jewish missionary acted in this way" (Barrett, *Epistle to the Romans*, 53). "It is anyway of course quite certain that there were many Jews in Paul's day who were not guilty of theft, adultery or temple robbing (or sacrilege) in the ordinary sense of the word" (Cranfield, *The Epistle to the Romans*, 1.168).

are strictly and radically understood, there is no man who is not guilty of all three."[60] Cranfield agrees, stating that "this seems more probable—that Paul is thinking in terms of a radical understanding of the law (cf. Matt 5.21–48)."[61] Dunn is correct in his assessment that the thesis of Barrett and Cranfield "is unnecessary, and in fact misses the point."[62]

Answering a perceived need to legitimate the charges, even commentators who view Paul's charges as other than literal cite numerous examples to demonstrate that at least some of Paul's Jewish contemporaries were guilty of the particular sins mentioned.[63] Stealing and adultery presumably need no supporting examples. Most commentators simply assume that these are common offenses in Israel as elsewhere.[64]

Idolatry and Temple Robbery:

But ἱεροσυλεῖν (temple robbery) evidently requires some explanation, and has occasioned numerous theories as

---

[60]Barrett, *Epistle to the Romans*, 54.

[61]Cranfield, *The Epistle to the Romans*, 1.169.

[62]Dunn, *Romans 1–8*, 114.

[63]Those, like Dunn, who believe a few representatives of evildoers simply undercut the pride of the rest of the Jews obviously only need a few examples to feel that Paul has made his rhetorical point (*Romans 1–8*, 116).

[64]These first two charges are almost universally passed over by commentators without attempts to provide examples of their commission by contemporary Jews, unlike attempts to find examples of temple robbery. The notable exceptions to this assumption are Goppelt and Krentz. Goppelt proposes that Paul's indictments originate in the context of gospel and Essene indictments against the Jerusalem priesthood. The scribes of the law *"circumvent the Law with the help of their interpretation of the Law."* Goppelt argues that Paul's interlocutor(s), possibly symbolically, "succumb to the two sins which they abhor as typically gentile: greed and indecency." The third indictment, temple robbery, is understood symbolically as the embodiment of the first two indictments. If greed and indecency are the essential features of gentile behavior, and if Paul speaks of the community and behavior as temple and worship (2 Cor 6:14–18), then by desiring adultery and theft, the Jew "robs the gentile temple" ("Der Missionar des Gesetzes," 142–43; emphasis his). This analysis requires quite a stretch to 2 Corinthians and is not convincing. Krentz believes greed, sexual impurity, and idolatry in 2:21–22 are specifically chosen to parallel the gentile sins of chap. 1 ("The Name of God," 437–38). The parallel is too limited to commend this explanation.

to how this could be literally, or even figuratively, true. Even given the fact of two possible uses of the word—either as temple robbery or as general sacrilege—the attribution of guilt to Jews has been a difficult interpretive problem.[65] Cranfield's assessment that "in Paul's time it could be confidently assumed that there was no longer any idolatry in Israel" is generally accepted.[66]

This is supported as early as Jdt 8:18: "For never in our generation, nor in these present days, has there been any tribe or family or people or town of ours that worships gods made with hands, as was done in days gone by." Rabbinic statements of Jewish pride in idolatry's eradication attest to this as well.[67] Edgar Krentz suggests that while this may have been true in Israel, "the situation in the diaspora may have been quite different."[68] However, Krentz gives no supporting evidence.

Garlington asks the appropriate question: "How could Israel *qua* Israel have been guilty of the sort of behaviour depicted by either sense of ἱεροσυλεῖν?"[69] Cranfield proposes some sort of generally sacrilegious behavior.[70]   Garlington, followed by Fitzmyer, proposes a figurative meaning.[71] Paul's

---

[65]G. Schrenk, "ἱεροσυλέω," *TDNT* 3.255. Krentz has compiled an impressive list of uses of the term in Greek literature from the Thesaurus Linguae Graecae data-base ("The Name of God," 433, n. 22). It most often appears as a component of lists of vices or crimes.

[66]Cranfield, *The Epistle to the Romans*, 1.169. Also Garlington, "ΙΕΡΟΣΥΛΕΙΝ," 142; Dunn, *Romans 1–8*, 114.

[67]Str-B, 3.111–12, gives numerous examples to support the contention that "the rabbinic scholars considered it an established matter that in their time idol worship no longer had a place in Israel." Those examples indicate that it had not existed since the Babylonian exile.

[68]Krentz, "The Name of God," 438.

[69]Garlington, "ΙΕΡΟΣΥΛΕΙΝ," 142.

[70]"[W]e may take him to be thinking not only of behaviour which is obviously sacrilegious, but also of less obvious and more subtle forms of sacrilege" (Cranfield, *The Epistle to the Romans*, 1.169–70).

[71]Garlington finds an idolatry motif from Genesis and Wisdom which ties Israel to the idolatry of Adam and all of humanity in general. This exposition on Adam and Israel then "implies that in Paul's mind there was a connection between Israel's idolatry and her ethnic, religious, and political self-awareness as the people of God" ("ΙΕΡΟΣΥΛΕΙΝ,"

accusation of idolatry followed by the statement that this person "boasts in the law," according to Garlington, "suggests most forcefully that for Paul *the new idol is the Torah!* The 'sacrilege' in question is *Israel's idolatrous attachment to the law itself.*"[72] The argument, among other problems, relies too heavily on identifying boasting in the law specifically with the preceding charge of idolatry. Boasting in the law would then logically also be expected to be identified with theft and adultery. Such a correlation is unlikely.

By far the more common approach is to take ἱεροσυλεῖν literally in some sense. Often mentioned but seldom supported is the possibility of robbery from the Jerusalem temple. Although a few texts, such as Mal 3:8–9, *Pss. Sol.* 8:11, and *T. Levi* 14:5, make such charges, they usually have to do with the more figurative withholding of tithes, or are not specific about the nature of the robbery. The idolatry-related context of Paul's text makes this connection unlikely.[73] An accusation related to pagan temples is more often suggested.

Derrett discusses evidence that Jews were "profiting...from a heathen religious endowment's assets," by accepting rents on idol-owned lands, selling stolen idol temple

---

148). Wright calls it the "idol of their own national identity and security" (*The New Testament and the People of God*, 475). He also speaks of the law in relation to the "idolatry of national privilege" in discussion of Romans 9 (*The Climax of the Covenant*, 240). See his extensive discussion of Paul's understanding of idolatry (ibid., 122–135).

In his commentary, though Garlington is listed in the bibliography for the section, Fitzmyer (*Romans*, 318) has evidently missed an attribution when quoting Garlington ("ΙΕΡΟΣΥΛΕΙΝ," 151): "[Israel has committed] the idolatry of elevating the Mosaic Law to a position of unwarranted devotion and of bestowing on it a permanence it was never intended to have in God's ultimate plan."

[72]Garlington, "ΙΕΡΟΣΥΛΕΙΝ," 144, 147–48; emphasis his. Garlington also approvingly views Cranfield's assessment that Paul is radicalizing the law in the same manner as Matthew 5 (ibid., 147 n. 30).

[73]Equally unlikely as the source of Paul's charge is the isolated incident in which four Jewish rogues in Rome defrauded Fulvia of her offering for the Jerusalem temple (Josephus, *Ant.* 18.81–84) proposed by F. F. Bruce (*The Epistle of Paul to the Romans: An Introduction and Commentary* [TNTC 6; Grand Rapids: Eerdmans, 1985] 93).

furnishings, or selling the idols themselves. According to Derrett, taking money either legally, or perhaps illegally, since there are two divergent legal strains in Judaism, is still against the "law of conscience."[74] Derrett's proposal is convoluted, relying on tenuous legal technicalities which display no relation to Paul's text. There is some evidence for a more direct plundering of idol temples and perhaps enrichment through the sale of the stolen items, as a number of commentators propose.[75] Even so, evidence of Jewish participation in temple robbery is minimal. Garlington points out the weakness of believing that Paul would impute these isolated occurrences to all Jews without more evidence.[76]

There is a still greater problem. Though the figurative interpretations such as those of Barrett, Cranfield and Garlington, and the financial gain hypothesis of Derrett attempt to address the issue, none of these proposals explains how ἱεροσυλεῖν is a counterpart to "you abhor idols."[77] Krentz is correct that "the question ought to conclude 'do you practice idolatry?' or 'do you worship cultic images?' But Paul instead

---

[74]Derrett"'You Abominate False Gods,'" 570–71. Schrenk says "[t]his probably means making profit out of such costly articles, e.g., votive offerings" ("ἱεροσυλέω," 256). Schrenk, like others however, also emphasizes the actual act of plunder of pagan shrines.

[75]They refer to, e.g., Acts 19:37; Josephus *Ant.* 4.207. For the rather limited evidence of the actual occurrence of Jews robbing idol temples, but at least often enough to merit comment by the rabbis and by Paul, see Str-B. 3.113–14. Supporters of this view include Schrenk, "ἱεροσυλέω," 256; Sanday and Headlam, *Romans*, 66; Lietzmann, *An die Römer*, 43; Dunn, Romans *1–8*, 114–15; Käsemann, *Commentary on Romans*, 71; Murray, *Epistle to the Romans*, 84; Krentz, "The Name of God," 434.

[76]Garlington, "ΙΕΡΟΣΥΛΕΙΝ," 143. Black's claim, that a worldwide charge against Jews as temple robbers was widely known, is unsubstantiated (*Romans*, 60).

[77]It is the necessity for some connection which leads most commentators to believe Paul's accusation has to do with idol temples rather than the Jerusalem temple. "Ἱροσυλεῖν must be understood in antithesis to 'you abhor idols,' meaning 'you rob *their* temples, so seize idols for yourself" (Goppelt, "Der Missionar des Gesetzes," 144). However, this still does not adequately explain how ἱεροσυλεῖν logically follows "you abhor idols."

accuses the Jews of temple robbery. The conclusion does not follow logically."[78] Any hypothesis to account for the charges Paul makes must deal adequately with the legitimacy and universal application of the charges, and the connection of idolatry with temple robbery which Paul implies.

The question is this: how is the interlocutor or someone identified with the interlocutor as a Jew, in Käsemann's words, "trapped" by accusations that have no application to most individual Jews?[79] More fundamentally and to the point of this study, why should Paul himself believe this to be the case? Commentators offer no convincing reason why this should logically follow. There must be some basis upon which these charges can stand, even if Paul is only making a hyperbolic rhetorical point.

A Basis for the Indictment:

The basis for his indictment is the OT passages which point out that Israel has broken the terms of the covenant. On the basis of the nation's history and its consequences as represented in OT texts, Paul makes a charge of law-breaking guilt against contemporary Jews. Paul intends no mere rhetorical hyperbole by attacking Jewish pride in their supposed superiority by possession of the law.[80] He is declaring that

---

[78]Krentz, "The Name of God," 433. A. Bischoff made the same point, "it is to be expected that βδελύσσεσθαι τὰ εἴδωλα would be contrasted to something like εἰδωλοταρεῖν" ("Exegetische Randbemerkungen," *ZNW* 9 [1908] 167). Bischoff is nearly alone in the belief that ἱεροσυλεῖν has to do with using pagan objects of worship in the expectation of supernatural help. It involves "the unlawful use of certain cultic issues, such as the presence of vessels and garments and the like ('you abhor idols and steal items of idol worship'). The appropriation of foreign items not out of greed (this would be κλέπτειν or συλᾶν), but because of supposed miracles, or because of their exceptional secrecy, is interpreted as parallel to idolatry and sorcery" (ibid.).

[79]Käsemann says only that rabbinic literature substantiates occurrences of such offenses, and describes the questions of vv. 21–22 as "a barrage which completely traps the one who is addressed" (*Commentary on Romans*, 69).

[80]So Dunn: "What is set in contrast, therefore, are the national pride of the typical Jew in the law, over against instances of transgression of the law by Jews. The argument is that the transgression of any

Jews as a people-group are guilty of sin equally with gentiles as a people-group: "Jews and gentiles are all under sin" (3:9). Paul uses the language in which ancient Israel as a nation was condemned in the prophets to carry forward that condemnation to those who trust in their relationship to the law as did Israel in Jeremiah's day.[81]

In both Jeremiah 7 and Rom 2:19 –23 those who trust (πέποιθάς/πείθω) in their relationship to God for special status protecting them from judgment are charged with sin. The charges to the Jew, κλέπτεις ("do you steal?"), μοιχεύεις ("do you commit adultery?"), ἱεροσυλεῖς ("do you rob temples?") all have their basis in Paul's reference to Jer 7:9–11.[82]

> Will you steal (κλέπτετε), murder, commit adultery (μοιχᾶσθε), swear falsely, make offerings to Baal, and go after other gods that you have not known, and then come and stand before me in this house, which is called by my name, and say, "We are safe !"—only to go on doing all these abominations (βδελύγματα)? Has this house, which is called by my name, become a den of robbers in your sight?

As Jeremiah's charges probably are meant to summarize the breaking of all the law, so are Paul's in his appropriation of those charges.[83] He adopts Jeremiah's assumption of Israel's covenant-breaking disobedience.

---

individual Jew is enough to call in question the Jewish assumption that as a Jew he stands in a position of privilege and superiority before God as compared with the Gentile" (*Romans 1–8*, 116). See also Pesch, *Römerbrief*, 35.

[81]"What is envisioned [in Deuteronomy 27–30 as it is appropriated by Paul in Galatians 3]...is not so much the question of what happens *when this or that individual sins*, but the question of what happens when *the nation as a whole fails to keep the Torah as a whole*. That Paul is familiar with this train of thought and exploits it at just this moment in his theology is clear from Romans 2.17–29 and 9.30–10.13" (Wright, *The Climax of the Covenant*, 146; emphasis his).

[82]There is another hook-word between the texts of Romans and Jeremiah: βδελυσσόμενος ("abhorring," the noun being "abomination" in some OT texts). The vocabulary of Deut 29:17: "their abominations and their idols" (τὰ βδελύγματα αὐτῶν καὶ τὰ εἴδωλα αὐτῶν) is reflected in Rom 2:22 as well (ὁ βδελυσσόμενος τὰ εἴδωλα).

[83]"[T]he crimes...are violations of the eighth, sixth, seventh,

The question of the connection between idolatry and temple robbery remains. Paul brings the idea of robbery in the temple from Jeremiah's charge of making the temple "a den of robbers," into a contemporary setting with the use of ἱεροσυλεῖν as described in chap. 3. But why doesn't Paul ask, "You who esteem the temple, do you rob temples?" Why does he ask a question related to idolatry at all? It is because idolatry is central to his reference in Jeremiah's text.

In Jer 7:9–11 it is specifically idolatry that is the culminating and overarching charge against Judah. Jeremiah concludes his accusation with the question, "Will you...make offerings to Baal, and go after other gods that you have not known?" The ultimate charge against Judah is the sin of idolatry.

Paul, however, cannot directly charge contemporary Jews with widespread idolatry. He cannot follow the model of the previous questions and ask, "You who say, 'Do not commit idolatry,' do you commit idolatry?" In fact, they "abhor idols." But the language of Jeremiah's charge of idolatry allows him to carry this most serious of charges into his contemporary setting in his address, "you who abhor idols...." The concept of idolatry is thereby introduced into Paul's text from Jeremiah. The connection of idolatry with temple robbery ("You who abhor idols, do you rob temples?") also originates in the connection between idolatry and "den of robbers" in Jeremiah. Paul retains the OT imagery and concepts, yet changes the language just enough to bring Jeremiah's charge into a contemporary setting.

The contemporary terms bridge the current generation to the charges of idolatry and temple desecration in Jeremiah. In his exegesis, if not on the surface of his argument, Paul connects his contemporary interlocutor—anyone who claims the title "Jew"—to the law-breaking recipients of Jeremiah's indictment. The charges point to the fact of the changed status of the covenant because of disobedience as described by

---

ninth, first, and second commandments, i.e., constitute an almost total breach of the covenant stipulations" (John Bright, *Jeremiah* (AB 21; New York: Doubleday, 1965) 56.

Jeremiah and the curses of Deuteronomy. A prophetic declaration of covenant-breaking against the entire nation is the
basis and legitimation for Paul's universal indictment in Rom
2:21–22, and for Paul's connection between idolatry and robbers in the temple.

Furthermore, the offenses in Jeremiah are repeatedly
characterized as offenses against the honor of God's name.
The sins are committed by people who "then come and stand
before me in this house, which is called by my name" (τὸ
ὄνομά μου, Jer 7:10), raising the question, "Has this house,
which is called by my name, become a den of robbers in your
sight?" (v. 11). It is precisely this dishonoring of the name of
God which becomes the focus of Paul's indictment in Rom
2:23, and which he supports with a citation of Isa 52:5/Ezek
36:20–23 in v. 24.[84] All of the charges, including the "comprehensive conclusion" of dishonoring God and blaspheming his
name, have their origin in Paul's exegesis of Jeremiah 7.[85]

The Summary Charge:

In the summary charge of Rom 2:23, "You who boast in
the Law dishonor God by breaking the Law," καυχᾶσαι ("you
boast") again surfaces from Paul's reference in Jer 9:23–24,
"let those who boast, boast in this." As in 2:17, here the boast
in relationship to God and the law is misplaced, the reasons
for that mistaken assumption now made clear. This summary
of v. 23 is most often correctly taken as a statement. This is so
not so much because of the change in sentence structure and

---

[84]Isa 52:5 and Ezek 36:20–23 both read τὸ ὄνομά μου, as does Jer
7:10. Paul makes the change to τὸ ὄνομα τοῦ θεοῦ to fit his context.

[85]Some might object that the origin of the citation from Isa 52:5 is
obviously the citation itself. However, the origin of the charge for Paul
more likely is in his exegesis of Jeremiah. Isaiah may be brought in at
even a third step as a concurring and supporting authority, its own
presence probably being a result of linking vocabulary from Paul's exegetical reference in Ezek 36:20–27. It is the web of themes and vocabulary deriving from Deuteronomy, Jeremiah, and Ezekiel that forms the
exegetical foundation for Paul's conclusions and upon which the entire
passage is dependent. This is not the case for Isaiah 52. It functions as a
simple proof-text.

Lietzmann says of v. 23, "The sentence is not a question, but with
v. 24 forms the comprehensive conclusion" (*An die Römer*, 43).

the grammatical switch to the relative pronoun and finite verb but because v. 23 and the citation from Isaiah in v. 24 flow together as one statement.

When the usual punctuation is removed and "as it is written" is placed at the end, as it stands in Greek,[86] the summary reads smoothly, "You who boast in the Law dishonor God by breaking the Law, for 'because of you the name of God is blasphemed among the gentiles,' as it is written." The inclusion of γάρ ("for") is not accidental or incidental.[87] The conjunction ought to be read as actively joining the two statements. It is scriptural statements (cited and uncited) of Israel's disobedience that lead Paul to the conclusion, and in the case of Isa 52:5 serve as his proof, that the Jews have broken the law to such an extent as to dishonor God. For Paul, that prophetic conclusion continues to be in effect for contemporary Jews.[88]

However, this is a complex mixture of reference and citation. In Isaiah the nations blaspheme God because Israel's captivity is taken as a sign of the weakness of their God.[89]

---

[86]Which Dunn, among many others, notes: "The formula of appeal...is, unusually, left to the end" (*Romans 1–8*, 115). Given that its unusual position in Paul's text ought to suggest some importance, it seems unaccountable that it is seldom translated so (e.g., NRSV; NIV; NEB; Käsemann, *Commentary on Romans*, 68; Fitzmyer, *Romans*, 5, 315). Placing the appeal formula in the middle of the sentence disrupts the logical connection the inclusion of the conjunction is meant to provide. "The appearance of the citation formula...at the end of the quotation rather than at the beginning, unique in the Pauline corpus, further reinforces the continuity between the citation and the words immediately preceding it" (Christopher D. Stanley, *Paul and the Language of Scripture: Citation Technique in the Pauline Epistles and Contemporary Literature* [SNTSMS 69; Cambridge: Cambridge University Press, 1992] 85 n. 9).

[87]It is entirely untranslated by, e.g., NIV; Fitzmyer, *Romans*, 5, 315. Even when translated it receives mention as noteworthy only rarely (e.g., Cranfield, *The Epistle to the Romans*, 1.170).

[88]See Wright, *The Climax of the Covenant*, 140–48.

[89]"In Paul's use of the verse, on the other hand, the meaning is just the opposite: it is the hypocritical deeds of the Jews themselves...that have caused the Gentiles to cast aspersions on the name of the God they profess to serve. The last words of Paul's extended indict-

The LXX adds δι' ὑμᾶς, but still does not direct the blame at Israel. Paul changes this emphasis in his appropriation of the passage.[90] Because of Israel's covenant-breaking disobedience ("by breaking the Law," διὰ τῆς παραβάσεως τοῦ νόμου, Rom 2:23) the nations hold God's name in contempt ("for because of you the name of God is blasphemed among the gentiles," τὸ γὰρ ὄνομα τοῦ θεοῦ δι' ὑμᾶς βλασφημεῖται ἐν τοῖς ἔθνεσιν, Rom 2:24).[91] How has Paul concluded that Israel is directly to blame for the dishonor of God's name?

As outlined in the previous chapter, the vocabulary evidence for Ezekiel 36 as a Pauline reference and the high concentration of phrases showing concern for the honor of God's name in Ezek 36:20–23 (a concentration shared with Jeremiah 7) make it unlikely that Paul was unaware of this parallel passage to the Isaiah quotation. There it is the "house of Israel" (οἶκος Ἰσραήλ) which has profaned the name of God. The charge is repeated directly, "you have profaned" (ἐβεβηλώσατε). The reason God's name is profaned in Ezekiel is the same as that in Isaiah—Israel's disobedience and exile have caused gentiles to hold Israel's God in contempt—but in

---

ment (2.23) charge the Jews with 'dishonoring God' by transgressing the very law they profess to uphold (2.23). Expressed in common Jewish parlance, it is God's 'name' that has been called into question by such behavior. The advancing of τὸ ὄνομα to a position of emphasis in place of the equally relevant δι' ὑμᾶς of the presumed original coincides perfectly with this concern for the honor of God's 'name' among the Gentiles" (Stanley, *Paul and the Language of Scripture*, 85). See also Fitzmyer, *Romans*, 318.

[90]"Assimilation to the Hebrew is unlikely; the LXX follows the word order of the MT at this point, while Paul's retention of the 'extra' language found in the LXX version...shows that he has relied on the standard Greek text for this quotation" (Stanley, *Paul and the Language of Scripture*, 84 n. 6). I.e., Paul's change in emphasis which places the blame on the Jews stems from his introduction of another text, not from following a different version of Isa 52:5.

[91]"The root βλασφημ– in the LXX has nothing clearly corresponding in the original" (Hermann W. Beyer, "βλασφημέω," *TDNT* 1.621). Isa 52:5 uses יְנֹאָץ, more accurately corresponding to "to hold in contempt," "to spurn," or "to despise" (BDB, 610–11).

Ezekiel the Jews themselves bring dishonor on the name of God, as Paul charges in Rom 2:23.[92]

It is not contemporary examples of law-breaking that make Paul's case. Prophetic statements of Israel's guilt do not simply provide a rhetorical flourish to confirm visible contemporary evidence. Paul concludes that Jews of his day remain guilty precisely because their guilt has already been established in the prophetic statements of scripture. Paul uses the juxtaposition of the parallel passages in Isaiah and Ezekiel to highlight his conclusion.[93]

The context of the quotation of Isa 52:5 is a recounting of exile and promise of return from exile. There is no evidence that Isaiah 52 functions exegetically as a reference for Paul. It serves the separate rhetorical function of a proof-text offering supporting authority for Paul's conclusion, which has its basis in Ezekiel 36. This is characteristic of Paul's use of quotations.[94]

Isa 52:5 provides the concise declarative statement Paul needs in order for the quotation to conform to the form of his

---

[92]Dunn describes Ezek 36:17–23 as sharpening the charge (*Romans 1–8*, 115). Thomas H. Tobin is more specific, stating that "Rom 2:24 is not an exact quotation of any OT text. The wording is closer to Isa 52:5..., but Paul's point in using the quotation seems closer to Ezek 36:20.... Only the text of Ezek 36:20 emphasize[s] the points that the Jews, because of their transgressions of the Law, were forced to leave their own land, and that this departure caused God's name to be dishonored among the Gentiles" ("Controversy and Continuity in Romans 1:18–3:20," *CBQ* 55 [1993] 311 n. 33).

In his study of the rhetoric of Pauline citation, David Earl Mesner concludes that Paul's modifications of citations are "extremely important for the advancement of Paul's argument, and should not be dismissed as loose technique" ("The Rhetoric of Citations: Paul's Use of Scripture in Romans 9" [Ph.D. diss. Northwestern University, 1991] 563). The change in the point of the quotation of Isaiah which follows the emphasis of Ezekiel is not accidental, but has argumentative import.

[93]Garlington, in regard to Paul's OT references in Galatians 3, comments that Paul "is indeed cognizant of the original intention of the passages" ("Role Reversal," 120). Paul consciously interprets the passages to turn them on their heads by his exegesis.

[94]This is not true in every case. At times quoted material is also an exegetical reference, e.g., the Abraham narrative in Romans 4 and 9.

indictment, but it does not make Paul's point. Ezek 36:17–23, which lacks the declarative statement which Paul could easily integrate into his indictment, provides the point Paul wishes to make. Because they are verbally linked, in Paul's contemporary exegetical world Isa 52:5 may in effect be interpreted by Ezek 36:17–23. Or, to put it the way the process more likely occurred, the language of Isa 52:5 may be used in connection with the exegesis of Ezekiel upon which Paul is dependent.

It is the prediction made by Moses in Deut 29:25–28 and 30:1–3 which Paul believes is fulfilled in the passages to which Paul refers from Jeremiah 7, 9 and Ezekiel 36. While vocabulary from the blessings and curses of the covenant from Deuteronomy 28–30 is only minimally reflected in Rom 2:17–24,[95] Paul believes it to be the text upon which the Jeremiah and Ezekiel references are dependent. Since Deuteronomy 29–30 (29:29; 30:6) also gives evidence of being a reference in Rom 2:25–29, the blessings and curses of Deuteronomy 29–30 with the predictions of Israel's failure to keep the covenant are almost certainly in the background of Rom 2:17–24.[96]

---

[95]The vocabulary of Deut 29:17 (βδελύγματα and εἴδωλα) in Rom 2:22 (ὁ βδελυσσόμενος τὰ εἴδωλα) being a minor exception.

[96]Not only in Romans 2 but elsewhere, e.g., Rom 10:6–8; 11:8; Gal 3:10. James Scott summarizes the evidence and concludes that "[i]n both his earlier and later correspondence, Paul appropriates a pervasive OT/Jewish tradition which we may refer to as the Deuteronomic View of Israel's History" ("Deuteronomic Tradition," 665). He notes Paul's particular reliance upon Deuteronomy 27–32. With regard to the passage's use in Romans 9–11, he concurs (ibid., 663) with Wright that "Paul is working out the exile-theology of Moses' closing speech in Deuteronomy, applying it to his new situation as others had applied it to the exile itself (Jeremiah) or the Maccabean crisis (Qumran, the apocalyptists), and would apply it to the events of AD 70 (4 Ezra, the Rabbis)" ("The Messiah and the People of God," 218; also, *The Climax of the Covenant*, 146–48). The evidence of this study shows that Paul also appropriates Jeremiah's and Ezekiel's own parallels to Deuteronomy for his own new situation. Stuhlmacher also points to Paul's dependence upon the deuteronomic tradition (*Letter to the Romans*, 48).

Paul attacks the assurance of those who "rely on the law" by appealing to the provisions of the law itself. Moses not only announced the institution of the covenant, but also foresaw the failure of Israel to uphold the requirements of the covenant. By his references to Jeremiah in particular, as well as Ezekiel, Paul arrives at the fact of Israel's fulfillment of that predicted failure, making Israel, like the surrounding nations, "uncircumcised in heart" (Jer 9:26). On the basis of these texts, whether or not his readers are aware of the exegesis upon which it rests, Paul can make his first case for the equality of Jews and gentiles before God; that is, both are guilty and in need of justification.[97] Any preferential status Paul's Jewish interlocutor might be thought to enjoy on the basis of being a Jew in relationship to the law is no longer applicable because of Israel's transgression of the covenant stipulations.

CIRCUMCISION AND GENTILE OBEDIENCE IN ROM 2:25–27

Paul next addresses circumcision as the other defining point of Jewish identity as the people of God.[98] Paul is progressing in stages to the core of Jewish self-identification. It is not that Paul attacks Jewish pride in the law by progressing from pride in the law in general (2:17–24) to pride in circum-

---

[97]The question of whether or not Paul's readers may have apprehended any or all of the exegetical background to Paul's conclusions will be taken up in the concluding chapter.

[98]It is the question of the identity of two groups competing for the distinction of being the people of God which Segal points out is central to Paul's understanding of the relationship between Jews and Christianity. In a discussion of the meaning of "works of the law," dependent upon Dunn, Segal states that this phrase as well is directed to the question of identity. "'Works of the law' means the ceremonial Torah, those special ordinances that separate Jews from gentiles....Paul uses the phrase to mean the typical ways Jews assert their identity (Rom. 3:19–20). This approach is associated with boasting (Rom. 3:27–8; 4:2), paralleling Paul's earlier attack on the Jews as people of the law (Rom. 2:17–20, 23), with circumcision serving as the primary sign of this identity (Rom. 2:25–9)....The distinction is between two different communities—those who keep the law as a mark of their identity and those who can be identified by faith" (*Paul the Convert*, 124).

cision as the cardinal representation of the law (2:25–29).[99] It is preferable to understand the argument to be a progression through the stages or bases of Jewish identity relied upon for covenantal blessing.[100] In vv. 17–24 Paul addressed Jewish identity as people of the law of Moses, and undercut the supposed privilege of that identity through scriptural references pointing to God's judgment on the Jews as law-breakers. But Paul recognizes that his interlocutor, even admitting the reality of law-breaking, may retreat to another, final, point of defense. The core of Jewish identity as God's people reaches back beyond Moses and the law to Abraham and the covenant of circumcision.

Dealing with the Issue of Circumcision:

Paul will address this point once again by his reference to scripture in 2:25–27. In the larger section of Rom 2:25–29 Paul relies on his intertextual references to Jer 9:25–26 and Gen 17:11–27. Rom 2:25–29 also continues to include references to Deuteronomy 29–30, already a basis for the charges of disobedience to the covenant in Rom 2:17–24. In vv. 25–29, however, Deuteronomy serves to reinterpret the command for circumcision from Genesis 17 in terms of heart circumcision. Jeremiah provides the determination that Israel has become no better than the surrounding nations, being "uncircumcised in heart."

This both underlines the charges of the preceding verses and forms the basis for Paul's argument against physical circumcision as surety of special status before God when the law has not been kept. In Paul's exegesis the blessings and curses of Deuteronomy show the circumcision of the Abrahamic covenant to be a heart circumcision, a spiritual renewal which Paul also finds in Ezekiel 36, and to which Jews and gentiles alike have access through faith, as did Abraham (Romans 3–4).[101]

---

[99]E.g., Barrett, *Epistle to the Romans*, 55; Dodd, *Epistle*, 40; Bruce, *Romans*, 89.

[100]So, e.g., Dunn, *Romans 1–8*, 119; Stuhlmacher, *Letter to the Romans*, 49.

[101]Segal, in reference to Paul's attitude toward gentile conversion

It is not clear that the subject of circumcision in Rom 2:25 is supposed to have been raised by the interlocutor, though it would reasonably be an interlocutor's objection that "at least we are circumcised, even if we do not observe the Law."[102] In any case circumcision is an unavoidable subject for Paul if he is to address supposed privilege based on identification as a Jew. This is particularly the case since his references deal with the status of the covenant. It is circumcision as the mark of a covenant with God even more than possession of the law which is viewed as the preeminent sign of Jewish identity as the elect people of God.[103] To address the

---

in general, states, "The problem raised by Paul was not one of universalism so much as the recommendation that the ritual distinctions between Jews and gentiles be removed entirely, which shocked Paul's fellow Christians" (*Paul the Convert*, 103). While the removal of ritual distinctions certainly is a part of Pauline theology and integral to the argument he is making, he goes beyond even this in Romans 2. For Paul, the ritual itself becomes meaningless without obedience, and obedience without the ritual becomes salvific.

[102]Fitzmyer, *Romans*, 320. Dodd (*Epistle*, 40) and Lietzmann (*An die Römer*, 44) also believe the subject is raised as a diatribal objection. There is no grammatical marker to indicate that this is the case. The γάρ of v. 25 ought to be read as a more strongly connecting conjunction, as Paul's references indicate that disobedience and uncircumcision are connected. The charge of disobedience resulting in dishonoring God's name in Jeremiah 7 and Ezekiel 36 (Rom 2:21–24) is not separate from the conclusion in Jeremiah 9 that Israel is "uncircumcised in heart" ("your circumcision has become uncircumcision," Rom 2:25). In other words, in the references, Jewish disobedience shows that they are "uncircumcised in heart." In Rom 2:21–27 Jewish dishonoring of the name of God shows that their "circumcision has become uncircumcision." This does not affect the way Paul reinterprets circumcision as heart circumcision. It shows that Paul takes up the topic of circumcision not only because he has to deal with Genesis 17, but because his other references already point toward a connection between disobedience and the efficacy of circumcision. Käsemann notes that Paul "disposes at once of a Jewish objection that has not in fact been made" (*Commentary on Romans*, 72).

[103]"In the Jewish view only circumcision grants a share in God's covenant with Israel" (Käsemann, *Commentary on Romans*, 72). *Jub.* 15:25–27 emphasizes the importance of circumcision: anyone not circumcised will "be destroyed and annihilated from the earth." Further, in vv. 33–34, some will "deny this ordinance," so that "there is therefore for them no forgiveness or pardon...from all the sins of this eternal error."

covenant one must ultimately address its origin with Abraham in the text of Genesis 17.[104]

Paul does address the Abrahamic covenant of circumcision, although he does not bring Abraham to the surface of the text as he does in Romans 4 and 9. The Abraham narrative functions as an unstated assumption about Jewish identity which Paul reinterprets through other texts, rather than functioning as a proof of the special status of the Jews. Paul's use of Genesis 17 as an intertextual reference has been established in the preceding chapter primarily on the basis of the repeated use of περιτομή and the rare, ἀκροβυστία. However, in this instance his reference would appear to be the basic supporting text for those who argue against Paul that circumcision is the definitive marker of one who stands to receive the blessings of the covenantal relationship. In Gen 17:10–14 God declares:

> Every male among you shall be circumcised. You shall circumcise the flesh of your foreskins, and it shall be a sign of the covenant between me and you. Throughout your generations every male among you shall be circumcised when he is eight days old, including the slave born in your house and the one bought with your money from any foreigner who is not of your offspring. Both the slave born in your house and the one bought with your money must be circumcised. So shall my covenant be in your flesh an everlasting covenant. Any uncircumcised male who is not circumcised in the flesh of his foreskin shall be cut off from his people; he has broken my covenant.

Since difficult texts are often the object of Jewish exegesis, Gen 17:10–14 gains Paul's attention as a text requiring reinterpretation. It appears to directly contradict his own po-

---

See also the willingness to die rather than forego circumcision in 1 Macc 1:48, 60–61; 2 Macc 6:10. Cranfield cites several later rabbinic statements concerning circumcision as a guarantee of salvation, among them, "Circumcised men do not descend into Gehenna" (*Exod. Rab.* 19 [81c]; *The Epistle to the Romans*, 1.172 n. 1).

[104]This is commonly mentioned in connection with Paul's argument. See, e.g., Dunn, *Romans 1–8*, 119; Fitzmyer, *Romans*, 321; Stuhlmacher, *Letter to the Romans*, 49.

sition, which he has arrived at largely because of his experience with gentile Christianity. It also conflicts with the call for heart circumcision in Deuteronomy. Paul will redefine circumcision as heart circumcision by reference to Deuteronomy, but how does he then deal with the specific command for circumcision in the flesh in Genesis? The answer is found in Ezekiel 36:16–27, a passage to which Paul has already referred and to which he will return in 2:29.

Immediately following the material concerning the profanation of God's name linked to Isa 52:5 in Rom 2:25 is Ezek 36:26: "and I will remove from your body the heart of stone and give you a *heart of flesh.*" As Paul may read this reference, for those who experience Ezekiel's prophecy of spiritual renewal ("in spirit," Rom 2:29), *hearts* become *hearts of flesh.*[105] Therefore, in Jewish exegetical practice one could argue that circumcision of the heart *is* circumcision of the flesh.

This is a clear example of what later became Hillel's 13th rule, wherein a conflict between two opposing texts (the command for "circumcision in the flesh" in Genesis 17 and the call for "circumcision of the heart" in Deuteronomy 30) is resolved by reference to a third text ("hearts of flesh" in Ezekiel 36:26).[106] In keeping with contemporary exegetical practice, Paul resolves the problem of how to argue for heart circumcision while still fulfilling the command for circumcision in the flesh.

Of course, Paul's argument in v. 25 is not that circumcision is not a mark of the covenant, "for circumcision indeed is of value if you obey the law." Paul's interlocutor would certainly accept the value of circumcision.[107] Rather, his point is that the efficacy of that mark of the covenant for salvation

---

[105]Paul's reference to Ezekiel 36 at this point is made more likely by a recurrence of Paul's dependence on this unique phrase (hearts of flesh) in 2 Cor 3:3. See Stockhausen, *Moses' Veil,* 46–49, 62–63.

[106]As usual for Paul, it is the prophetic text which interprets the narratives.

[107]Dunn, *Romans 1–8,* 121. However, Barrett is probably correct that the interlocutor would dispute a contrast between circumcision and doing the law since circumcision *was* doing the law (*Epistle to the Romans,* 55).

from wrath is lost if the covenant is not kept: "but if you break the law, your circumcision has become uncircumcision."[108]

Circumcision becomes Uncircumcision:

To reach this conclusion he relies in part again on Jer 7:4, 8, where a marker of relationship with God was rendered worthless because of disobedience. In Rom 2:25 circumcision, the preeminent identifier of the covenant and symbol of the law "profits" or "has worth" (ὠφελεῖ) if the law is kept. But if the law is not kept, it becomes worthless "uncircumcision." In Jer 7:4, 8, Israel has trusted in deceptive words, relying on another prominent identifier of relationship to God: the presence of the temple of the Lord. But because of Israel's disobedience their reliance on the temple becomes worthless to them (οὐκ ὠφελήσουσιν and οὐκ ὠφεληθήσεσθε).

The OT text again makes precisely the point Paul makes in Romans. The markers of covenant relationship with God become worthless when the covenant has been broken. When that is the case, as Paul's other Jeremiah reference, Jer 9:26, instructs, Jewish περιτομή (circumcision) is found to be no better than gentile ἀκροβυστία (uncircumcision).[109]

---

[108]And Paul's references already tell him that the covenant has not been kept. He is in the process of reconstructing a new model both of covenant-keeping and of Jewish identity based on it. According to Sanders, contrary to the conception of a legalistic works-centered religion, in Judaism obedience and repentance *preserve* but do not *earn* a place in the covenant (*Paul and Palestinian Judaism*, 205, 450). One has a place in the covenant purely on the basis of election as long as one does not totally reject the covenant relationship. Paul is stating that breaking the law puts one under the judgment of God's wrath as though one were not a circumcised person of the covenant.

[109]Black comments that in v. 25, "'become as though you had not been circumcised,' γέγονεν in rabbinic use can mean 'is reckoned as,' and so be considered more literally parallel to λογισθήσεται in the following verse" (*Romans* 60). Contra Käsemann who says, "γέγονεν of v. 25 is not construed with the dative and the particle of comparison ὡς, and it cannot then be equivalent to כ נחשב in the sense of 'is reckoned as...although λογισθήσεται in v. 26 corresponds to it" (*Commentary on Romans*, 73). Since there is this correspondence in the parallel statements it is clear that what Paul means is that circumcision will be counted as, or reckoned as, uncircumcision. Käsemann admits as much in his addition to his translation "your circumcision becomes uncircum-

More than that, he will argue that the uncircumcised may be reckoned as circumcised if they keep the law, in preference over the circumcised Jew. This is an unorthodox position.[110] The point concerning the uncircumcised being reckoned as circumcised stems from the figure of Abraham himself, and from texts reinterpreting Genesis 17. Paul, as he does elsewhere, uses interpretive texts to take a text which would seem to support his interlocutor and turns it to support his argument.[111]

At this point Paul depends upon his reference to Jer 9:25–26. If Genesis 17 is the difficult text for Paul's position, Jer 9:25–26 is the difficult text for the interlocutor's position.[112] It appears to make Paul's very point that the Jews were "no better than their pagan neighbors" and, like Deuteronomy, establishes heart circumcision as the redefining ele-

---

cision (before God)" (parenthesis his). How that addition differs from "is reckoned as" is difficult to tell.

The use of "circumcision" and "uncircumcision" is general here, referring to categories of Jews and gentiles and circumcision or uncircumcision as the mark thereof. Making the observation that "circumcision" can mean the act of circumcision, the condition of being circumcised, or the community of the circumcised, is Michel (*Der Brief an die Römer*, 132). For a study of the various meanings of circumcision, see Joel Marcus ("The Circumcision and the Uncircumcision in Rome," *NTS* 35 [1989] 67–81).

[110]Käsemann, *Commentary on Romans*, 72. Dunn remarks: "The second half of Paul's assertion would be more controversial....But that such failure could cost a circumcised Jew his place in the covenant and in the blessings of the new age was a prospect that devout Jews did not care to contemplate" (*Romans 1–8*, 121). Cranfield discusses the equation of circumcision with participation in the blessings of the covenant (*The Epistle to the Romans*, 1.172 n. 1).

[111]He has done much the same thing with Genesis 15 and 21 in Galatians. See Garlington, "Role Reversal," 114.

[112]Bright calls the passage, "cryptic and difficult to interpret" (*Jeremiah*, 79). Andrew Blackwood remarks, "This is a bewildering passage. The essential message seems to be that the mere physical rite of circumcision is of no spiritual benefit without the circumcised heart" (*Commentary on Jeremiah* [Waco: Word, 1977] 109). Blackwood notes the similarity with the warning against trusting in the temple and sacrifice in chap. 7, Paul's other Jeremiah reference.

ment.[113] Bruce notes that these points were "already taught by Jeremiah."[114] Fitzmyer is more to the point, recognizing that "in the background of Paul's thinking about this matter is Jer 9:22–25."[115] However, more than just being in the background of Paul's thinking, Jer 9:22–26 has been shown to be Paul's exegetical reference, on the basis of which he reaches his conclusion. Jer 9:25–26 in particular can be shown to provide the basis for Paul's assertion in Rom 2:25b: "but if you break the Law, your circumcision becomes uncircumcision."[116]

It is easy to see how Jer 9:25–26 could be a difficult passage for interpreters to exegete:

> The days are surely coming, says the Lord, when I will attend to all those who are circumcised (περιτετμημένους) only in the foreskin (ἀκροβυστίας):[117] Egypt, Judah, Edom, the Ammonites, Moab, and all those with shaven temples who live in the desert. For all these nations are uncircumcised (LXX adds σαρκί, "in flesh"), and all the house of Israel is uncircumcised in heart.

Paul appropriates this judgment in Rom 2:25, then addresses questions inherent in the passage. How is the circumcision of Israel to be lowered to the ineffectual status of the circumcision of the surrounding nations of Egypt, Idumea, Edom, Ammon, and Moab, and even equated with the uncircumcision of all the gentiles?[118] Paul will present an answer

---

[113]R. K. Harrison, *Jeremiah and Lamentations: An Introduction and Commentary* (TOTC 19; Downers Grove, IL: Inter-Varsity, 1973) 92.

[114]Bruce, *Romans*, 89.

[115]Fitzmyer, *Romans*, 320. Fitzmyer quotes through v. 26 under this statement.

[116]Martin argues that there was a more liberal strain of Diaspora Judaism upon which Paul is dependent which supported an ethical code defining Jewish identity more in moral than legal/cultic terms ("The Righteousness of God," 320–25, 351–54). He argues that Paul uses that "accepted premise" in 2:25b to expand to the more controversial conclusion of 2:26. How "common" the "Jewish belief that Jewish identity alone does not guarantee salvation" actually was remains unclear. Paul appears to engage any definition of Jewish identity not grounded in faith, and the statement of 25b is certainly scripturally based no matter how accepted it may have been in a particular strain of Judaism.

[117]Or "I will visit upon all the circumcised their uncircumcision."

[118]Dunn makes the point that though the Jews would not have

in Rom 2:28–29 through his references to Jer 9:26, Deut 29:29 and 30:6, and Ezek 36:26–27 with their calls to an inward spiritual obedience that is a circumcision of the heart.

Paul finds a bridge from the fact of Israel's disobedience to the concept of heart circumcision in Jer 9:26. First, he establishes Israel's disobedience in Rom 2:17–24 by reference to Jeremiah 7. Paul concludes that the result in Jer 9:26 is that breaking the law results in being regarded as uncircumcised, that is, in no better position than the gentiles. Second, the same statement in Jer 9:26 points out that while Israel may have been physically circumcised, it was heart circumcision which was required. Heart circumcision in fact becomes the interpretive hook-word from Deuteronomy 28–30, which narrates the giving of the law and reaffirmation of the covenant and the prophecy of Israel breaking the covenant.

Gentiles Judging Jews:

Paul questions the value of circumcision, then goes further in Rom 2:26–27. As Israel in Deut 30:10 will enjoy covenant status if they keep the commandments (φυλάσσεσθαι), so will the uncircumcised one who keeps the law (φυλάσσῃ) have his uncircumcision be considered circumcision (ἡ ἀκρο-βυστία αὐτοῦ εἰς περιτομὴν λογισθήσεται). That is, the uncircumcised will be considered as having the covenant status the Jews had thought reserved only for themselves.

This extension of Paul's logical argument also stems from Abraham and legend surrounding Abraham, as it fills a part in a parallel between Rom 2:12–16 and 25–29.[119] As gen-

---

disputed the fact of failure to adhere to the law, the idea of loss of covenant status as a result of that failure would have been much more difficult (*Romans 1–8*, 121). While the point has already been established that the covenant has been broken and Israel's privileged position is not what it was, Richard B. Hays notes that "Israel's covenant relation with God remains intact, as many other passages both in Isaiah and in Romans will insist" (*Echoes*, 46). The theme of restoration, also found in Deuteronomy and the prophets, appears in Romans 9–11. While the curses of the covenant from Paul's perspective have been and remain invoked, that fact has not ended Israel's covenant relationship with God.

[119]For Abraham as faithful for fulfilling the law, see Gen 26:5, "because Abraham obeyed my voice and kept my charge, my command-

tiles who do not have the law yet keep the law show themselves to have the law written on their hearts, their consciences bearing witness at the judgment (vv. 14–16), so the uncircumcised who keep the law will be regarded as circumcised and be present in judgment upon law-breaking Jews (vv. 26–27).[120]

Such a parallel also in part accounts in v. 27 for the assertion that law-keeping gentiles will judge law-breaking Jews. In direct contrast to the interlocutor's assumption of standing in judgment upon the lawless gentiles (2:1–3), the law-keeping gentile whose conscience witnesses in defense at the judgment (2:15–16) will judge the law-breaking Jew. "In a fitting climax to the argument the tables are neatly turned on the interlocutor, and the counsel for the prosecution (2:1–3) finds himself [or herself] in the dock."[121]

Ezekiel 36 is important here. There is verbal correspondence at this point only in the presence of κρίνω, but the passage has already been seen to be a reference in the parallel to Isa 52:5, that is, Ezek 36:19. In the verse preceding that parallel, the nations are to be judged "according to their conduct and actions." Although the judgment concerning the nations in Ezekiel is a negative one, Paul appropriates the unstated corollary. Proper conduct by the uncircumcised puts them in a privileged position. They will judge those who are people of the covenant with its identifying markers (τὸν διὰ γράμματος καὶ περιτομῆς) if they prove to be lawbreakers.[122] Paul doesn't

---

ments, my statutes, and my laws," and Sir 44:20, "He kept the law of the Most High." For Abraham in a position of judgment, see the Parable of the Rich Man and Lazarus in Luke 16:19–21. For Abraham as present at the eschatological judgment, see, e.g., *Testament of Abraham* 9–10; *Apocalypse of Abraham* 22–29.

[120]See esp. Pesch, *Römerbrief*, 36. Also, e.g., Käsemann, *Commentary on Romans*, 72; Dunn, *Romans 1–8*, 119; Snodgrass, "Justification by Grace—To the Doers," 80.

[121]Dunn, *Romans 1–8*, 127.

[122]Cranfield's view of κρινεῖ may be near the mark: not that the gentiles will participate in purposeful condemnation of Israel, but that their righteousness will stand as a witness against the unrighteousness of Israel (*The Epistle to the Romans*, 1.174). This ties in well with the parallel of vv. 14–16.

develop it yet, but he introduces one side of his antithesis between γράμμα and πνεῦμα, to be drawn out in v. 29, as well as in 7:6 and 2 Cor 3:6.[123]

C. H. Dodd, however, rightly understands Paul's statement as simply equating the positions of Jews and gentiles before God on the basis of their behavior, or more properly in this context, their lack thereof. "[Paul's] main point is not that the pagan, if he does right, will escape the Wrath, but that the Jew, unless he does right, will certainly not escape it....that being so, they have not a shadow of hope on the ground of their position of national privilege."[124] Paul would probably have a difficult time supporting, or even coming to, such a view without the underlying exegesis of these OT texts.[125] Their use, however, enables Paul to reach this conclusion in a way that is exegetically, if not theologically, legitimate in his contemporary context.

REDEFINING JEWISH IDENTITY IN ROM 2:28–29

Still, Paul's "apparent surplus" to his argument, reaching an "inexplicable crescendo" in his assertion that law-keeping gentiles will judge law-breaking Jews, is not clarified until vv. 28–29.[126] These verses provide the reasoning for the

---

[123]The antithesis in 2 Cor 3:6 is also closely related to an intertextual reference to Ezekiel 36 and Jeremiah, as Stockhausen has shown (*Moses' Veil*). The connection is extensively discussed by Scott J. Hafemann (*Paul, Moses, and the History of Israel: The Letter / Spirit Contrast and the Argument from Scripture in 2 Corinthians 3* [WUNT 81; Tübingen: Mohr, 1995] esp. 145–73). Paul appears to rely on certain groups of references together in different places. This provides evidence of recurrence not only of individual references, but of complexes of references.

[124]*Epistle*, 40–41.

[125]"But the fact that Paul extensively relativizes circumcision, which was viewed by the Jews as the seal of the Abrahamic covenant (cf. Gen. 17:1–27), and elevates those gentiles who follow God's will as judges over the Judaism which departs from the Law goes beyond even the most radical Jewish texts on judgment" (Stuhlmacher, *Letter to the Romans*, 49). Also, Dodd, *Epistle*, 41; Cranfield, *The Epistle to the Romans*, 1.173.

[126]The descriptions of v. 27 are Käsemann's (*Commentary on Ro-*

assertion and are the summation of the entire argument of 2:17–29.[127] There Paul gets to the heart of the issue: who, in fact, is a Jew? This is a question he will return to and deal with extensively in chaps. 4 and 9–11.

Rom 2:17–29, then, has multiple functions. On the one hand Paul's immediate task is to call into question assurance on the basis of identification as a Jew by making the case that Jews as well as gentiles are under judgment. Yet at the same time Paul upholds a special place for Israel in God's economy and denies that God has broken any promises to Israel (3:1; 9:6).

The second function is to lay the groundwork for redefining who is the true Israel, the children of Abraham (chaps. 4 and 9). A foundation is laid in Rom 2:28–29. Not only is being born a Jew and circumcised on the eighth day no assurance of being a recipient of covenant blessing, it is not even assurance of being a Jew: "for a Jew is not one outwardly [in the visible], nor is circumcision external and physical [in what is visible] in the flesh" (οὐ γὰρ ὁ ἐν τῷ φανερῷ Ἰουδαῖός ἐστιν οὐδὲ ἡ ἐν τῷ φανερῷ ἐν σαρκὶ περιτομή).[128]

The interlocutor's assumption that the circumcised descendants of Abraham will judge the uncircumcised is accurate. However, Paul concludes from his exegesis that it is the circumcised in heart who are truly circumcised: "a person is a Jew who is one inwardly [in secret]." They are the descendants of Abraham's faith who will judge the uncircumcised in heart. It is the interior, or hidden, things which concern God.

These conclusions, too, are based on Paul's references. A pivotal reference for Paul throughout his argument has been Deuteronomy 29–30, the reaffirmation of the covenant and the giving of the blessings and curses of the covenant.[129]

---

mans, 74).

[127]The use of γάρ in v. 28 indicates explanation of what precedes.

[128]This translation is more literal than the NRSV in order to clarify the similarities with Deuteronomy.

[129]While Paul may read Deuteronomy 27–32 as a unit (James Scott, "For as Many," 194), and the entire passage may influence his argument at certain points, it is in chaps. 29–30 that verbal connections with Rom 2:17–29 are found.

There Israel's failure is prophesied by Moses (29:22–28), which Paul believes Jeremiah confirms. He applies that failure to his interlocutor. There circumcision of the heart is specified (30:6, MT), for Paul again confirmed by Jeremiah. In combination with the reference to "heart of flesh" in Ezek 36:26 this allows Paul to reinterpret the Abrahamic covenant of Genesis 17 in those terms in Rom 2:29 without violating the command for circumcision in the flesh.

In v. 28, however, Paul picks up some obscure and special vocabulary from Deut 29:29 which also informs his argument: "The secret things (τὰ κρυπτά) belong to the Lord our God, but the revealed things (τὰ δὲ φανερά, "visible things") belong to us and to our children forever." Jews contemporary with Paul may have considered the hidden things of that passage (τὰ κρυπτά) to be a reference to the mysteries of God that they were not to know about. The revealed things (τὰ φανερά), the words of the law, were the things with which they were to be concerned.[130]

Paul takes this passage, in conjunction with the nearby mention of heart circumcision (30:6), as evidence of the fact that God looks upon what is unseen: the secrets (Rom 2:16), the inward heart (2:28–29). Rather than seeking the praise of people (οὐκ ἐξ ἀνθρώπων) who see only what is visible or outward (ἐν τῷ φανερῷ), it is "the praise...from God" (ὁ ἔπαινος...ἐκ τοῦ θεοῦ) that is to be sought. Therefore, the hidden things (ἐν τῷ κρυπτῷ) about which God is concerned, the things of the heart, are those which ought to be the concern of God's people. In fact in vv. 28–29 there is a redefinition of the Jew (Εἰ δὲ σὺ Ἰουδαῖος ἐπονομάζῃ, "If you call yourself a Jew," v. 17). Jewish identity—as God's people, the people of the covenant, the circumcised, whom God will praise—now includes those who are so inwardly, in the hidden sense about which Deut 29:29 says God is concerned. There are in effect "hidden" Jews, who also "belong to the Lord" (Deut 29:29). They are those who are considered cir-

---

[130]See, e.g., J. A. Thompson, *Deuteronomy: An Introduction and Commentary* (TOTC 5; Downers Grove, IL: Inter-Varsity, 1974) 283–84.

cumcised people of the covenant on the basis of a spiritual circumcision of the heart.

The reference to circumcision of the heart in Deut 30:6 is verbally linked to the other reference evident in Rom 2:29: Ezek 36:26. As noted in the previous chapter, the promise of restoration after disobedience in Deut 30:6, "the Lord your God will circumcise your heart," is changed in the LXX to "and the Lord will cleanse your heart" (καὶ περικαθαριεῖ κυ-´ριος τὴν καρδίαν σου).[131] In keeping with contemporary Jewish exegetical practice, Paul exploits the translational ambiguity between the Hebrew text and the LXX in Deuteronomy to link that text to Ezekiel.

The promise of restoration in Ezek 36:25–26 also says "and I will cleanse you" (καὶ καθαριῶ ὑμᾶς). This is immediately followed by the promise of a new heart (of flesh) and a new spirit in v. 26, which language Paul appropriates in 2:29. Through Ezekiel 36 Paul introduces the idea that circumcision (cleansing) of the heart is a matter of spiritual restoration ἐν πνεύματι.[132] It also fulfills the command for circumcision in the flesh from Genesis 17, because the hearts that are circumcised are "hearts of flesh" (Ezek 36:26). All of this in Ezekiel will reemerge later in Romans in Paul's discussion of Israel's restoration. The point in Romans 1–4 is

---

[131]This is accompanied by various promises of blessing. Israel will be restored to the promised land (30:5), will obey and follow the Lord's commands (30:8), and will enjoy numerical and agricultural prosperity (30:9). The deuteronomic promises of restoration blessing in Ezek 36:27–30 mirror much of the language of Deut 30:5–9. Israel will be restored to the land, and will enjoy numerical and agricultural prosperity. The common material and exploitation of the translational difference lead Paul to link these texts in his exegesis.

[132]The contention of Käsemann (*Commentary on Romans*, 75), Cranfield (*The Epistle to the Romans*, 1.175), and Hafemann ("The Spirit of the New Covenant," 88–89) that the holy spirit of God is meant ("circumcision of the heart *by* the spirit") gains credibility when the use of "spirit" in its Ezekiel context is taken into account. The emphasis there is upon the action of God's spirit in the vision of Israel's restoration in Ezekiel 37. Contra Barrett (*Epistle to the Romans*, 58). In any case, whether God's spirit is to be understood as the circumciser of hearts or not, the point has to do with inward spiritual obedience.

that this spiritual circumcision of the heart is available to, and needed by, both Jews and gentiles.

AN EXEGETICAL BASIS FOR ROM 2:17–29

The preceding intertextual analysis demonstrates the fact that Paul reaches his conclusions in Rom 2:17–29 on the basis of his exegesis of OT texts. The passage is only a part of a larger logical argument from 1:18–3:20 establishing that "both Jews and gentiles are all under sin" (3:9). Paul goes on to establish the case for justification by faith apart from the law in 3:21–4:25.

To make the case that Jews specifically are under sin, Paul must address Jewish possession of the law and circumcision, supposed to be identifiers of the Jews as a people enjoying the benefits of a special status before God. By undercutting Jewish reliance on the covenant of the law (2:17–24), questioning the value of circumcision when the law is broken (2:25–27), and specifying meaningful circumcision as circumcision of the heart (2:28–29), Paul in effect redefines the meaning of "Jew" to be a spiritual, rather than simply an ethnic or national, definition.[133] In so doing, ethnic or national Jews are consigned to the same position regarding God's wrath as are gentiles.

THE RESULTS OF PAUL'S EXEGESIS

Paul's charges of Jewish law-breaking, his devaluation of circumcision, and his use of heart circumcision to redefine what it means to be a Jew are conclusions so radical that one should not assume Paul reaches them without serious consideration and without some basis.[134] Familiarity with Paul's let-

---

[133]The question of the status of national Israel is addressed again by Paul in Romans 9–11. Paul is not saying that ethnic Jews are no longer Jews. For further discussion see chapter 4, and Cranfield, *The Epistle to the Romans*, 1.176.

[134]Regarding the conclusions through Romans 3 Jouette M. Bassler comments, "scholars have recognized that Paul needed some warrant for these rather dramatic assertions" ("Divine Impartiality In Paul's Letter to the Romans," *NovT* 26 [1984] 43). Divine impartiality

ters points to the scriptures as most often the basis for his arguments and conclusions. This analysis provides evidence regarding the scriptural basis to which Paul has recourse for his radical conclusions in Rom 2:17–29.

Two of the passages which give evidence of being Pauline reference texts in Rom 2:17–25, Jer 7:2–11 and 9:23–26, address those who trust in and boast of their supposed relationship with God. They are warned that their trust is misplaced because of their covenant-breaking disobedience. The nation of Israel has become no better than the surrounding nations. In fact, these passages assume the curses of the covenant also mentioned in Deuteronomy 29–30 to have been invoked. Paul mirrors the language of these passages and concludes from them that the Jews are guilty of covenant-breaking disobedience, bringing disrepute upon the name of God. Identification as a Jew under the covenant of the law is not assurance of deliverance from wrath when the covenant has been broken.[135]

The Abrahamic covenant is redefined in Paul's references to Deut 30:6, Ezekiel 36:26, and Jer 9:26. In Rom 2:25–27 he addresses the value of circumcision in the face of the evidence of covenant-breaking disobedience, concluding also on the basis of Jer 9:26 that under that circumstance circumcision is of no value in assuring Jews a privileged position before God. Paul goes a step further by stating that law-keeping gentiles will be considered circumcised when law-breaking Jews are not. To make this statement he must come

---

summarized in the important statement of Rom 2:11 is certainly a major theological conclusion of Paul, as Bassler shows. However, Paul's assertion of impartiality cannot itself be the basis for his more dramatic conclusions. The assertion of divine impartiality also requires some warrant, which Paul finds in his intertextual references. See also, e.g., Barrett, *Epistle to the Romans*, 55; Käsemann, *Commentary on Romans*, 73; Dunn, *Romans 1–8*, 121.

[135]Again, the fact of a broken covenant does not imply the eradication of the covenant relationship. The question of restoration is developed elsewhere in the epistle, though it is implied in 2:28–29 by the reference to Ezekiel 36.

to grips with Gen 17:11–27, which specifies physical circumcision as the mark of the covenant and promise.

Deut 30:6, Ezekiel 36:26, and Jer 9:26 provide a reinterpretation of circumcision in Genesis 17 as heart circumcision (in "hearts of flesh"). This interpretation of the Abrahamic covenant, together with evidence of God's concern for internal "hidden" rather than external things (Deut 29:29), and the tie between the heart and spirit (Ezek 36:16–27) allow Paul to propose a redefinition of a Jew including one who is one inwardly, whose circumcision is spiritual. These "hidden" Jews also belong the the Lord (Deut 29:29). By these arguments, supported by his OT references, Paul at the same time undermines Jewish assurance on the basis of identification as a Jew and directs his readers to a spiritual obedience which can result in salvation for gentiles as well as Jews, later to be defined as based upon faith.

THE COURSE OF PAUL'S EXEGESIS

One should not assume that Paul's exegesis necessarily followed the course of his argument in Rom 2:17–29. There are a variety of exegetical scenarios which may be proposed. One which is not unlikely begins with Paul's earlier use of the Abraham narrative and the topic of circumcision from Genesis 12–22, and the blessings and curses of the covenant in Deuteronomy 27–32 (Galatians 3, 4). Genesis 17 with its support of the institution of circumcision as the mark of the covenant is a difficult text for Paul's position. To interpret Genesis 17 Paul goes to Deuteronomy 29–30 and the reaffirmation of the covenant to find a redefinition of the requirement of circumcision as heart circumcision, and evidence of God's concern for what is not visible. He relies on the phrase "hearts of flesh," to which he has had recourse in the past (Ezek 36:26; 2 Cor 3:3) to fulfill the command for circumcision in the flesh.

The linking vocabulary identified in the previous chapter ties Deuteronomy to the indictments of Jeremiah, which indicate, first, that Israel has broken the covenant and lies under the curses specified in Deuteronomy for disobedience and, secondly, that Israel's failure to be circumcised in heart has rendered physical circumcision ineffective as a covenant sign. Vocabulary links also tie these texts to Ezekiel 36, confirming Israel's disobedience, calling for inward change "in heart," and requiring spiritual obedience.[136] This is one possible exegetical road Paul may have followed.

Not all of these references are equally visible in the text of Romans 2. Jeremiah 7, 9, Exekiel 36, and Deuteronomy 29–30 provide Paul's primary conclusions, with the interpretive prophetic texts being most evident. Genesis 17, while present as a reference, is not obviously recalled in Rom 2:17–29. It is substructure not near the surface of the text. This is probably purposeful. Paul, showing some rhetorical sophistication, does not start his argument with the giving of the covenant, but with its breaking. He saves the giving of the covenant, its confirmation, and its modification until chap. 4, so that his readers may see its inception in the light of Paul's interpretation of its true meaning and effect.

The radical conclusions of Rom 2:17–29 are not merely hyperbolic examples presented to make a point, nor are they the unsubstantiated and overstated views of a vociferous opponent of Judaism. They are not even simply a well reasoned and logical argument. The evidence of this analysis shows that they are the conclusions of a student of scripture based upon his exegesis of scriptural texts. This understanding explains both the nature of the conclusions and the way the writer may have legitimately considered them to be true. An intertextual analysis of Rom 2:17–29, in short, makes sense of a text which has continually presented interpreters with difficulties. The task remaining is to see whether or not the conclusions of this analysis make sense in the larger context of the epistle to the Romans.

---

[136]The links also introduce the concept of Israel's restoration, to be developed later in Romans.

4

Rom 2:17–29 in Intertextual and Epistolary Context

The preceding analysis has shown how intertextual references lead Paul to the conclusions he reaches in Rom 2:17–29. In the scriptures Paul finds evidence of covenant-breaking disobedience on the part of the Jews, which makes their status as God's people regarding wrath no better than that of the gentiles. In the scriptures Paul also finds evidence that the Abrahamic covenant of circumcision calls for spiritual circumcision of the heart, so that a Jew is actually one who is so circumcised. For Paul, this fulfills the command for circumcision in the flesh, and may include ethnic gentiles as well as Jews.

Contextual analysis will determine if such a proposal comports with the context of Romans, and if it may shed light on its interpretation. First, the place of the reference texts found in Rom 2:17–29 in the web of intertextual references underlying the entire epistle will be examined. This will ascertain whether or not the proposed references in the passage are well integrated into that intertextual web. Secondly, the relationship of Rom 2:17–29 to the overall argument of the epistle will be examined. This will provide support for the conclusions reached in the preceding chapters about Pauline methods and statements in Rom 2:17–29.

AN INTEGRATED INTERTEXTUAL CONTEXT

Paul's epistle to the Romans is filled with OT allusions and quotations used to provide authoritative support for his arguments.[1] However, Paul also uses OT texts exegetically.[2] Thematic and verbal correspondence between OT references reveal what might be described as a web of mutually interpretive texts "beneath the surface" of Romans. They provide the basis for several themes which together form a foundation for Pauline conclusions.

Some of the most important OT texts underlying Romans prove to be those also in evidence as exegetical references in Romans 2:17–29: the blessings and curses of the covenant from Deuteronomy 29–32 (especially in Rom 2:1–16 and chap. 10), and the Abraham narrative of Genesis 15–22 (especially in Romans 4 and 9). Interwoven with the prophetic texts of Jeremiah 7, 9 and Ezekiel 36 evident in Rom 2:17–29 are vocabulary and themes throughout Romans from a variety of prophetic sources.

These texts provide Paul with six themes that are central particularly to Romans 2–4, and 9–11:

1. The theme of the giving of the covenant, both from the Abraham narrative and Deuteronomy 29–32, is evident in Romans 2 and in chaps. 4, 9–10. For Paul this theme is an obvious and assumed prerequisite.

2. The theme of faith/faithfulness as a covenant stipulation derives from the Abraham narrative, Deuteronomy 29–30, and supporting prophetic texts. Beyond the call for heart circumcision in Romans 2 it finds expression in Romans 4, 9, and 10.

3. The theme of the broken covenant is supported by Deuteronomy 29–30 in combination with linked prophetic texts. The assumption of the broken covenant underlies Romans 2 and is carried forward to Romans 9–10.

4. The theme of a "second line" of Abraham's descendants through Ishmael (the displaced first-born) is derived from the Abraham narrative and worked out in Romans 9. It is foundational for the development of the next theme.

---

[1]E.g., the strings of quotations at 3:10–18, 9:22–29, 15:9–12, and the Abraham narrative in chaps. 4 and 9.

[2]As already seen in 2:17–29. This is also the case in some of those passages where OT proof-texts are used, particularly in Romans 4, 9.

5. The theme of the reconciliation of the second line/inclusion of the gentiles into the people of God is creatively developed from the Abraham narrative and linked prophetic texts. That reconciliation underlies Paul's assertions not only in Romans 9–11 but also those about "the true Jew" in Romans 2:28–29 and the parallel definition of "Abraham's children" in Rom 4:16–17.

6. The theme of the restoration of a remnant of Israel stems from Deuteronomy 29–30 and linked prophetic texts. This theme is not explicitly dealt with until Romans 9–11, but is assumed in Paul's references underlying Romans 2:17–29.

This analysis will necessarily be cursory, merely touching on some of the major evidence for the use of intertextual references in many passages of Romans. Sufficient attention to intertextual references throughout Romans will be given to demonstrate the place of Rom 2:17–29 in the intertextual context.[3]

DEUTERONOMY IN ROMANS 2 AND 9–11

Pauline references to the reaffirmation of the covenant in Deuteronomy 29–32 most obviously confirm the integration of the OT references of Rom 2:17–29 into the intertextual web of Romans. It has already been mentioned that the reaffirmation of the covenant in Deuteronomy 29–32 forms an intertextual bridge between Rom 2:1–16 and 17–29. There are notable vocabulary links between Rom 2:1–16 and Deuteronomy 28–30, as noted in chap. 2.[4]

---

[3]The analysis will proceed through the OT reference texts in order to emphasize intertextual and thematic continuity, rather than through the order of Romans. The analysis of Rom 2:17–29 in its epistolary context will provide that level of continuity.

[4]Again, these include θλῖψις and στενοχωρία ("trouble and distress," Rom 2:9) in Deut 28:53, 55, 57; forms of ὀργή ("anger") and θυμός ("wrath") and their combination (Rom 2:5, 8) in Deut 29:20, 24, 28; τὰ κρυπτά ("the hidden/secret things," Rom 2:16) in Deut 29:29; and a parallel to τὰ τοῦ νόμου ποιῶσιν ("doing the things of the law," Rom 2:14) in Deut 29:29 (ποιεῖν πάντα τὰ ῥήματα τοῦ νόμου τούτου, "to do all the words of this law"). See James Scott "For as Many," 213–14 n. 88.

In the first half of Romans 2 the references to Deuteronomy serve primarily to remind the interlocutor of the consequences of disobedience, and to introduce a redefinition of "doing the law" which is "written on the heart" and "secret" (2:15–16). Paul will further define it in terms of faith/faithfulness as a covenant stipulation, using the language of heart circumcision from Deuteronomy. The presence of these references from Deuteronomy in Rom 2:1–16 provides confirmation of the evidence that those references also exist in Rom 2:17–29.

The presence of linking vocabulary and themes between references points to the likelihood that Deuteronomy 29–30 also echoes in the argument of Romans 9.[5] The entire theme of judgment and restoration in the Isaiah quotations of Rom 9:27–29 is present in Deut 30:1–10. Although the nation will experience the curses of the covenant, banishment, and famine, their fortunes will be restored. This echo is all the more likely given the fact that Paul almost immediately appeals to the very next verses in Deuteronomy in his citation of 30:11–14 — the reassurance that "The word is near you," etc. — in Rom 10:6–8. The larger context of Deuteronomy 29–32 is quoted at Rom 10:19 and 11:8. The recurrence of Deuteronomy 29–30 both in Rom 2:1–16 and chaps. 9–11 con-

---

[5]The presence of Deuteronomy 29–30 in Romans 9 may or may not meet the criteria for identification as an exegetical reference. But it does echo in Paul's argument and is finally quoted as a reference in Romans 10. The Genesis references upon which Paul depends in Rom 9:6–17 have verbal connections to Deuteronomy 29–30. Abraham, Isaac, and Jacob are mentioned in references to Genesis in Rom 9:7–13. They are mentioned as well in Deut 29:13, "as he promised you and as he swore to your ancestors, to Abraham, to Isaac, and to Jacob." Pharaoh, who appears in Rom 9:17 in connection with a quotation from Exod 9:16, interestingly also is mentioned at Deut 29:2. The quotations from Hos 2:23 and 1:10 at Rom 9:25–26 parallel the language of Deut 29:12 (LXX), where God appoints Israel to himself as a people, and himself to them as a God. Although this language is formulaic, the concentration of vocabulary from Deuteronomy ought not to be entirely discounted.

firms the evidence that these passages also occur as a reference in Rom 2:17–29.[6]

ABRAHAM IN ROMANS 4 AND 9

While there is only one narrative in Genesis 15–22, there are really two story-strands to which Paul refers. There is first the story of Abraham and the covenant with Israel through Isaac. But there is also a sub-plot, forming an entirely different story-strand for Paul. It concerns the relationship to the covenant of the displaced first-born son, Ishmael. This strand becomes representative of the gentiles in Romans 9.[7] It provides one of his bases for inclusion of gentiles as children of Abraham in chap. 4 and as heart-circumcised "inward" or "hidden" Jews (ὁ ἐν τῷ κρπτῷ Ἰουδαῖος) in chap. 2. The Abraham narrative is also foundational for Paul's arguments concerning faithfulness/heart-circumcision as the covenantal requirement in chaps. 2 and 4.

The Nature and Timing of the Covenant in Romans 4:

In chap. 4 Paul concludes from the Abraham narrative that Abraham was justified not by the law, but by faith.[8] The

---

[6]In keeping with Jewish exegetical principles, it is possible that the renewal of the covenant, in essence a second law-giving, in Deuteronomy 29–32 is a pattern which opens the entire concept of the covenant and the people of God to reinterpretation for Paul. Narrative repetitions which introduce variation in the narrative invite reinterpretation. For Paul, this appears to be particularly the case with the covenant renewal narrative. Rom 10:6–8 shows that Paul interprets that renewed covenant in terms of faith.

[7]The theme of the displaced first-born (Ishmael and Esau) is beneath the surface of Rom 9:6–17. James D. G. Dunn discusses the place of Esau in the argument (*Romans 9–16* [WBC 38b; Dallas: Word, 1988] 541–49). The theme of the inclusion of the gentiles/reconciliation of the displaced second line in the plan of God informs Rom 9:22–26. The displaced ones (gentiles represented by the displaced firstborn sons Ishmael and Esau) are to be reconciled and reinstated as God's people. See Cranfield, *The Epistle to the Romans*, 2.498.

[8]The issue introduced by Rom 4:1 is the question of the identity of Abraham's descendants (Richard B. Hays, "'Have We Found Abraham to be Our Forefather According to the Flesh?' A Reconsideration of Rom 4:1," *NovT* 27 [1985] 76–98). Abraham and questions concerning God's promises to him and his descendants provide the main line of continuity

foundational proof-text which summarizes the entirety is Rom 4:3 (Gen 15:6): "Abraham believed God, and it was credited to him as righteousness." Paul then introduces the theme of the inclusion of the gentiles at Rom 4:9 by referring to Abraham and asking if the blessing of forgiveness for sin was "only on the circumcised, or also on the uncircumcised?" In what has been called a "brilliant exegetical insight,"[9] Paul simply points out the chronology of the narrative and exploits it for application to his argument. Abraham was credited with righteousness by his belief and obedience of God (Gen 15:6) before the sign of circumcision was given (Gen 17:10).[10]

Paul interprets this chronology to have theological import: "in order for him to be father of all who believe while uncircumcised," εἰς τὸ εἶναι αὐτὸν πατέρα πάντων τῶν πιστευόντων δι' ἀκροβυστίας (Rom 4:11), as well as father of those who are circumcised and believe with the faith of Abraham before he was circumcised (4:12).[11] Paul adds the point that even the circumcised are children of Abraham by faith, not by virtue of their circumcision. He first broached this point in 2:28–29 when he redefined a Jew as one who is circumcised in heart. It is repeated here in 4:12 and will receive

---

for Romans 2–4 and 9–11. For a discussion of Romans 4 as Paul's means "to show why gentiles can be considered members of God's people," see Michael Cranford, "Abraham in Romans 4: The Father of All Who Believe," *NTS* 41 (1995) 73–88. Abraham's justification on the basis of faith before he was circumcised makes him "the father of all who believe," specifically inclusive of gentiles.

[9]Anthony J. Guerra, "Romans 4 as Apologetic Theology," *HTR* 81 (1988) 276.

[10]Barrett discusses the sign as a seal connoting "confirmation" (*Epistle to the Romans*, 86–87).

[11]I depart from the NRSV at this point because its translation of 4:11b is unusually paraphrastic, although it does accurately communicate the meaning of the verse: "The purpose was to make him the ancestor of all who believe without being circumcised."

Guerra states that "[Paul] pleads their [gentile Christians'] case that the one God justifies them as well as Jewish Christians, that the promise to Abraham included them and that they represent the many nations of which Abraham is the father" ("Romans 4," 270). While this is true, Guerra does not deal with the connections of Romans 4 with Romans 2 and 9–11 and the place of the Jews as God's people.

further emphasis in 9:6–7, "Not all who are of Israel are Israel, nor because they are Abraham's seed are they his children."

The covenant/promise comes by faith to all of Abraham's σπέρμα, which includes not just Jews but all those who have faith (Rom 4:16). Paul finds support for this conclusion in a passage which allows identification of the gentiles with the second line of the displaced first-born, Ishmael.

The original form of the giving of the covenant included the promise, "I will make of you a great nation" (Gen 12:2). Paul, however, does not rely on that verse. Instead, he quotes the pluralizing expansion of the promise given to Abraham immediately following the birth of Ishmael (Gen 17:5). The choice of this version of the promise is significant and intentional. Abram receives a new identity from God. The change in his status, and in the terms of the covenant itself, requires that he be renamed Abraham, "for I have made you a father of many nations" (πλήθους ἐθνῶν). The promises of the covenant are immediately reaffirmed in 17:6–8. There is an assumption of the inclusion of Ishmael and his descendents in the promise:

> I will make you exceedingly fruitful; and I will make nations of you, and kings shall come from you. I will establish my covenant between me and you, and your offspring after you throughout their generations, for an everlasting covenant, to be God to you and to your offspring after you. And I will give to you, and to your offspring after you, the land where you are now an alien, all the land of Canaan, for a perpetual holding; and I will be their God.

Paul has interpreted Gen 17:5–8 to include gentiles in the promise as children of Abraham, albeit on the basis of Abraham's faith.[12]

The promise concerning Ishmael and his descendents is immediately followed by the specific command for circumci-

---

[12]See e.g., Fitzmyer, *Romans*, 386. The passage is reinterpreted elsewhere, e.g., Sir 44:21: "Therefore the Lord assured him with an oath that the nations would be blessed through his offspring."

sion in the flesh in Gen 17:9–14. This is the difficult reference in Rom 2:25–27 for which Paul has found an answer in Eze- kiel 36:26: "and I will remove from your body the heart of stone and give you a heart of flesh." This allows Paul to con- clude that heart circumcision is circumcision in the flesh.

In Rom 2:25–27 on the surface of the text the issue was the true nature of circumcision and gentile inclusion in the people of the covenant. Here in Romans 4 the surface issue is righteousness apart from circumcision and gentile inclusion in the promise. The conclusions on the basis of Paul's exegesis of Genesis 17 inform Paul's argument in both cases. In Ro- mans 4 Abraham's example of righteousness before his cir- cumcision and the inclusion of Ishmael in the promise form the foundation of the argument. The conclusions Paul has reached on the basis of Ezekiel 36 in Romans 2 are unstated in Romans 4, but are already assumed.

The God "who gives life to the dead and calls into exis- tence the things that do not exist" (4:17) is a reference to Gen 17:17 and 18:11–12. Abraham and Sarah each find the prom- ise of a son incredible at their advanced age. Paul makes this explicit in 4:19 by describing Abraham and Sarah's reproduc- tive capabilities to be as good as dead. In reference to God's life-giving ability Paul extends his statement to encompass the resurrection of Jesus from the dead in 4:24–25.

In his reference to the Abraham narrative, in Romans 4 Paul finds several of the themes also evident in the references supporting Rom 2:17–29: the theme of the covenant and its blessings; the theme of faithfulness as a covenant stipulation; a hint of the breaking of the covenant and its consequences;[13] and the theme of the inclusion of the gentiles among God's people/the children of Abraham. These themes begin to dem- onstrate the intertextual cohesiveness of Romans. Paul's de- pendence upon one passage in Genesis 17 in both Romans 2

---

[13]Although this element is present in Gen 17:14, Paul does not in- troduce it into Romans 4. At this point he is interested in proving Abra- ham's righteousness before he was circumcised, not in establishing Jewish guilt. That theme is developed in Rom 2:17–29 and Romans 9–11 from reference texts in Deuteronomy and the prophets.

and 4 shows that those passages are inextricably bound together.

Promise and the Displaced First-born in Romans 9:

Romans 9 is also dependent on the Abraham narrative. With Romans 10, these chapters have been called the "greatest of all repositories of Pauline scripture citation and allusion."[14] Beginning with Rom 9:6–32, Paul enters a complex exegetical argument employing diatribe and intertextual exegesis.[15] Rom 9:6–7 confronts the identity of Abraham's descendants on a fundamental basis with the statement that "not all the ones from Israel [are] Israel" (οὐ γὰρ πάντες οἱ ἐξ Ἰσραὴλ οὗτοι Ἰσραήλ) nor are they all Abraham's children (τέκνα) just because they are his descendants, (σπέρμα).[16] It is not the natural children who are Israel, but those of the promise.[17]

Paul's distinctive emphasis on the promise, rather than the covenant, is one way he is able to redefine both children of God and children of Abraham in Romans 4 and 9, and true Jews in Romans 2.[18] But the interlocutor with whom Paul is

---

[14]Witherington, *Paul's Narrative Thought World*, 45.

[15]9:1–5 are not properly part of the argument, but introduce the question of the propriety of God's treatment of Israel. Käsemann, among others, emphasizes the elements of diatribe (*Commentary on Romans*, 261), while William R. Stegner points out Paul's use both of diatribe and midrash ("Romans 9:6–29 — A Midrash," *JSNT* 22 [1984] 42). The ambiguity of the term "midrash" has already been addressed.

[16]For discussion of the chaiastic structure of the entire passage see Dunn, *Romans 9–16*, 537, but especially Jean-Noël Aletti, "L'argumentation Paulinienne en Rm 9," *Bib* 68 (1987) 41–56.

[17]This is similar to the distinction between children of the law and children of the promise in Romans 4.

[18]Paul in Romans consistently substitutes ἐπαγγελία for διαθήκη in reference to the Abrahamic covenant of blessing for Abraham and his descendants. Διαθήκη appears in Romans only at 9:4 where it is parallel with ἐπαγγελία, and at 11:27, which is a conflated quotation dependent in part upon Jer 31:33–34. The word ἐπαγγελία appears in the OT only in 2 Chr 35:7, Ps 55 (56):9, Esth 4:7, and Amos 9:6 and is unrelated to the Abrahamic covenant. Paul apparently chooses ἐπαγγελία because it does not have the restrictive connotation applying only to Israel. The distinction is useful if Paul understands the covenant as reaching its "climactic moment" in Jesus Christ, as discussed by Wright (*The Climax*

at odds mistakenly thinks in terms of natural descent, assuming "being Israel" means national Israel, the descendants of Isaac, the son of the promise.

But Paul's point is just the opposite.[19] In his appeal to Gen 21:12 in Rom 9:7, far from equating children of the promise with national Israel, Paul is proving that election depends on God's choice alone for his reasons alone, and not on descent from anyone (Rom 9:11–15). If it depended upon descent, Ishmael and Esau, rather than being displaced, would specifically have been the elect because they were the firstborn sons.[20]

The reference to Gen 21:12 (Rom 9:7) is particularly important. The quotation, "Your descendants will be reckoned (called) through Isaac," is in the context of Sarah's thrusting of Hagar and Ishmael from the camp. Abraham is troubled because it concerns his son. In the next verse, God then tells Abraham not to be troubled. He will make Ishmael into a great nation (ἔθνος μέγα) because he is Abraham's child (σπέρμα, Gen 21:13).

If Paul has only the words he quotes in mind, then a reaffirmation of the priority of Isaac could be understood. But if, as usual, Paul is contextually aware, he is saying something about the outcome of Ishmael and his descendants as Abraham's descendants (σπέρμα 'Αβραάμ, Rom 9:7–8). It is signifi-

---

of the Covenant, xi, 235–50, 263–67). Paul certainly understands the covenant/promise as inclusive of gentiles, and the law as fulfilled in Christ, whether or not the covenant itself reaches its fulfillment in Christ. In Romans, however, Paul still appears to prefer the term "promise" over "covenant" for application beyond Israel. Difficulties and ambiguities concerning Paul's understanding of "covenant" may be comparable to those concerning his understanding of "law." On Paul referring to promise rather than covenant, see Morna D. Hooker, "Paul and 'Covenantal Nomism,'" *Paul and Paulinism: Essays in Honour of C. K. Barrett* (ed. Morna Hooker and S. G. Wilson; London: SPCK, 1982) 51–53; reprinted in *From Adam to Christ*, 158–69.

[19]So Dunn, *Romans 9–16*, 545.

[20]Barrett understands these consequences of Paul's argument (*Epistle to the Romans*, 171). Dunn concurs, "their founding fathers disprove rather than prove the equation" (*Romans 9–16*, 547). The choosing of the second-born over the first-born makes just that point.

cant that in Romans 2, 4, and 9 Paul's references from the
Abraham narrative are taken from material in which the
promise to Ishmael is central. Abraham's true descendants
are those of the promise. The promise was confirmed specifically in relation to Ishmael, the displaced firstborn, representative of the gentiles for Paul. The course of Paul's continuing
argument concerning the place of gentiles in God's plan confirms this. The displaced firstborn is still included in God's
promise.

In Paul's exegesis Ishmael represents the first in a line
of displaced first-born children who make up a "second line" of
inheritance estranged from the covenant. They are estranged
until Paul weaves his reference texts together to show how
the second line regains status as children of God/children of
Abraham in Romans 9. Paul does not include Ishmael in the
promise in so many words. But he does include gentiles, for
whom Ishmael serves as the first representative, shown by
the fact that the themes Paul develops in Romans 9 are em-
bedded in Ishmael's story.[21]

What emerges from Genesis is a sense of ambiguity concerning Ishmael's relationship to the covenant.[22] He appears

---

[21]Cranfield notes the presence of the Ishmael sub-plot: "So we
must not read into Paul's argument any suggestion that Ishmael...is
therefore excluded from the embrace of God's mercy" (*The Epistle to the
Romans*, 2.475). Donaldson denies this type of connection between the
promise to Abraham and the salvation of the gentiles, missing the references to Ishmael. "Nowhere in the rhetoric of Romans...is the salvation
of the Gentiles seen as the product of God's faithfulness to a promise
made to Abraham" (*Paul and the Gentiles*, 98). The Ishmael strand of
the Abraham references indicates an inclusion of gentiles in the promise
in some sense. Donaldson does understand Paul's argument in Romans
4 to say that "believing Gentiles are to be included among the heirs of
the promises" (ibid.), and he is correct that gentile salvation is not "explicitly" connected to the promise (ibid., 99). But the Ishmael reference
in Romans 9 makes a stronger connection between Ishmael/gentiles and
the promise than Donaldson concludes.

[22]This sense of ambiguity concerning the status of those outside
the covenant extends beyond Paul's exegesis of Genesis. The discussion
within Judaism contemporary with Paul provides an already existing
stage for his exegetical approach to the question of gentile inclusion.
"[T]he literature of Second Temple Judaism displays no single clear and

to be both included and excluded. He is included as a son of Abraham, yet not included as the son of the covenant.[23] It is in Romans 9 that Paul ends the ambiguity by showing scripture to include all of God's children in mercy, the chosen as well as the displaced (Rom 9:6–24). What then ironically becomes ambiguous is the relationship of the physical descendants of Isaac—the children of the covenant—to the promise to all of Abraham's children (Rom 9:30–10:21). These conclusions from the Abraham narrative in Romans 4 and 9 resonate in the reference to Genesis 17 in Rom 2:17–29. Dependence in particular upon the material concerning Ishmael shows how intertextually integrated these chapters in Romans are to one another.

PROPHETIC THEMATIC LINKS IN ROMANS

As has already been demonstrated, vocabulary and thematic links tie together otherwise disparate strands of the intertextual web underlying Romans. This is so to an even greater extent with prophetic texts. With the narratives, some broad themes are encapsulated in a relatively few major texts which recur as reference texts repeatedly in Pauline material.

---

agreed-on position regarding the Gentiles themselves—their status vis-à-vis God in the present or their destiny in the eschatological future. Not that there were no opinions on the matter;...the literary and other remains of the period bear witness to a lively interest in the issue, and a rich range of approaches. But most of these are consistent with covenantal nomism, and none of them can be taken as normative" (Donaldson, *Paul and the Gentiles*, 75). On covenantal nomism see Sanders, *Paul and Palestinian Judaism*, 422–23. Paul in effect delves into the middle of a theological conundrum confronting Judaism. There is "a tension inherent in the covenant idea itself: in that Israel's God is the creator and sovereign of all, the Gentiles cannot be excluded from God's purposes; but in that Israel has been chosen in distinction from the other nations, the Gentiles cannot simply be included without the potential of a threat to Israel's special status" (Donaldson, *Paul and the Gentiles*, 75). Paul's attempt to include gentiles as children of the promise while preserving an advantage to being a Jew goes to the heart of these questions. The story of Ishmael provides Paul's interpretive answer.

[23]Even though Ishmael was circumcised and named "man from God," Isaac takes precedence thereafter as the special son of the covenant, while Ishmael is driven into the desert.

In the case of the prophetic references a wide variety of texts similar to one another point to a body of themes. As a reference text shares vocabulary and themes with other referent texts, it is integrated into the intertextual web.

As seen earlier, the links of Jeremiah 7 and Ezekiel 36 to the references from Deuteronomy 27–30 already show those prophetic texts found as references in Rom 2:17–29 to be intertwined with a narrative text which provides major themes at a number of points in Romans. As they are used by Paul to re-present and interpret the narrative text of Deuteronomy as it appears in Romans, they are integrated into the larger intertextual whole.

A Broken Covenant: Isaiah 59, Jeremiah 11, and Jeremiah 7 in Romans:

Besides the narrative of Deuteronomy, prophetic links also integrate Jer 7:2–11 into the intertextual web of Romans. At Rom 3:15–17 Paul quotes Isa 59:7–8.[24] The quotation includes the phrase "They rush swiftly to shed blood" (τρέχουσιν ταχινοὶ ἐκχέαι αἷμα, Isa 59:7). A similar phrase occurs in the warnings of Jeremiah 7: "[and if] you do not shed innocent blood" (αἷμα ἀθῷον μὴ ἐκχέητε, Jer 7:8).

Likewise, in the near context of Isaiah it is said of Israel that "they rely (trust) on emptiness and they speak empty [words]" (πεποίθασιν ἐπὶ ματαίοις καὶ λαλοῦσιν κενα, Isa 59:4). Trust in useless words is also a theme in Jeremiah: "Do not trust in these deceptive words" (μὴ πεποίθατε ἐφ᾽ ἑαυτοῖς ἐπὶ λόγοις ψευδέσιν, Jer 7:4).

While the vocabulary links are not exact, these passages share concerns about the shedding of blood, trusting in useless speech, and other forms of violence and injustice. Both passages are part of the web of texts establishing the themes of Israel's failure to abide by the terms of the covenant, warning of the consequences of continued disobedience, and in

---

[24]Paul quotes again from Isa 59:20–21 at Rom 11:26, conflated with Jer 31:33–34.

Paul's argumentative interpretation establishing the fact that Israel's status before God is no better than that of gentiles.[25]

Jeremiah 7 is also linked to Jeremiah 11, which provides the imagery for breaking branches off from the olive tree of Israel at Rom 11:17–21 (Jer 11:16).[26] Although Jeremiah 7 warns Judah to reform or suffer the consequences, as has been noted previously, Jer 7:16 says, "As for you, do not pray for this people, do not raise a cry or prayer on their behalf, and do not intercede with me, for I will not hear you." Preceding the olive branch imagery by two verses, at Jer 11:14, the instruction seen in Jeremiah 7 is repeated, "As for you, do not pray for this people, or lift up a cry or prayer on their behalf, for I will not listen when they call to me in the time of their trouble."

Both passages are concerned with following other gods and burning incense to Baal (7:9; 11:10, 12–13), and with trusting in worthless corrupted temple worship (7:4, 10–11, 14; 11:15).[27] They share the theme of a covenant broken through disobedience.[28] The context of Jeremiah 11:16 shares

---

[25]Hosea 1–2, serving as a reference at Rom 9:25–26, also embodies these themes, although the theme of restoration is primary in Hosea. While there is no significant vocabulary correspondence with Jeremiah 7, the presence of both as references in Romans is consistent with the pattern of thematic coherence.

[26]See, e.g., Dodd, *Epistle*, 180. Vocabulary links between Jeremiah 11 and Romans 11 include ἐλαία "olive tree," κλάδος "branch." Rom 11:17 and 19 read ἐξεκλάσθησαν (ἐκκλάω) κλάδοι. In the LXX of Jer 11:16 the branches are not broken off, but cut off, περιτομῆς αὐτῆς. Since περιτομή proves to be such a significant link between many of the texts in Romans this may be one of the links of this passage in Jeremiah 11 to other reference texts. However, Paul probably avoids the translation because of the confusion it would introduce into his imagery. The MT does read, רֵעוּ (רעע), "broken."

[27]There are a number of statements in these passages concerning the temple which may function to support Paul's effort to diminish or eliminate the importance of ceremonial law for gentiles, including temple worship.

[28]Jer 11:10 confirms what Jeremiah 7 warned of: "they have gone after other gods to serve them; the house of Israel and the house of Judah have broken the covenant that I made with their ancestors."

vocabulary and themes integrating Jeremiah 7 into the larger intertextual web of Romans.

Unfaithfulness and Heart Circumcision: Isaiah 28–29, Jeremiah 31, and Jeremiah 9 in Romans:

The reference to Jer 9:23–26 in Rom 2:17–29 is also tied to the text of the Deuteronomy references in Romans by the important vocabulary link of heart circumcision. It is linked to the text of Genesis 17 by forms of περιτέμνω, ἀκροβυστία, and σάρξ. But the integration of Jeremiah 9 into the intertextual web is further confirmed by links to two prophetic reference texts appearing in Romans, Isaiah 28–29 and Jeremiah 31.

Paul quotes from Isa 28:16 at Rom 9:33 (conflated with Isa 8:14), and again at Rom 10:11: "See, I am laying in Zion a foundation stone, a tested stone, a precious cornerstone, a sure foundation: 'One who trusts will not be humiliated'" (Rom 9:33).[29] He also quotes from Isa 29:10 (πνεύματι κατανύξεως) at Rom 11:8 (πνεῦμα κατανύξεως),[30] and Isa 29:16 at Rom 9:20.

Not surprisingly, given the nature of much prophetic material, Jeremiah 9 and Isaiah 28–29 share the theme of a broken covenant in indictments of disobedience and lawbreaking. There is a concern for justice and righteousness in both passages (Isa 28:17; Jer 9:24). The vocabulary of setting aside the wisdom of the wise is present as well (Isa 29:14; Jer 9:23). In Isaiah as in Jeremiah 9 fulfillment of the ritual requirements of the law is again repudiated in favor of faithful-

---

[29]The NRSV translation of καταισχύνω as "panic" is not followed here. See R. Bultmann, "αἰσχύνω," *TDNT* 1.189–90.

[30]"God gave them a sluggish spirit, eyes that would not see and ears that would not hear, down to this very day" (Rom 11:8). The Pauline quotation is conflated with Deut 29:4, also a part of one of the primary strands of the intertextual web.

Perhaps in oblique and undeveloped echo of what Paul has said in Rom 2:29 regarding the "secret" Jew (ἐν τῷ κρυπτῷ), and tied to Deut 29:29 where "the secret things belong to the Lord" (τὰ κρυπτά), in Isa 29:10 those who are given the spirit of slumber and closed eyes are the prophets and rulers, "the ones seeing secret things" (οἱ ὁρῶντες τὰ κρυπτά).

ness as the true covenant stipulation: "These people...honor me with their lips, but their heart is far from me; they worship me in vain, teaching the commandments and doctrines of men" (Isa 29:13, LXX).[31]

An additional note of support for the integration of Jeremiah 9 into the intertextual web is found in the fact that Jer 9:23–26 recurs as a reference in other Pauline literature, in a quotation of 9:24 at 1 Cor 1:31. There Paul links the passage from Jeremiah to Isa 29:14 (1 Cor 1:19).[32] He employs the same two linked texts in Romans and in 1 Corinthians.

Jeremiah 9 is also linked to Jeremiah 31. Jer 31:33–34 serves as a reference in a conflated quotation along with Isa 59:20–21 and 27:9 at Rom 11:26–27.[33] The language of Jer 31:33 also stands behind Rom 2:15, "written on their hearts," while Rom 11:2 may refer to Jer 31:37, where God affirms that he will not reject Israel.[34] The passages from Jeremiah 9 and 31 share language concerning interior spirituality of the heart (καρδία, 9:26; 31:33), and an admonition to know the Lord (γνῶθι τὸν κύριον, 31:34; γινώσκειν ὅτι ἐγώ εἰμι κύριος, 9:24). The theme of a broken covenant is shared with Jeremiah 9 in the assumption of 31:32, "because they did not remain in my covenant" (ὅτι αὐτοὶ οὐκ ἐνέμειναν ἐν τῇ διαθήκῃ μου). These texts and themes show Jer 9:23–26 to be well integrated into the intertextual web of Romans.

Restoration: Isaiah 52, Jeremiah 31, Joel 2, and Ezekiel 36 in Romans:

Ezek 36:16–27, the final reference from Rom 2:17–29, is integrated into the intertextual web of Romans. Ezekiel 36 is

---

[31]The larger context of Jeremiah 9 shows extensive parallels with Isaiah 59 as well. Both bring repeated charges of lying and deception, and both promise God's justice and righteousness in the face of the injustice and unrighteousness of God's people. Such general thematic coherence is not entirely without merit.

[32]O'Day, "Jeremiah 9:22–23 and 1 Corinthians 1:26–31," 259–67. Jer 9:24 appears in 2 Cor 10:17 as well.

[33]See Fitzmyer, *Romans*, 625.

[34]"If the heavens above can be measured, and the foundations of the earth below can be explored, then I will reject all the offspring of Israel" (Jer 31:37).

also part of the deuteronomic blessings and curses like Deuteronomy 27–30 and is already intertextually linked to other reference passages in Romans from this standpoint, as noted above. Ezekiel 36 is also linked to Isaiah 52, first by the parallel to the quotation of Isa 52:5 at Rom 2:24. The context of Isaiah 52, also quoted at Rom 10:15 (Isa 52:7) and 10:16 (Isa 53:1), is tied to Israel's restoration in Romans 10–11, which is in thematic coherence with Ezekiel 36. Both passages also emphasize the cleansing of Israel and the display of God's salvation before the nations.[35]

Ezekiel 36 also recurs as a reference in Pauline literature in 2 Cor 3:1–6, in a complex of texts that includes Jeremiah 31 (LXX 38).[36] Again it can be seen that two reference texts appear with links to one another in two different places in Paul's epistles, since the passage from Jeremiah 31 also links Ezekiel 36 to the larger intertextual web in Romans.

Ezek 36:26 promises a new heart (καρδίαν καινήν) and new spirit (πνεῦμα καινόν). In Jer 31:31 the promise is for a new covenant (διαθήκην καινήν). In Ezekiel the memory of former sins is reason for distress: "Then you shall remember your evil ways" (καὶ μνησθήσεσθε τὰς ὁδοὺς ὑμῶν τὰς πονηράς, Ezek 36:31). The emphasis in Jeremiah is more positive, but dealing with the memory of former sins is part of restoration there, too: "for I will be merciful to their iniquities,

---

[35]"And you will be cleansed from all of your uncleanness" (καὶ καθαρισθήσεσθε ἀπὸ πασῶν τῶν ἀκαθαρσιῶν ὑμῶν, Ezek 36:25); "Do not touch an unclean thing...separate yourselves" (ἀκαθάρτου μὴ ἅπτεσθε...ἀφορίσθητε, Isa 52:11).

"And the nations will know that I am the Lord" (καὶ γνώσονται τὰ ἔθνη ὅτι ἐγώ εἰμι κύριος, Ezek 36:23); "And the Lord shall reveal his holy arm in the sight of all the nations, and all the ends of the earth shall see the salvation of God" (καὶ ἀποκαλύψει κύριος τὸν βραχίονα αὐτοῦ τὸν ἅγιον ἐνώπιον πάντων τῶν ἐθνῶν, καὶ ὄψονται πάντα τὰ ἄκρα τῆς γῆς τὴν σωτηρίαν τὴν παρὰ τοῦ θεοῦ, Isa 52:10).

[36]Stockhausen, *Moses' Veil*, 48–49, 68–71. In 2 Corinthians, Jeremiah 31 and Ezekiel 36 function together to interpret a narrative text. In Romans the passages are simply linked with themes and vocabulary. They are not used together exegetically in the way they are in 2 Corinthians.

and remember their sins no more" (ὅτι ἵλεως ἔσομαι ταῖς ἀδικίαις αὐτῶν καὶ τῶν ἁμαρτιῶν αὐτῶν οὐ μὴ μνησθῶ ἔτι, Jer 31:34).

In both passages the restoration is complete when the deuteronomic blessing is fulfilled: "And you will be my people, and I will be your God" (καὶ ἔσεσθέ μοι εἰς λαόν, κἀγὼ ἔσομαι ὑμῖν εἰς θεόν, Ezek 36:28); "And I will be their God, and they will be my people" (καὶ ἔσομαι αὐτοῖς εἰς θεόν, καὶ αὐτοὶ ἔσονταί μοι εἰς λαόν, Jer 31:33).

The passages are linked by the theme of faith/faithfulness as a covenant stipulation. The keeping of the law is an interior matter of the heart: "A new heart I will give you, and a new spirit I will put within you; and I will remove from your body the heart of stone and give you a heart of flesh. I will put my spirit within you..." (καὶ δώσω ὑμῖν καρδίαν καινὴν καὶ πνεῦμα καινὸν δώσω ἐν ὑμῖν καὶ ἀφελῶ τὴν καρδίαν τὴν λιθίνην ἐκ τῆς σαρκὸς ὑμῶν καὶ δώσω ὑμῖν καρδίαν σαρκίνην. καὶ τὸ πνεῦμά μου δώσω ἐν ὑμῖν..., Ezek 36:26–27). "I will put my laws in their minds and write them on their hearts" (δώσω νόμους μου εἰς τὴν διάνοιαν αὐτῶν καὶ ἐπὶ καρδίας αὐτῶν γράψω αὐτούς, Jer 31:33).

Finally, parallels between Joel 2 and Ezekiel 36 are remarkable in their characterization of Israel's restoration. Joel 2:32 is quoted at Rom 10:13. Joel also emphasizes interior spirituality and faithfulness: "rend your hearts, and not your garments" (διαρρήξατε τὰς καρδίας ὑμῶν καὶ μὴ τὰ ἱμάτια ὑμῶν, 2:13). Both passages promise the returned prosperity of the land (Joel 2:21–26; Ezek 36:29–30). They both assure the removal of Israel's shame for the desolation of the land. In Joel, the result is this: "And never again will my people be ashamed" (καὶ οὐ μὴ καταισχυνθῇ ὁ λαός μου εἰς τὸν αἰῶνα, Joel 2:26, repeated in v. 27). Ezek 36:30 also ties renewed prosperity to a removal of shame. Israel's crops will increase, "so that you not bear the shame of famine among the nations" (ὅπως μὴ λάβητε ὀνειδισμὸν λιμοῦ ἐν τοῖς ἔθνεσιν, Ezek 36:30).[37]

---

[37]The idea is expanded upon in vv. 33–36.

Ezek 36:26 promises a new heart and new spirit, adding, "And I will put my spirit (πνεῦμα) in you." This is paralleled in Joel 2:28, 29, "Then afterward, I will pour out my spirit on all flesh" (Καὶ ἔσται μετὰ ταῦτα καὶ ἐκχεῶ ἀπὸ τοῦ πνεύματός μου ἐπὶ πᾶσαν σάρκα). The expansion of the promise of the spirit to those beyond Israel is appropriated by Paul in his argument when he quotes Joel 2:32, "And everyone who calls on the name of the Lord will be saved" (Rom 10:13). The reference to Ezekiel 36 in Romans 2 is clearly in concert with Paul's use of Isaiah 52, Jeremiah 31, and Joel 2 elsewhere in Romans, supporting its integration into the intertextual web upon which Paul is dependent.

This analysis has not included some OT references and themes developed in Romans which have no direct bearing on Rom 2:17–29.[38] It has been the purpose of this analysis to present evidence that the intertextual references and themes evident in Rom 2:17–29 are consistent with and an integral part of a larger sub-structure of interrelated texts. This analysis is the first confirmatory step, showing that the references upon which Paul is dependent in Rom 2:17–29 are integrated into the intertextual web of Romans. The final step is to determine if the proposal concerning Paul's conclusions in Rom 2:17–29 based upon his intertextual references comports with the rest of the epistle.

ROM 2:17–29 IN EPISTOLARY CONTEXT

The preceding analysis has confirmed that the intertextual references identified in Rom 2:17–29 are consistent with the larger intertextual web in Romans. The following brief overview of important connective themes in Romans will demonstrate how Rom 2:17–29, together with the references identified there, fit into and help explain the overall context of the epistle.

The composition of the Roman church and Paul's intended audience have already been touched upon because

---

[38]E.g., the use of the Adam narrative. See Hooker, "Adam in Romans I," 297–306.

they both address and are addressed by the exegesis of Rom 2:17–29. This analysis will confirm a Pauline address to both gentile and Jewish Christians.[39] It will also point toward a purpose of the epistle tied more to the situation of the Roman congregation than to Paul's travel plans.[40] This does not exclude a desire on Paul's part to gain good favor in the furtherance of his mission to the west. However, it will indicate that such a concern is more peripheral than is sometimes proposed.[41] Instead, it will show that Rom 2:17–29 is an integral part of Paul's argument addressing the relationship of Jews

---

[39]In agreement with, e.g., Dunn (*Romans 1–8*, xliv–liv), Michel (*Der Brief an die Römer*, 7–14), Fitzmyer (*Romans*, 32–34), Cranfield (*The Epistle to the Romans*, 1.18–21), Dodd (*Epistle*, xxviii), and Kümmel (*Introduction to the New Testament*, 309–10).

[40]Guerra opts for both purposes. "Most important to Paul is the encouragement of mutual respect between Jewish and Gentile factions in the Roman community....Paul is concerned also with lessening the likelihood of the kind of direct opposition to his projected missionary labors which he had frequently encountered in the East and which was certainly one of the primary impediments to his work there" (*Apologetic Tradition*, 41, see also 177–79).

[41]The conclusion of Krister Stendahl in his more recent work overemphasizes Paul's remarks concerning his apostolate to the gentiles and underemphasizes evidence of Paul's desire to promote unity in the local church at Rome. "Romans is Paul's final account of his theology of mission.... It is not a pastoral letter dealing with the specific problems in Rome, as the Corinthian correspondence is with respect to Corinth.... But he was anxious that they have a clear understanding of his apostolic mission as he planned to leave the East and go West to Spain. Thus Romans is Paul's account of how his mission to the Gentiles was grounded not only in his call to be Apostle to the Gentiles but also in Scripture" (*Final Account*, ix). Paul's desire to promote a unified church inclusive of both Jewish and gentile Christians is certainly related to his continuous defense of his gentile mission (see the work of Segal, *Paul the Convert*) but the evidence of Romans also points to a situation in Rome to which Paul speaks. As Stendahl says, the letter does not have the specificity of the pastoral letters to Corinth. However, since Paul's knowledge of individuals in the church at Rome is limited, it might be expected not to address issues relating to specific individuals, but community-wide issues. This does not preclude Paul from speaking to matters of Christian belief on a more general level which are current issues in Rome.

and the law to Christ and the increasingly gentile church in Rome.

GENTILES AND JEWS SHARE SIN AND FAITH: ROMANS 1–4
Scripture and God's Righteousness:

Paul begins his epistle by pointing out that the gospel was "promised beforehand through his prophets in the holy scriptures" (1:2). This unusual addition to the normal Pauline greeting should not be overlooked, and provides the initial indication of Paul's desire to emphasize the relationship of the church of his gentile mission to Jewish belief grounded in the scriptural law.[42]

The emphasis continues in chaps. 1 and 2. Arguments from scripture culminate in the assertion that Jews are under the same judgment as gentiles in Rom 2:17–29. In chap. 3 salvation for both groups is tied to scripture. Salvation is found in Christ, faith in whom brings about the righteousness from God "to which the law and the prophets testify" (3:21). Giving this emphasis its full due is important to a correct un-

---

[42]The word "promised beforehand" (προεπηγγείλατο) appears elsewhere in the NT only in 2 Cor 9:5. This is the only appearance in the NT of the phrase "holy scriptures." Michel is right in asking if Paul's grounding of the gospel in the OT implies something concerning the Roman congregation (*Römerbrief*, 37). Often that implication is overlooked, seeing v. 2 only as a general acknowledgment of the gospel's relation to salvation-history (Fitzmyer, *Romans*, 233), or in relation to a promise and fulfillment motif (Käsemann, *Commentary on Romans*, 9). Tobin stresses that Paul's appeal to scripture is given as evidence that his position has "traditional" precedent ("Controversy and Continuity," 299). There is, however, no acknowledgment that Paul's appeal to scripture also serves to justify scripture's own pronouncements. Dunn, more to the point, concludes that the allusion to the promise of scripture is made "perhaps because it is precisely the role of the law within the divine purpose which he seeks to clarify in this letter, and almost certainly because he wants to strike the note...of God's promise and his faithfulness to that promise" (*Romans 1–8*, 10–11). More broadly, Paul seeks to clarify the role of the law and of Jews in the overall plan of God in relation to Christ, faith, and the church of his gentile mission.

derstanding of the epistle and of Paul's reliance on OT references in Rom 2:17–29 and elsewhere.[43]

In the thesis statement of 1:16–17, Paul's own reason for not being ashamed of the gospel points again to the relationship of both Jews and gentiles to the gospel: "it is the power of God for salvation to everyone who has faith, to the Jew first and also to the Greek." Paul does not simply end with, "to everyone who has faith," because he is beginning an argument concerning God's impartial treatment of Jews and gentiles alike, of which Rom 2:17–29 and its references are a part.[44]

The thesis statement lays the foundation for Paul's discussion of God's righteousness being worked out in the history of the Jews and the law, as well as for gentiles and the church, through the all encompassing medium of faith/faithfulness.[45] The epistle is a defense of the right(eous)ness of God in working out his salvation for both Jews and gentiles as children of Abraham. The establishment of Jewish guilt and gentile inclusion in the people of God in Rom 2:17–29 is foundational for the argument by placing Jews and gentiles in equal standing before God.

---

[43]"Paul, as it seems, is constantly concerned to show that God's gospel, which he is now preaching, 'was promised beforehand'" (Samuel Byrskog, "Epistolography, Rhetoric and Letter Prescript: Romans 1.1–7 as a Test Case," *JSNT* 65 [1997] 41). Byrskog points out that it is the use of scripture in Romans which makes the case, in the words of Richard Hays, "that the gospel is the fulfillment, not the negation of God's word to Israel" (*Echoes*, 34).

[44]See esp. Bassler, *Divine Impartiality*.

[45]See Douglas Campbell, "Romans 1:17—A *Crux Interpretum* for the ΠΙΣΤΙΣ ΞΡΙΣΤΟΥ Debate," *JBL* 113 (1994) 280–85. Here in Rom 1:17a and the quotation from Hab 2:4 in 17b, Campbell's reading of "faithfulness of Christ" rather than the faith of individuals is entirely correct. However, see the critique by Brian Dodd, that Campbell oversteps the evidence in attributing this understanding of πιστις too broadly to other passages ("Romans 1:17— A *Crux Interpretum* for the ΠΙΣΤΙΣ ΧΡΙΣΤΟΥ Debate?," *JBL* 114 [1995] 470–73). Campbell responds ("False Presuppositions in the ΠΙΣΤΙΣ ΧΡΙΣΤΟΥ Debate: A Response to Brian Dodd," *JBL* 116 [1997] 713–19) and defends his position on the basis of earlier work ("The Meaning of ΠΙΣΤΙΣ and ΝΟΜΟΣ in Paul: A Linguistic and Structural Perspective," *JBL* 111 [1992] 91–103).

Gentiles and Sin:

At 1:18 Paul begins the argument with an assertion of God's righteousness in wrath for the disobedience of gentiles. The argument will continue to include Jews as well (2:9–10), and the need for salvation from wrath for both groups. The description of human sinfulness in chap. 1 is again bound up with the Jewish scriptures, at this point from the Adam narrative of Genesis 2–3 and Wisdom 11–15.[46] The fact that gentile humanity is sinful and under God's wrath was not a point of dispute, but the introduction of the interlocutor in chap. 2 indicates that the Jews also being under the wrath of God requires some explanation.

Whether or not the interlocutor is meant to stand in for persons in the Roman church, the true purpose of the device is to allow Paul to offer an explanation of how God's chosen people, to whom faithfulness had been pledged, find themselves at odds with the gospel of that same God. Chap. 2 is a necessary step in the explanation. He must first show why the gospel of faith is also necessary for the people of the covenant.[47]

---

[46]Hooker, "Adam in Romans I," 297–306. Among others, Dunn, *Romans 1–8*, 53.

[47]Segal points out that Paul's new view of what faith entails is basic to his understanding of the need for Jewish conversion. "But faith means more to Paul than remaining faithful and steadfast to the covenant. It is not something that Judaism or Jewish Christianity exhibits, but it is inherent in gentile Christianity....By faith Paul essentially means a radical reorientation and commitment." Christian faith is not, however, to be understood in antipathy to the law, rather, as Segal continues, "[Paul] is trying to show that those who have faith can also count themselves as part of the covenant relationship with Abraham" (*Paul the Convert*, 121). Segal frames Paul's arguments opposing law in the context of ceremonial regulations differentiating Jews from gentiles.

Cf. Donaldson, who concludes that Torah and faith "are somehow mutually exclusive....the unexpressed premise in [3:30] is not simply that Torah is not to be imposed on Gentiles; rather, there is one way for circumcised and uncircumcised alike to relate to God, and this way is not the Torah" (*Paul and the Gentiles*, 85). More strongly than Segal, Donaldson's view emphasizes Paul's new conception of the law. While it has, or had, its purpose which Paul defends, it is "not to be imposed as a condition of salvation in Christ," because Christ "displaces the law from

Jews and Disobedience:

In 2:1–16 Paul levels a general indictment against those who "pass judgment" on others while doing "the same things." The argument begins to include the Jews, to be explicitly dealt with in 2:17–29.[48] Paul asserts that both Jews and gentiles who do evil will receive God's wrath, while those who do right will receive reward. Starting with v. 12 Paul states that it is doers, not hearers, of the law who will be justified before God, whether Jew or gentile.[49] The establishment of divine

---

the role it plays within covenantal nomism" (ibid., 165–66). Donaldson speaks in terms of the "elimination of the Torah" (ibid., 169). This perhaps overstates the case. He, too, understands "works of the law" as boundary markers of differentiation. Christ and Torah are antithetical rival boundary markers (ibid., 171–72). "Paul's Christ-Torah antithesis is rooted in a perception that Christ and Torah represent mutually exclusive boundary markers, rival ways of determining the community of salvation" (ibid., 172). Paul's is not a displacement of the law in every aspect, however, but in its specifically salvific capacity. That displacement also entails fulfillment, not simply elimination. On the other hand, Paul's defense of the role of the law in Romans is not intended to support its continued relevance, but to defend God's institution of it in the first place. Paul still asserts that "the law is good" (Rom 7:16). See also, Dunn, "Paul's Conversion," 92. On Paul's perception of his pre-Christian zeal for Torah as a marker of Jewish identity see N. T. Wright, "Paul, Arabia, and Elijah (Galatians 1:17)," *JBL* 115 (1996) 689.

[48]See, again, Dunn, *Romans 1–8*, 76; Lietzmann, *An die Römer*, 38; Käsemann, *Commentary on Romans*, 168; Schlier, *Der Römerbrief*, 38; Cranfield, *The Epistle to the Romans*, 1.163; Dodd, *Epistle*, 30; Black, *Romans*, 54.

[49]This has some precedent in Jewish thought. Cranfield's citation of *'Abot* 1:17 is perhaps the most comparable to Paul's statement, "not the expounding [of the Law] is the chief thing but the doing [of it]; and he that multiplies words occasions sin" (*The Epistle to the Romans*, 1.154).

Sanders points out incongruities and unexpected statements arising in this entire section of Romans (1:18–2:29) which often become the focus of attention. "Paul takes over to an unusual degree homiletical material from Diaspora Judaism, ...consequently the treatment of the law in chapter 2 cannot be harmonized...The Gentiles are condemned universally and in sweeping terms in 1:18–32, while in 2:12–15, 26 Paul entertains the possibility that some will be saved by works....2:12–15 and 2:26 do not square well with the conclusion that all are under the power of sin (3:9, 20) ...(2:17–24) also causes some surprise, since in

impartiality in God's treatment of Jews and gentiles is critical to Paul's argument.[50]

In 2:17–29, Paul makes the corresponding case that like the gentiles, the Jews are also under God's wrath. As discussed in the previous chapters, through references to Jer 7:2–11 and 9:23–26 Paul determines that Jewish trust in their relationship to the law is misplaced because of their covenant-breaking disobedience. On the basis of OT statements Paul assumes the curses of the covenant of Deuteronomy 29–30 to have been invoked, and the covenant to have been broken. It follows that identification as a Jew under the covenant of the law is no longer assurance of salvation from God's wrath.[51] Paul at the same time undermines Jewish assurance based upon identification as a Jew and directs his readers to a spiritual obedience which can result in salvation

---

Rom. 10:2 he characterizes his kin as zealous for the law, and in Gal. 2:15 he contrasts Jews with 'Gentile sinners.'...[T]he description of Jewish behavior in 2:17–24 is unparalleled" (*Paul, the Law*, 123–24). Some of these issues are resolved with an understanding that Paul addresses different issues at different points in different ways. Others, however, remain in unresolved tension. Sanders does not take into account the scriptural background of Paul's statements. I do not believe the difficulties of Romans 2 are as great as Sanders supposes (ibid., 126–32). On the apparent contradiction between 2:13 and 3:20, see Hendrikus Boers, "'We Who are By Inheritance Jews; Not From the Gentile Sinners,'" *JBL* 111 (1992) 273–81.

For the disputed question as to whether Paul really believes in the efficacy of works, and whether or not he is only speaking hypothetically of gentiles being able to "do the things of the Law," see Snodgrass, "Justification by Grace—To the Doers," 72–93, esp. 80–82. Paul's chief concern is that "works of the law"—meant to identify Jews in particular as God's people—are not effective for justification. Yet he affirms the value of "keeping the law" as an act of obedience and faithfulness for both Jews and gentiles. See, e.g., Boers, "We Who are by Inheritance Jews," 275–76.

[50]See Bassler, *Divine Impartiality*, 121–56. Bassler makes important points concerning the unity of chaps. 1 and 2 which are only touched on briefly here.

[51]Again, the covenant relationship is not completely disavowed. Chaps. 9–11 take up the continuation of that relationship.

for gentiles as well as Jews.[52] Rom 2:17–29 and the underlying exegesis of OT references is pivotal in the larger argument.

These conclusions place Jews and gentiles together under God's wrath and in need of salvation, as Paul makes explicit in Rom 3:9.[53] However, in denying the Jews the special status once assumed he has raised a question directly connected to his assertion of God's righteousness (1:16–17). If Jews are not in a better position before God, what is the point

---

[52]"The obedience of faith" (Rom 1:5). Paul's position is also dependent upon his broader understanding of the need for transformation or conversion beyond the scope of Romans 2, as described by Segal. "Paul is suggesting that Jews as well as Gentiles need to undergo a significant transformation before they can enter the new community. This would contrast with the position attributed to James, who felt that the teaching of Jesus and his messianic mission can be accommodated within the sphere of traditional Judaism. It means for Paul, as it cannot for James, that to be a Jew who has accepted Christ is not enough. For Paul, the Jew as well as the gentile must be converted, and the new community that Jesus founded must be a community of converts" (*Paul the Convert,* 113). Paul's indictment presupposing a broken covenant places Jews in a position requiring conversion no less than gentile converts to Christianity. For Paul, as Segal affirms, conversion did not require an entire abandonment of Judaism. "Paul did not understand himself as a convert from one religion to another" (Stendahl, *Final Account,* 2). It did, however, require a significant transformation as Segal describes at length, which re-interpreted and re-contextualized his Jewish belief.

Francis Watson affirms the conclusion that Paul addresses questions of relationship between Jewish and gentile Christians, exhorting Jewish Christians meeting as a separate congregation to join with gentile Christians (*Paul, Judaism, and the Gentiles: A Sociological Approach* [SNTSMS 56; Cambridge: Cambridge University Press, 1986] 94–98; "The Two Roman Congregations: Romans 14:1–15:13," *The Romans Debate,* 203–15). However, Watson reaches the unlikely conclusion that Paul knows "this would inevitably mean a final separation from the synagogue" (*Paul, Judaism, and the Gentiles,* 178). The evidence indicates that this is precisely what Paul wishes to prevent and that he certainly does not believe it is inevitable. His efforts ultimately proved unsuccessful, and in fact he may have unintentionally helped precipitate the eventual separation (Segal, *Paul the Convert,* 205).

[53]Cambier identifies this idea as "the principle center of interest of this Pauline passage" ("Le jugement de tous les hommes," 212).

of being a Jew (3:1)? Is God's faithfulness to those claimed as God's own people suspect (3:3–4)?[54] Paul reasserts that there is advantage in being a Jew and that God is faithful, although without much explanation at this point (3:2, 4). His defense of God's righteousness will unfold throughout the rest of the epistle, but it is in chaps. 9–11 that he will return to the largely unanswered question of Israel's current place in God's plan, which was raised in Rom 2:17–29.

Faith and Abraham:

Paul continues referring to the scriptures, finding attestations in the law and the prophets (3:21) for evidence that righteousness always was a matter of faithfulness. Now a new righteousness apart from the law comes "through the faithfulness of Jesus Christ to all who believe" (3:21–22). People are, as the scriptural texts make clear to Paul, justified by faith/faithfulness (3:28).[55] This corresponds to the spiritual obedience called for by Paul's references in Rom 2:17–29. The theme of gentile inclusion is reaffirmed from Rom 2:25–29, since Jews and gentiles have the same God and are justified by the same faith (3:29–30).[56]

As noted in the section on intertextual context, Paul is dependent on the Abraham narrative of Genesis in Rom 2:17–29 and Romans 9 as well as in chap. 4, where Paul shows that Abraham was not justified by the law, but by faith. The use of Abraham in the argument "is not merely an

---

[54]Cranfield points out that "this is no frivolous objection....it would call in question the truthfulness of the OT or the faithfulness of God" (*The Epistle to the Romans*, 1.176).

[55]For πίστις in 3:21–30 as referring to the faithfulness of Jesus see, e.g., Richard Hays (*The Faith of Jesus Christ* [SBLDS 56; Chico, CA: Scholars Press, 1983] 157–92), Luke T. Johnson ("Rom 3:21–26 and the Faith of Jesus," *CBQ* 44 [1982] 80), Stanley K. Stowers ("EK ΠΙΣΤΕΩΣ and ΔΙΑ ΤΗΣ ΠΙΣΤΕΩΣ in Romans 3:30," *JBL* 108 [1989] 667), Hooker (*From Adam to Christ*, 165–86), and Douglas Campbell (*The Rhetoric of Righteousness in Romans 3:21–26* [JSNTSup 65; Sheffield: JSOT, 1992] 58–69, 214–18).

[56]Käsemann notes the "incomparable audacity of this thesis" since it opposes a central tenet of rabbinic teaching: that God is god of Israel alone (*Commentary on Romans*, 103). The proof of Abraham in chap. 4 provides Paul's support for his thesis.

adventitious example, for it is quite likely that Abraham had been used by the Pharisees as a role model for potential converts, as he was thereafter by rabbinic Judaism."[57]

Paul takes the existing example of Abraham as convert and describes the circumstances of his conversion to Paul's advantage. Abraham is found to be our father not according to the flesh, but according to faith (4:1).[58] By referring to Abraham as declared righteous in his uncircumcised state, Paul allows gentile inclusion in God's plan, supporting the statements already made on the basis of other references in Rom 2:25–29. "So then, he is the father of all who believe," both Jews and gentiles (4:11).[59] The covenant/promise comes by faith to all of Abraham's σπέρμα, which includes not just Jews but all those who have faith (4:16).[60]

The defense of God's righteousness in dealings with God's people taken up at 1:16–17 has progressed through establishing the sinfulness of Jews and gentiles alike (1:18–3:20), to establishing faith as the basis for salvation for all, including gentiles as well as those born under the covenant (3:21–4:25). Rom 2:17–29 and its references, particularly the Abraham narrative, are fully integrated into the argument.

---

[57]Segal, *Paul the Convert*, 121. He continues: "Because Abraham left his gentile home and made the great journey to the one God, rabbinic and Philonic Judaism, as well as Christianity, use him as an example of conversion" (ibid.).

[58]Again, see Hays, "'Abraham," 76–98. Also, Witherington, *Paul's Narrative Thought World*, 42–43.

[59]For gentile inclusion as one of the main points of this section see Krister Stendahl ("Paul Among Jews and Gentiles," *Paul Among Jews and Gentiles: And Other Essays* [Philadelphia: Fortress, 1976] esp. 26–30). Also, Stowers, "ΕΚ ΠΙΣΤΕΩΣ," 667. Their emphasis that the passage is almost solely about the availability of salvation for gentiles probably overlooks Paul's desire to show God's righteousness in dealing with both people-groups on the basis of faith. See Dunn, *Theology of Paul*, 44–46.

[60]Paul appears to use σπέρμα in Romans primarily to identify children of the promise as opposed to children of the flesh. See Rom 9:7–8.

CHRIST, THE LAW, AND THE CHILDREN OF GOD:
ROMANS 5–8

In chaps. 5–8 Paul explains how the new righteousness from God founded in faith works in relationship and in contrast to the law. The defense of the role of the law is part of the defense of God's righteousness in dealing with the Jews. It continues to address the question of the law as inadequate to identify God's people raised in Rom 2:17–29.[61] In these chapters Paul clarifies the true role of the law.

Adam and the Human Relationship to the Law:

Having established universal sinfulness and righteousness through faith for Jews and gentiles alike, Paul goes on to address the place of the law in dealing with sin.[62] To do so he returns to scripture references and the beginning of sin in Adam (5:12–14).[63] Sin began with Adam, resulting in death

---

[61]Sanders decribes the Jewish conception of the righteous as the people of God: "Thus we have seen, on the one hand, that *the righteous are those who are saved*: they are those who receive their reward in the world to come and who walk in the garden of Eden with God...On the other hand, the *righteous are those who obey the Torah and atone for transgression*...[T]hose who accept the covenant, which carries with it God's promise of salvation, accept also the obligation to obey the commandments given by God in connection with the covenant. One who accepts the covenant and remains within it is 'righteous,' and that title applies to him *both* as one who obeys God *and* as one who has a 'share in the world to come,' but the former does not earn the latter" (*Paul and Palestinian Judaism*, 204). Paul declares that the law has not made Jews righteous in these terms, and that a new righteousness on the basis of faith defines the people of God who will receive mercy.

[62]"Perhaps the most important point about the whole section is the significance of διὰ τοῦτο at the start of 5.12. The most natural way to read this is at face value, meaning 'for this reason,' 'so it comes about that.' Paul invites his readers to stand back and see the result of the argument so far" (Wright, *The Climax of the Covenant*, 35). See Dunn for more discussion on this point (*Romans 1–8*, 271–72). Morna Hooker goes so far as to suggest 5:12–19 is "the key to Romans, summing up the argument of the previous chapters in terms of the contrast between Adam and Christ" (*From Adam to Christ*, 27). Her assessment oversteps the evidence.

[63]Wright discusses Jesus taking the place of Israel as the second Adam, dependent upon Jewish apocalyptic tradition (*The Climax of the Covenant*, 35–40). Hooker summarizes the parallels: "five times over,

before the existence of the law, and the law "multiplied the trespass" (5:20). The sin of Adam described in Romans 5 supports the statements concerning universal sinfulness in Romans 2. The continuity of chaps. 5 and 6 in the defense of God's righteousness is found in Paul's description of the sinful human condition in need of some means of reconciliation with God which was established in chap. 2. The law has played its part in establishing human guilt (6:20) rather than serving as an identifier of the people of God, in keeping with the statements of Rom 2:17–27.

The Place of the Law:

In Rom 2:28–29 Paul's OT references form the basis for his argument against the importance of external law-keeping in preference to spiritual obedience. The ceremonial aspects of the law are not decisive for identifying one as a Jew. This relates to the arguments of chap. 7, which also address those aspects of the law that were understood as markers of those whom God declares righteous.

In the analogy of the legal contract of marriage ending with the death of one of the partners (Rom 7:1–6), the believer, having died with Christ, is no longer bound by the law, as the obedient gentile in Rom 2:25–29 is not bound by ritual circumcision in the flesh.[64] Paul then comes to a crucial point

---

first negatively and then positively, everything which happened 'in Adam' is more than counterbalanced by what happens 'in Christ'" (*From Adam to Christ*, 28).

[64]"Paul is not primarily interested in the legal ramifications of the principle...Paul states only that the Torah is no longer the medium of justification and salvation. By this Paul does not necessarily negate the importance of Torah. Paul still understands Torah as the sacred story of Israel's salvation. What he negates is the value of observing Torah for the purpose of defining who is part of the community of the saved" (Segal, *Paul the Convert*, 139). The question of exactly what Paul means by "law," and what his attitude toward it is in any particular case remains a matter of scholarly debate. Sanders observes "that the different things which Paul said about the law depend upon the question asked or the problem posed. Each answer has its own logic and springs from one of his central concerns; but the diverse answers, when set alongside one another, do not form a logical whole, as might have been expected had he set out to discuss the problem of law as such" (*Paul, the*

in the argument in Rom 7:7–13. In order to defend God's righteousness and impartiality, Paul has to show not only God's salvation under grace apart from the law but also the positive role the law has played.[65]

Continuity and the Children of God:

The question of who are recognized as the righteous people of God, raised in Rom 2:28–29, is addressed again initially in Romans 8. The condemnation brought about by the law of sin and death has been set aside by the law of the spirit of life (Rom 8:12). For those who walk in the spirit, God accomplishes through Christ what the law was unable to do—fulfillment of the law's requirement of righteousness (8:3–4). This corresponds to the spiritual obedience and circumcision of the heart by the spirit Paul finds in his references underlying Rom 2:29. Those in whom the spirit of God dwells and who are led by the spirit are the adopted children

---

Law, 4). If there is any place in which Paul addresses "the question of the law as such" it is in Romans. There the law is both defended and described as ineffective for salvation and superseded by grace (3:20–21, 6:14). Paul at least attempts to answer the most significant questions concerning the place of the law in relation to the gospel as a logical whole. Yet even this most comprehensive of Pauline discussions on the law takes its form and direction only as part of a larger argument, still dependent "upon the question asked or the problem posed."

[65]The position of Segal on Paul's conception of the purpose of the law requires modification. "Paul suggests to the Galatians that the relationship between the two experiences [Jewish faith and Christian faith] is chronological. God intended Torah to have sole validity for a time as the Jewish-gentile dichotomy was valid for a time. He intended to replace it by the appearance of Christ" (*Paul the Convert*, 125). This is probably an overstatement for Galatians and is certainly not the case in Romans. Rather, Paul's exegesis suggests to him first that faith has always been the valid way to salvation, even for the Jews under the law, and second that gentiles have been included in the promise from its inception.

Sanders sheds light on Paul's attitude toward the law but says that Paul engages in a "negative argument against the law" and that the "argument for faith is really an argument against the law" (*Paul and Palestinian Judaism*, 491). More accurately, Paul argues against the law as an identifier of the people of God/the righteous elect. Sanders later softens his view with the clarification that "the law is not an entrance requirement" (*Paul, the Law*, 17–48).

of God, in the same way that those who are spiritually obedient and circumcised in heart are true Jews in Rom 2:28–29.

It is sometimes supposed that Romans 5–8 is discontinuous with the course of the discussion in Romans 1–4 and 9–11. This is not the case as points of the argument have been traced here. It is also sometimes supposed that Pauline OT references are "almost completely absent" from these chapters, again in contrast to chaps. 1–4 and 9–11.[66] If "reference" is taken as open citation, this may be so, but OT references more broadly defined are in evidence throughout the section. Hays notes allusions to Adam and Moses in chap. 5, an "echo" of Isa 53:11 in Rom 5:19, an illustration drawn from Exod 20:17/Deut 5:21 in Rom 7:7, and numerous allusions in Rom 8:3–4, 20–21, 32 along with citation of Psalm 44 in Rom 8:36.[67] Sylvia Keesmaat points out numerous verbal links from Deuteronomy 32 in 8:14–17.[68] Although brief, D. T. Tsumura's study of Rom 8:22 confirms Paul's dependence upon Gen 3:16–17 at that point.[69]

Moreover, many links intratextual and intertextual between chaps. 5–8 and 1–2, 9–11 have already been noted. The connections of chap. 8 to what follows are noteworthy as well. At 8:14 it is those who are led by the spirit who are the children of God (υἱοὶ θεοῦ). At 9:8 it is the children of the promise who are the children of God (τέκνα τοῦ θεοῦ).[70]

At 8:15 believers received the spirit of adoption (υἱοθεσίας). At 9:4, to Israel belongs the adoption (υἱοθεσία). At 8:28, Paul speaks of those "called according to [God's] pur-

---

[66]Beker, "Echoes and Intertextuality," 66.

[67]Hays, "On the Rebound," 88–89. Walter Diezinger points to possible references to Psalm 87 (LXX) and Genesis 15 ("Unter Toten Freigeworder: Eine Untersuchung zu Rom III–VIII," *NovT* 5 [1962] 268–98). The reference to Psalm 87 seems less likely.

[68]"Exodus and the Intertextual Transformation of Tradition in Romans 8.14–30," *JSNT* 54 (1994) 29–56. She also argues for the presence of themes from Isaiah 63, Jeremiah 38, and Exodus, but the evidence is much weaker in these cases.

[69]"An OT Background to Rom 8.22," *NTS* 40 (1994) 620–21.

[70]Käsemann says that the phrases are "obviously interchangeable" (*Commentary on Romans*, 229). They are certainly so in 8:14, 16.

pose" (τοῖς κατὰ πρόθεσιν κλητοῖς οὖσιν), further describing them as "God's elect" (ἐκλεκτῶν θεοῦ), in v. 33. At 9:11–12 Rebekah is told of the fate of her children by God "who calls," (τοῦ καλοῦντος), in order that it be according to the purpose of God's election (κατ᾽ ἐκλογὴν πρόθεσις τοῦ θεοῦ).

The continuity is clear. But the conclusions in chap. 8 regarding the identity of the people of God return to some serious questions Paul left unanswered beginning in 2:17–29 and continuing through chap. 4. Who are those whom God has called and chosen? What about those who were thought to be called, but whose chosen position Paul has determined to be forfeit in Rom 2:17–29? Paul does not even allow the interlocutor to raise the question. With "great sorrow and unceasing anguish" (9:2) Paul preempts the objection by showing the depth of his own concern about that very problem.

PROMISE, ELECTION, AND THE CHILDREN OF ABRAHAM: ROMANS 9–11

Romans 9 continues the argument by addressing the question of who God's people are. If the covenant with Israel is broken and Israel's special status is abrogated, as the references in Romans 2 lead Paul to conclude, he must address God's righteousness in dealing with Israel.[71] He does not let his interlocutor conclude either that the word of God has failed (9:6) or that God is unjust (9:14). Paul has already established a defintion of a Jew which includes having an interior spirituality defined as circumcision of the heart in chap. 2. In chap. 4 faith defines Abraham's descendants. In chap. 9 Paul expands his assertion of gentile inclusion in the children of God as the reconciliation of the second line of Abraham's descendants.[72] Romans 10 and 11 return to the question of

---

[71]As has been mentioned, many of Paul's conclusions concerning Israel's failure and subsequent restoration, not only in Romans 9–11 but in a number of Pauline passages, are shown by James Scott to depend upon "a pervasive OT/Jewish tradition which we may refer to as the Deuteronomic View of Israel's History" ("Deuteronomic Tradition," 665).

[72]Barnabas Lindars remarks: "Of course the reader of Romans already knows from the earlier treatment of the faith of Abraham in chapter 4 that the children of the promise are to be identified with Gentiles

national Israel, with Paul struggling to define the nation's continuing place in God's plan in light of the gospel.

Election and Abraham's Children:

In 9:4–5 Paul reaffirms the fact of the giving of the covenants to Israel, as he did in 2:17–20.[73] He then returns to the Abraham narrative to explain that the descendants of Abraham are children of the promise whom he identified in chap. 4 as those who have faith (9:6–8).[74] The second story-strand of the narrative which concerns Ishmael—the sub-plot discussed earlier in this chapter and identified with gentiles—is also beneath the text, being the source for the citations that Paul uses in 9:7–9. This is reaffirmed by the introduction not only of Jacob but of Esau as well. Esau's "non-election" was purely an act of God's own choosing.[75]

---

as well as Jews" ("The Old Testament and Universalism in Paul," *BJRL* 69 [1987] 515). Paul makes a distinction between σπέρμα as descendants of the promise and τέκνα as children of the flesh in chap. 9. However, in chap. 8 τέκνα is used to describe the adopted children of God. There is a certain amount of ambiguity concerning exactly what Paul means by "Israel" in chaps. 9–11. He has included heart-circumcised gentiles among the Jews (2:29) and defined "children of Abraham" as those who have faith (4:16, 9:6–8). Yet he apparently is speaking of ethnic or national Israel in Romans 10–11. For discussion on this issue, see Sanders, *Paul, the Law*, 173–76.

[73]On the plural "covenants" see chap. 2 n. 27.

[74]Dunn states that "the explicit reference back to God's promise of a son to Abraham when he was yet childless would again recall the force of the last point made in the argument of chap. 4...Although he has not mentioned either law or faith Paul's line of argument is clear: scripture confirms Paul's earlier exegesis" (*Romans 1–8*, 548).

[75]"[Paul] cites the stories of God's pleasure with Isaac and Jacob and his displeasure with Ishmael and Esau as evidence that election and promise matter, but ancestry does not. Paul's usage is chiastic, opposite to the interpretation that a rabbinic Jew would have made: for the Jew, the positive fact that God chose Isaac and Jacob is important; for Paul the converse is equally important: God disinherited Esau and Ishmael in spite of their ancestry" (Segal, *Paul the Convert*, 277). Paul's affirmation that election is a matter of God's choice alone without regard to merit conforms to one of the reasons given in rabbinic literature for the election of Israel (Sanders, *Paul and Palestinian Judaism*, 87–88).

Paul's point is that God's purpose involves not exclusion of Jews but inclusion of gentiles as well as Jews (9:22–24). The inclusion of the gentiles among the people of God initially addressed in Rom 2:26–29 is reaffirmed here, but without the theme of judgment against the Jews found in chap. 2. In chap. 9 the overriding theme is inclusion. Those who were not chosen, the "not my people" (gentiles), are also to be included as the objects of God's mercy, to be called "children of the living God" (9:25–26). Paul's exegetical references in chap. 2 point toward inclusion of heart-circumcised gentiles among the people of God. The references in chap. 9 inform him that the inclusion of the gentiles in the promise to Abraham is the reconciliation of the second line consisting of the displaced first-born.

Paul then returns to the conclusion implied by chap. 2, where he had left the Jews as condemned because of disobedience. He again asks if the Jews have really not attained righteousness (9:30–31). He concludes that the Jews "did not strive for it on the basis of faith" (9:32). However, fully to address God's fidelity to his promise, Paul cannot leave the question of Israel's status just yet. In the Deuteronomy texts to which Paul referred in Romans 2, and from which Paul will quote shortly in chap. 10, there was also the promise of restoration. This is the thread Paul has already picked up in his prophetic references in 9:25–29.[76]

---

[76]For a discussion of the rhetorical structure of Rom 9:30–10:13 in particular, see Pattee, "Stumbling Stone or Cornerstone?," 59. Paul's appropriation of these prophetic passages, particularly his contra-contextual interpretation of them in reference to gentiles, is another study entirely. See, e.g., Mesner, "The Rhetoric of Citations."

To address the question only briefly, Donaldson refers to a question asked by Cerfaux concerning "the priority of conviction over exegesis. In a discussion of Paul's attempts to justify the gentile mission on scriptural grounds, Cerfaux wonders aloud 'whether the texts led Paul to formulate his theory, or if the theory impelled him to search the Bible to find them there.' The latter is clearly the case" (*Paul and the Gentiles*, 101). While true, it is not novel. It is a reflection of the exegetical tradition of which Paul is a part. Donaldson says that "Paul's conviction that salvation is for the Gentiles is not to be seen in any simple way as the product of his reading of the scriptures. To be sure, his convictions are

Failure, Promise, and The Status of Israel:

In chap. 10 Paul shows that Christ is evident in the law in Deut 30:13–14 (Rom 10:6–10), a reference underlying Rom 2:17–29 as well. By failing to have faith in Christ the Jews continue to fail to accomplish the stipulation of the covenant. It is faith in Christ, not performance of their own idea of the law (10:3), that brings righteousness, for "Christ is the fulfillment (τέλος) of the Law" (v. 4).[77] Paul is making more ex-

---

at every point so intertwined with his reading of scripture that we are not to suppose that he would have been able to differentiate the two. Nevertheless, his use of scripture is governed by and in the service of his convictions, rather than the other way around" (ibid., 103).

On the other hand, the content of Paul's convictions about a range of issues, including the gentiles, ought to be understood to derive from reading scripture differently, through the lens of his conversion. From the fact of his experience of Christ and his witness of gentile conversion, Paul returns to scripture and finds there different answers than he had seen before. In this way the content of Paul's convictions is a product of his reading of scripture, although the relationship of his experience which forms his convictions and his reading of scripture is ultimately dialogic. Donaldson proposes a sequence of stages culminating in a situation wherein Paul's convictions are reconfigured: "a reconfigured set of convictions and perceptions, one in which selected elements of the old world are retained, but organized now with reference to a new center and pattern" (ibid., 295). Certainly Paul's reading of scripture plays a part in that sequence leading to convictional reconfiguration.

[77]Barrett speaks of "fulfillment" of the law, but still does not emphasize Christ as the completion *of the law* (*Epistle to the Romans*, 184). Instead the emphasis seems to be on Christ as something different, having "brought to an end the old order." In an extensive study of τέλος in uses ranging from classical Greek to Jewish, Robert Badenas determines that "τέλος with genitive is generally used in expressions indicating result, purpose, outcome, and fate, not termination....τέλος νόμου and related expressions are indicative of the purpose, fulfillment, or object of the law, not of its abrogation" (*Christ the End of the Law: Romans 10:4 in Pauline Perspective* [JSNTSup 10; Sheffield: JSOT Press, 1985] 79). See also the suggested translation, "Christ *was* the goal of the law," by Julian V. Hills ("'Christ was the Goal of the Law...' [Romans 10:4]," *JTS* NS 44 [1993] 585–92). Hills notes that "it is hazardous to attempt a demonstration that an absent word is to be 'translated' one way rather than another" (ibid. 586). However, his suggestion certainly gets to the point of Paul's statement that Christ was intended to be the goal or fulfillment of the law all along. Contra Sanders, who says Christ "put an

plicit the reasoning behind the similar conclusion concerning true law-keeping he reached in chap. 2. The theme of the breaking of the covenant established through his references to Rom 2:17–25 continues in the Jews' rejection of Christ. Quoting Isaiah's indictment of Israel, Paul reaffirms Israel's status as disobedient (Rom 10:21).

The central question around which the defense of God's righteousness revolves is finally asked at 11:1: "Has God rejected his people?" Paul rejects that possibility, as the references from Deuteronomy, Ezekiel, and Isaiah in chaps. 2 and 9 concerning restoration have already implied. He returns to the concept of a remnant to be saved (11:6). He asserts that the failure is not permanent (11:11).[78] This affirms the position present in a reference passage underlying Rom 2:17–29 and 10:6–8 (Deut 30:1–10).

Paul attempts a final statement on the status of Israel, stating that "all Israel will be saved" (11:26).[79] Paul is un-

---

end" to the the law (*Paul and Palestinian Judaism*, 550; *Paul, the Law*, 39).

[78]Donaldson argues against understanding Paul's logic as defining a "spatial displacement" of Israel. Instead, Paul produces "the temporal logic of delay" ("'Riches for the Gentiles,'" 92–94). This accords with the view that disobedience brings wrath, but not loss of status as one of the elect. Paul's caveat "as long as they do not continue in unbelief" (11:23) may parallel the rabbinic exceptions for totally renouncing the covenant given by Sanders (*Paul and Palestinian Judaism*, 147–48).

[79]Reidar Hvalvik says that there is "general agreement" that ethnic Israel is meant ("A 'Sonderweg' for Israel: A Critical Examination of a Current Interpretation of Romans 11.25–27," *JSNT* 38 [1990] 100). Bruce Longenecker concurs ("Different Answers to Different Issues: Israel, The Gentiles, and Salvation History in Romans 9–11," *JSNT* 36 [1989] 96–97). Sanders, however, disagrees and argues that "all Israel" is parallel to "the full number of Gentiles," which includes those saved on the basis of faith (*Paul, the Law*, 196). James W. Aageson appears to defend this position as well (*Written Also for Our Sake: Paul and the Art of Biblical Interpretation* [Louisville: Westminster/John Knox, 1993] 100–101). On "all Israel will be saved" (11:26) as referring to a percentage (larger than that of gentiles) of Jews who will be saved on the basis of faith, see Ferdinand Hahn, "Zum Verständnis von Römer 11.26a: '...und so wird ganz Israel gerettet werden,'" *Paul and Paulinism*, 221–36.

willing to relinquish a place for ethnic Israel in God's redemption, yet qualifies this belief with the requirement for faith (11:23, "if they do not persist in unbelief"). This corresponds to the requirement for heart circumcision established in chap. 2. Paul's own understanding of Israel's disobedience as an act of God's mercy for all people (11:30–32) is captured in his doxological summation: "how inscrutable are his ways!" (11:33).[80]

Rom 2:17–29 in the Completed Argument:

The defense of God's righteousness in his dealings with his people begun at 1:16–17 is essentially complete at this

---

Perhaps Paul concludes that all of ethnic Israel will eventually respond in faith. This is the view of most commentators, although an eschatological salvation is often preferred. Sanders contends that this will include only part of ethnic Israel (*Paul, the Law*, 194–95). See the contrasting view of Stendahl that Israel will be saved apart from faith in Christ ("Paul Among Jews and Gentiles," 4). He is joined by Mary Ann Getty ("Paul and the Salvation of Israel: A Perspective on Romans 9–11," *CBQ* 50 [1988] 459, 464).

[80]Segal summarizes the issues of Romans 9–11, and the tensions in Paul's argument. "First, he propounds that the failure of Israel to convert is not incompatible with God's promises to Israel (Romans 9). Second, he maintains that the hardening of Jewish hearts is due to their own lack of faith and is a response to their own guilt (9:30–10:21). Third, Paul maintains that the Jewish rejection of Christ will not last forever, for God will eventually show mercy and save all Israel (Romans 11)....These statements are offered independently, and it is not clear that they can all be held simultaneously. But philosophical consistency was not the purpose of Paul's remarks; rather, they express Paul's sorrow that the rest of Israel has not followed him in seeing the truth of the Christian message, combined with his desire to protect the promises of the Hebrew Bible from the allegation of inconsistency, based on his novel interpretation of them....His basic answer is that God has not changed his mind about the promises offered to Israel; they are still valid. But the way in which they are valid must be seen in a different light after Christ" (*Paul the Convert*, 276, see also 280–81).

See also Donaldson's comments on differentiating between Paul's "argumentative logic" and his "convictional logic" ("'Riches for the Gentiles,'" 88–90). These tensions in Paul's thought may be seen as parallel to those often noted concerning his attitude toward the law (Heikki Räisänen, *Paul and the Law* [WUNT 29; Tübingen: Mohr, 1983] 11–15, 264). Räisänen, however, tends to overemphasize the perceived tensions and inconsistencies, while ignoring evidence and explanations which reduce that perception of tension in Paul's statements.

point. Paul has established the universal sinfulness of gentiles as well as Jews in chaps. 1–3. In 2:17–29 his OT references indicate that the covenant with Israel has been broken, leaving Israel's status before God no better than that of gentiles. He has introduced the idea of the law's ineffectiveness in giving definition to the people of God. Interior spirituality is the mark of God's people, which implies the possibility of gentile inclusion in the children of God. Chapter 4 proves that interior spirituality defined as faith was the essential ingredient in the covenant relationship all along, even for Abraham, upon whom Paul continues to depend from chap. 2 onward.

In chaps. 5–8 justification brought about by faith results in life in the spirit, corresponding to circumcision of the heart by the spirit in Rom 2:29. The law was unable to provide life because of sin. Having called into question Jewish identity as the people of God in Rom 2:17–29, in chaps. 9–11 Paul shows that the Jews have not been abandoned in favor of the gentiles, whom Paul now also proclaims as God's children. God's righteousness will be proven by his salvation of "all Israel." Paul has no reason to be ashamed of the gospel: "for it is the power of God for everyone who has faith, to the Jew first and also to the Greek" (1:16).[81]

---

[81]Donaldson's comments on the status of Israel are worthy of repetition. "In the light of this conclusion [concerning a positive role for Israel in Rom 15:8–9 and elsewhere] to the argument of the epistle, the statement with which Paul begins—"to the Jew first and also to the Greek" (1:16)—may suggest a priority for Israel going beyond merely the right of first refusal....The collection project is a means for the Gentile Christians to acknowledge the debt incurred when the Jewish Christians shared with them their spiritual blessings in Christ (Rom 15:26–27). Gentile Christians have been grafted in 'among'...the Jewish Christian branches to share in the life of the vine of Israel (11:17)" (*Paul and the Gentiles*, 32). Paul does not offer an entirely new vocabulary concerning the people of God, but continues to use the language and images of Israel's relationship with God in his descriptions. The continued use of this vocabulary suggests that Paul does not conceive of the kingdom of God without Israel as an integral element, at least in some sense and however redefined.

PRACTICAL CONSIDERATIONS: ROMANS 12–15

As is usually the case with parenesis, Rom 12:1–15:13 gives general hortatory instruction. To assume, however, that this section of Romans is only general ethical instruction, without relation to the rest of the epistle or to the Roman situation, is a mistake.[82] Much that is included in the general parenesis of other Pauline epistles is missing here.[83] On the other hand, much that is included in the parenesis of Romans deals with unity, functioning together as a body, and tolerance for differences—exactly the kind of material one would expect in an epistle dealing with questions about the relationship of Jews and gentiles in the church.

Beginning in 2:17–29 and continuing in chap. 9, Paul has redefined those who are called as children of God. He has outlined the place of Jews and gentiles in God's plan and the results of justification for all. Paul addresses the possibility that some in the church—whether it be Jews because of their relationship with God as his chosen people or gentiles as those who might believe they have taken over that role—might consider themselves to have an elevated position of importance (12:3). The admonition to sober self-judgment is in keeping with Paul's indictment of the misplaced trust of the Jews in a supposed position of privilege before God in Rom 2:17–25. In chaps. 12–15 Paul turns to the practical considerations of conduct which result from the fact of equality before God and enjoins mutual acceptance.

---

[82]Although his explanation for the purpose of the epistle is different than my own, Jeremy Moiser concludes rightly that Paul addresses "the problems of the law, Judaism and the Christian gospel," and that Paul seeks to "reconcile the differences between Jewish and gentile Christians at Rome" ("Rethinking Romans 12–15," *JSNT* 36 [1990] 571–73). He calls the epistle, "an answer to an urgent and delicate situation" (ibid.). This includes chaps. 12–16. Fitzmyer recognizes that at least some of the material is situational and related to the earlier "doctrinal" section (*Romans*, 637–38). Dunn regards chaps. 12–13 as general parenesis (*Romans 9–16*, 705–6), but considers it linked as a "necessary corollary" to the earlier portions of the letter, as does Käsemann (*Commentary on Romans*, 323).

[83]See Moiser for examples, including themes of marriage and sex, slavery, and working hard ("Rethinking Romans," 572).

Paul continues a call to love one another in the Christian community at 13:8–10 with a reminder that "love is the fulfilling of the law," a point intimately connected to his preceding argument about the relationship of the law and the gospel. It is parallel to and the practical application of the conclusion that law-keeping is an interior matter of the heart as established in Rom 2:28–29.

These issues of behavior address an "actual problem in Rome."[84] The discussion concerning the weak and the strong and the warning against causing others to stumble have often been understood at least in part to address practices of Jews and gentiles in the Roman church.[85] The issue is obviously more complicated than that.[86] The practices mentioned are not all easily identified with any particular group, and Jews or gentiles might be the weak or the strong, depending upon the specific practice concerned. In either case, however, Paul's assertions concerning the value of external law-keeping in Rom 2:17–29 have a direct impact upon matters of behavior and conscience. The claim that the person who is spiritually circumcised receives praise from God rather than others (2:29) and the statement that "each of us will be accountable to God" (14:12) are parallel.

The admonition for tolerance comes to completion in chap. 15. After establishing the fact of equality before God and the possibility of gentile inclusion among the people of God in Rom 2:17–29, Paul punctuates his admonition with a prayer asking that God grant his readers "to live in harmony with one another" (15:5).[87] The purpose of the whole is that

---

[84]Ulrich Wilckens, *Der Brief an die Römer: Röm 12–16* (EKKNT 6, vol. 3; Neukirchen-Vluyn: Neukirchener Verlag, 1982) 79. Also, Dunn, *Romans 9–16*, 795.

[85]Barrett, *Epistle to the Romans*, 235–36; Cranfield, *The Epistle to the Romans*, 2.695; Fitzmyer, *Romans*, 687–88; Dunn, *Romans 9–16*, 795; Marcus, "The Circumcision and the Uncircumcision," 68.

[86]See, e.g., Robert J. Karris ("Romans 14:1–15:13 and the Occasion of Romans," *The Romans Debate*, 65–84).

[87]By the use of such a "prayer-wish" Paul is bringing the argument to a close (Käsemann, *Commentary on Romans*, 383). But the con-

they together glorify God (15:6), which is Paul's ultimate concern.

Paul's Summary and Conclusion:

Paul then offers a summary statement of his instruction toward unity which further confirms the fact that Jewish and gentile relationships within the church are a central concern throughout the epistle. In 2:26–29 heart-circumcised Jews and gentiles are both counted as God's people. That fact is reaffirmed in a christological context in Paul's summary. The readers are enjoined to "welcome one another" because "Christ has become a servant of the circumcision on behalf of the truth of God...and [a servant] with respect to the gentiles on behalf of mercy in order to glorify God" (15:7–9).[88] The scriptural proofs of Rom 15:9–12 affirm the inclusion of both Jews and gentiles as God's accepted people in the same way that Paul's references in Rom 2:26–29 identified heart-circumcised Jews and gentiles as God's people.

The explanation of the place of both Jews and gentiles in the church and their respective roles in God's plan—which forms the central argument of the letter—exists for the purpose of enabling unity between the two groups in the Roman Christian community. A wish of peace concludes the section and the central argument of the epistle (15:13).

This summary of both the intertextual and epistolary contexts of Romans has, of course, left many issues concerning the interpretation of Romans untouched. In some cases the issues have no bearing on the outcome of the larger scenario presented here, and in others the assumptions of this presentation rule out certain possibilities. However, this

---

clusion is lengthy, including a doxology (vv. 7–14) and a postscript justifying his approach (vv. 14–21).

[88]The translation is based on that of J. Ross Wagner in a recent article ("The Christ, Servant of Jew and Gentile: A Fresh Approach to Romans 15:8–9," *JBL* 116 [1997] 481–82). The summary is parallel to the thesis statement of 1:16. The gospel is "the power of God for salvation...to the Jew first" (a servant of the circumcision), "and also to the Greek" ([a servant] with respect to the gentiles). Wagner's insightful clarification confirms this passage as a key statement for the entire epistle.

summary has provided a framework of interpretation for the epistle which is consistent with the conclusions reached earlier concerning Rom 2:17–29. The intertextual references from Deuteronomy 29–30, the Abraham narrative of Genesis, Jeremiah 7 and 9, and Ezekiel 36 are well integrated into the larger intertextual web of Romans by verbal and thematic coherence. Themes of the place of the Jews and the law in the plan of God, the status of the Jews, and the integration of the gentiles among the people of God—all issues raised in 2:17–29—are seen to be integral to the overall argument and context of Romans. The interpretation of Rom 2:17–29 to which this research points is consistent with and illuminates a coherent and logical discussion dealing with the relationship between Jews and gentiles in the church at Rome.

5

Implications and Conclusions

This study indicates that Paul engages in intertextual exegesis in Rom 2:17–29. He does so as part of a comprehensive dependence upon the OT which forms a basis for the conclusions he reaches throughout Romans. There are a number of implications of this research, both for Pauline studies as a whole and for the study of the epistle to the Romans in particular.

IMPLICATIONS FOR PAULINE STUDIES

A greater appreciation for the depth of Pauline scriptural reference and allusion has been gained in recent decades, most notably in the work of Richard Hays.[1] The discovery of meaningful scriptural allusion in Pauline material not restricted to the forms of quotation or paraphrase has revealed a rich field for research. Recognizing links between scriptural references as an interpretive tool used by Paul has clarified the foundations of Pauline theology.[2]

PAULINE EXEGESIS OF UNCITED TEXTS

Hays has concluded, however, that Paul has no "systematic exegetical procedures" and that Paul's readings are

---

[1] See, e.g., Hays, *Echoes*; Dodd, *According to the Scriptures*; Ellis, *Paul's Use of the Old Testament*; Stockhausen, *Moses' Veil*; Evans and Sanders, *Paul and the Scriptures of Israel*; Witherington, *Paul's Narrative Thought World*.

[2] Hays, *Echoes*, 20–24.

"unpredictable."[3] Interpreters then were left with little way to tell whether the more subtle echoes of scripture are intentional on Paul's part, or may simply grow out of the interpreter's imagination.[4] These conclusions are contrary to other studies which show Paul relying on existing exegetical procedures where there is quotation or significant specialized vocabulary.[5] Beyond those studies, this research provides the means to identify Pauline intertextual exegesis in a passage where the OT references have not been immediately evident.

Hays heard the echo of OT references in Romans 2 and gave a cursory analysis of the passage.[6] This study more fully explains the scriptural basis for Paul's "bitterly controversial" opinions in Rom 2:17–29 concerning the culpability and identity of the Jews and the admissibility of gentiles among the circumcised who will receive praise from God.[7] The results of this research indicate the need for a reexamination of Pauline passages previously assumed not to contain exegetically significant references.

MUTUALLY INTERPRETIVE REFERENCES
IN AN INTERTEXTUAL WEB

The mutually interpretive character of a web of OT texts in Pauline material is another area in which further study is likely to be beneficial. This is part of an important change that Alan Segal points out has likely occurred in Paul's exegetical method as he was transformed from a Jewish Pharisee to a Jewish Christian convert, no longer relying on strictly legal interpretations of texts. "In post-Pauline rabbinic terms, Paul reveres Torah as *aggadah*, story, and prophecy, but he ceases to practice it as *halakah*."[8] Evidence of an intertextual web beneath an entire document can reveal the extent of the

---

[3]Ibid., 160.

[4]Ibid., 23.

[5]E.g., William R. Stegner, "Romans 9.6–29—A Midrash," 37–52; Stockhausen, *Moses' Veil*.

[6]Hays, *Echoes*, 44–46.

[7]Ibid., 44.

[8]Segal, *Paul the Convert*, 139.

writer's scriptural frame of reference and theological foundations. Continued study of ancient Jewish exegesis and ways it may have been modified by Paul will bring greater understanding of Pauline methodology and theology.

While there are important Greek influences on Paul's thought and writing, this study implies a greater reliance upon scripture in Pauline material than is sometimes supposed.[9] Jewish scriptures and exegetical customs are an integral and primary part of Paul's thought world.[10] Previous studies indicate that this is the case with some non-Pauline material as well, for which this method may be useful.[11]

THE RHETORICAL IMPACT OF PAUL'S EXEGESIS

This study also raises questions about the rhetorical impact of Paul's exegesis. How does Paul's intertextual exegesis relate to his rhetorical argumentation? That is, do these texts function only exegetically as background material, or do they serve a convincing rhetorical function as part of the ar-

---

[9]Greek rhetorical influence, especially, is often noted in the work of, e.g., H. D. Betz (*Galatians* [Hermeneia; Philadelphia: Fortress, 1979] 14–25) and Robert Jewett ("Following the Argument of Romans," *The Romans Debate*, 265–77; "Romans as an Ambassadorial Letter," *Int* 36 [1982] 5–20). However, Stowers is correct to remember Bultmann's finding, that "Jewish and Greek elements in Paul's letters could not always be easily separated" (*Diatribe*, 19).

[10]Pattee comes to the same conclusion, summarizing that "Paul's theology is at least partly the product of his interpretation of a network of OT texts which extends beyond those he explicitly cites...The networking of texts through verbal and thematic parallels...is consistent with the practices employed by other interpreters of scripture in Paul's day" ("Stumbling Stone or Cornerstone?," 27–28). Witherington goes even further, claiming that "all Paul's ideas, all his arguments, all his practical advice, all his social arrangements" are grounded in a narrative thought world largely deriving from scripture (*Paul's Narrative Thought World*, 2). This oversteps the evidence by ignoring Greco-Roman influence.

[11]See, e.g., Stendahl, *The School of St. Matthew*; Donald Senior, *The Passion Narrative According to Matthew: A Redactional Study* (BETL 39; Leuven/Louvain: Leuven University, 1975); Frédéric Manns, "Un Midrash Chrétien: Le Récit de la Mort de Judas," *RevScRel* 54 (1980) 197–203; Berkley, "OT Exegesis and the Death of Judas," 29–45.

gument of Romans?[12] For any writer it is probably impossible for the two to be entirely divorced from one another. It is helpful here to present some preliminary observations about whether or not Paul intends his exegesis of OT texts to be rhetorically convincing to his audience.

In the cases of OT quotation as proof-text,[13] the use of scripture as example or typology,[14] doxology and summation,[15] or even simply as the appropriation of an apt phrase,[16] the overt rhetorical function of OT quotation and allusion is self-evident.[17] However, in the cases of less obvious intertextual references any rhetorical function is not as evident.

Whether or not Paul's exegesis itself, rather than the argument derived from his exegesis, has a rhetorical effect is in part dependent upon the exegetical sophistication of his readers. Their familiarity with exegetical methods applied to scripture, or their lack thereof, will determine whether or not the unstated exegesis has a rhetorical impact upon them. Likewise, for Paul to intend rhetorical effectiveness from his exegesis would require his own knowledge of the exegetical sophistication of his readers. He would then be expected to give some indication that the exegesis itself has rhetorical import. Whether he intends his exegesis to be rhetorically effective or not, Alan Segal makes the important point that "after becoming a Christian he does not abandon his previously

---

[12]Martin states: "Intentional exegesis is being done by Paul as part of his argument" ("The Righteousness of God," 35). The question of how that exegesis functions "as part of his argument" is more complex and is not the same in every case of Pauline exegesis. The question of the rhetorical impact of OT references is also raised by Fields ("Paul as Model," 315).

[13]E.g., Rom 3:10–18; 2 Cor 9:9.

[14]E.g., 1 Cor 10:1–11; Gal 4:21–31.

[15]E.g., Rom 15:9–12.

[16]E.g., 1 Cor 15:32.

[17]The pervasive reference to the OT in the NT and post-apostolic writings is ample evidence of the authority and familiarity scripture quickly gained even among predominantly gentile congregations. Marcion and his followers are the notable exception. Kugel and Greer discuss both biblical and extra-biblical material (*Early Biblical Interpretation*, 137–50).

learned methodology, even when his predominantly gentile audience would not understand his references."[18]

The fact that Paul leaves his exegesis unstated in Rom 2:17–29 shows that his rhetorical effectiveness is not dependent upon an understanding of the exegesis behind his argument. If Paul had intended the underlying exegesis of the OT texts to which he refers to serve a convincing rhetorical function, he would have included the steps of that exegesis in the surface of his presentation. He did not. He does not so much argue for his interpretation of scripture as he does simply present the results of that new interpretation.[19] In Rom 2:17–29 it is the results of his exegesis rather than the exegesis itself which is rhetorically effective.

However, the familiar themes and language which echo in Paul's text may be evident when the exegesis is not, even for a predominantly gentile audience. This may be the case with Rom 2:18–22, where bits of language from reference texts defining the Jews and indicting Israel give a ring of scriptural authenticity to Paul's statements.[20] While this may add to the rhetorical effectiveness of Paul's argument, his case is not dependent upon his readers' apprehension of the scriptural basis of those themes and language. To answer the original question, Paul's reference texts function primarily as exegetical background. Paul's exegesis may have a convincing rhetorical effect on any exegetically sophisticated readers in Paul's audience, but that is not intended or required.

IMPLICATIONS FOR THE STUDY OF ROMANS

The study has some implications concerning the audience and situation to which Paul writes. His purpose in writ-

---

[18]Segal, *Paul the Convert*, 118. Segal makes this comment in a discussion of Gal 3:6–14, but it is applicable to all of his exegesis to any audience.

[19]A point made by Segal, *Paul the Convert*, 120. There are exceptions, where the exegesis itself works into Paul's argument, e.g., the Abraham narrative in Romans 4 and Gal 4:21–31. Even in these cases there is exegesis left unstated.

[20]The question of persuasive impact is also raised by Beker ("Echoes and Intertextuality," 65).

ing and some elements of his theology are also clarified when this understanding of Rom 2:17–29 is read in the context of the entire epistle.

PAUL'S AUDIENCE IN ROME

Conclusions about Paul's address to both gentile and Jewish Christians in Rome have already been discussed. Arguments for a totally or almost totally gentile congregation and readership are insufficient to account for the material of Romans 2. They must rely on an entirely different understanding of the point and purpose of the epistle.[21] This analysis recognizes the internal cohesiveness of the epistle and the centrality of chaps. 2–4 and 9–11 to the conclusive call for unity between Jewish and gentile Christians in chap. 15.

This study shows that Paul's intertextually sophisticated argument in Rom 2:17–29 is necessary to address the issue of Jewish guilt to a partially Jewish audience. Such an argument would not be necessary against a diatribal "straw man" for an entirely gentile audience. This conclusion confirms the opinion that the epistle addresses the relationship of Jewish and gentile Christians at Rome.[22] The emphasis is on relationship, rather than the opposition of Christ and faith to the Jews and the law.[23]

---

[21]E.g., Stowers (*Rereading*, 21–33) and Lampe ("The Roman Christians of Romans 16," 225 n. 38).

[22]E.g., Cranfield, *The Epistle to the Romans*, 1.18; Fitzmyer, *Romans*, 32–34; Dunn, *Romans 1–8*, xliv–liv; Käsemann, *Commentary on Romans*, 384; Kümmel, *Introduction*, 309–10. A rhetorical analysis of the letter opening confirms this judgment (Marty L. Reid, "A Consideration of the Function of Rom 1:8–15 in the Light of Greco-Roman Rhetoric," *JETS* 38 [1995] 181–91).

[23]The suggestion of Jacob Jervell—that the positive view of Jews and the law in Romans is due to the fact that Paul intends this to be his defense when he arrives in Jerusalem with the collection—assumes an uncharacteristic inapplicability of the epistle to the situation at Rome ("The Letter to Jerusalem," *The Romans Debate*, 53–64). Sanders likewise defends the view that Paul is concerned with questions outside of Rome having to do with his "impending trip to Jerusalem and then to the West and Paul's worry about the Jewish-Gentile problem, informed by his recent difficulties" (*Paul and Palestinian Judaism*, 488). He does

PAUL'S PURPOSE IN WRITING

This study indicates that Paul writes Romans to promote unity among Jews and gentiles in a church where there may have been some question concerning proper relationship, if not a certain amount of conflict. Alan Segal describes a broader dissonance regarding the nature of conversion which has an impact upon the development of Christianity and Paul's epistles: "Paul began as a highly committed Pharisee and became a highly committed member of an apocalyptic form of Judaism, whereas his converts began as pagans and entered a new, ambiguous group whose relationship to Judaism shortly became a vexing issue."[24]

The general ambiguity Segal outlines is heightened by a specific situation in the churches at Rome. But Paul's concern

---

not address the question of why Paul should have written *this* letter to *this* audience.

[24]Segal, *Paul the Convert*, 74–75. Donaldson makes an interesting proposal that Paul's concern for gentile salvation did not begin with his conversion. He argues from Paul's self-description in Gal 5:11 as someone "preaching circumcision" that Paul had already been "interested in attracting proselytes to Judaism" before he became a Christian. He further argues that Paul's persecution of the church stemmed from "his perception that Christ was being presented as a rival boundary marker [to the Torah] for the people of Israel." After his conversion, Paul understands Christ as the legitimate boundary marker, and the Torah as the rival. Thus, "the *form* of Paul's convictions about the Gentiles remained the same through his conversion experience....But the *substance* of his conviction was reconfigured" (*Paul and the Gentiles*, 78, 249–60, 273–92). In Romans Paul continues to debate the validity of boundary markers for the people of Israel.

As Donaldson contends, his hypothesis is not only plausible but does much to account for unanswered questions about the origin of Paul's convictions. However, he acknowledges that he is at "risk of running in a circle" in attempting to reconstruct Paul's pre-Christian convictions (ibid., 289). This strong hypothesis is just that: a hypothesis with a certain amount of ambiguity attached to the evidence. Therefore Donaldson's proposal, while convincing and plausible on the whole, will probably be a matter of debate before any concensus can be established. I find it attractive, and believe it may accurately describe Paul's case. However, the proposal would benefit greatly from a higher level of hard evidence in its support.

for unity between Jews and gentiles in Rome, where the problem is more acute, speaks to a tension developing throughout the church.[25]

The uncertainty about God's relationship to the Jews in the light of the gospel raises a question about God's righteousness in dealing with the chosen people. Paul's argument leads to his admonition of 15:7, which enjoins his readers to mutual acceptance. The practical admonitions of Romans 12–14 further stress the importance of unity. The defense of God's righteousness in his dealings with his people functions to instruct the Roman church concerning the legitimate place in God's salvation of all of those who claim Christian faith.[26]

A ROMAN OCCASION

Such a purpose for the epistle also implies possibilities about the occasion for its writing. As the history of attempts at solving the problem shows, any suggestion as to an occasion for the epistle is necessarily hypothetical. Even so, the epistle itself gives some indication of a possible occasion.

It is most likely, given the occasional nature of all of Paul's other epistles, that Paul is addressing at least some issues that exist in the church at Rome regarding the relationship of Jewish and gentile Christians.[27] The removal of Jews from Rome under the ban of Claudius (49 CE) and their sub-

---

[25]Paul's attempts in Romans, Galatians, and elsewhere to promote unity had an unanticipated and ironic result. "Paul's solution to the inner Christian fight, that Jewish rules—ceremonial Torah—would not be significant for any Christian's justification, inevitably and logically meant Christianity's exclusion from Judaism. It confirmed Christianity's status as a Jewish heresy....Several generations were to pass before new borders could be clarified. These new borders, representing new definitions of the terms Christians and Jew, were not apparent until after the death of Paul" (Segal, *Paul the Convert*, 205).

[26]See, e.g., Dunn, "Formal and Theological Coherence," 250; Stendahl, "Paul Among Jews and Gentiles," 2–3; Philip R. Williams, "Paul's Purpose in Writing Romans," *BSac* 128 (1971) 62–67.

[27]Placing the burden of proof on those who think the letter does not deal with a Roman situation is entirely correct, as Karl Donfried has pointed out ("False Presuppositions in the Study of Romans," *The Romans Debate*, 103–4).

sequent return (c. 54 CE) certainly affected the make-up of the Jewish population in Rome and in the Roman church at the time the epistle was written.[28]

Inside the church this would mean the reintroduction of Jewish Christians into entirely gentile churches that had been functioning without direct Jewish influence for some years.[29] Further complicating the reintegration of Jews into

---

[28]Michel, *Der Brief an die Römer*, 7–8; Dunn, *Romans 1–8*, xlix–li. This would be true even if the ban was not totally successful. Thielman (*Paul & The Law*, 162–65) and Stuhlmacher (*Letter to the Romans*, 7–8) present different approaches to such a proposal. However, Stuhlmacher adopts Weizsäcker's thesis that Paul is opposing Judaizers who are trying to introduce a "gospel of the law" in Rome (*Letter to the Romans*, 5). Wolfgang Wiefel takes the ban seriously, but fails adequately to explain the character of the material in the epistle ("The Jewish Community in Ancient Rome and the Origins of Roman Christianity," *The Romans Debate*, 85–101). The letter is not simply an apology for Jewish Christians in the light of their social situation. Pattee argues from the fact of the ban and the presence of Pauline acquaintances in Rome that "Paul had been informed of and needed to address problems caused by a rapidly disintegrating situation in Rome between Christians and Jews" ("Stumbling Stone or Cornerstone?," 332–34). More likely the reintroduction of Jews into the church and the city has raised a number of questions. While Pattee's argument for Paul's conversation with Roman Christians is substantially sound, "a rapidly disintegrating situation" is probably an overstatement.

[29]Segal points to the question of the ceremonial law as being behind much of Paul's discussion in Romans. "The legitimate question posed to the gentile Christian is, How much of the ceremonial law should I perform? Now that they are halfway to Judaism by becoming God-fearers, should they not go all the way? Paul answers: 'No.' Paul says nothing about the value of law-abiding or moral behavior. If asked, he would certainly be in favor of Torah as a standard for moral behavior. He is advocating a new definition of community in which the performance of the special laws of Judaism does not figure. This new definition is an attempt to enfranchise the community in which he lives, the community in which he learned the value and meaning of his religious conversion" (*Paul the Convert*, 124–25). While this issue is certainly of importance to Paul's overall theology and has some application to Romans, Segal's analysis is more appropriate to Galatians in its specificity. The tensions proposed in this study more adequately account for the nature of Paul's argument in Romans. There, although he addresses the differences between the Jews and Christians as people of God in regard to the law, he also is concerned to show the connective relationships and

the Roman churches might be differences between Pauline and non-Pauline Jewish Christians arriving in Rome.[30] Added to this would be the renewed presence in Rome of non-christian Jews demonstrating hostility to the church. Paul's planned visit and the situation in the Roman church are most likely interrelated occasions for the writing of the epistle.

This could have some impact on the epistolary categorization of the letter. If Paul is not giving hypothetical or general instruction, but is addressing real concerns in the church, viewing it as an ambassadorial or friendly letter is problematic.[31] The style of the letter is ambiguous. Paul seems aware that the Romans might think it should be a friendly letter in which he is not expected to fill a role of authority. Yet he himself struggles not to push too far in asserting some apostolic authority in the instruction he obviously intends to give.[32]

---

the place of the law.

[30]Chap. 16, accepted here, argues for the presence of Jewish Christians from Pauline communities. The discussion of the weak and the strong in chap. 14 argues for the presence of Jewish Christians not yet tolerant of Pauline "freedom."

[31]For definitions, see Stanley K. Stowers (*Letter Writing in Greco-Roman Antiquity* [Library of Early Christianity 5; Philadelphia: Westminster, 1986] 58–60, 91–108) and Jewett ("Ambassadorial Letter," 5–20). The occasional nature of the letter as proposed here also argues against the protreptic category as it is suggested by Stowers (*Letter Writing*, 112–14) and David E. Aune ("Romans as a *Logos Protreptikos*," *The Romans Debate*, 278–96). Aune in particular misses the cohesiveness of the letter when he argues that "The main section of the letter (1:16–11:36) consists of a chain of interconnected theological arguments and positions for which little if any connection can be found with the specific situation of the Christian communities in Rome" (ibid., 289). He argues that chaps. 9–11 constitute a digression (ibid., 118). These assumptions are challenged by Guerra, who defends a protreptic categorization of the letter but makes a strong argument for its logical cohesiveness as well (*Apologetic Tradition*, 9–12, 22–42, 170–78). Guerra argues that Romans is protreptic, which "functions as an invitation to a way-of-life, espousing a comprehensive world view setting forth its advantages and replying to objections. The aim of protreptic writers is to bring their readers to a new or renewed commitment to pursue a particular life path" (ibid., 170). Unlike Aune, however, he argues that it is also occasional (ibid., 41–42).

[32]The conclusion of L. Ann Jervis that "the function of Romans is

Paul's past relationship with some of those mentioned in Romans 16 makes it likely that they would be receptive to a letter of instruction, admonition, or advice. This would not necessarily be true of the entire Roman church, however. Paul is in a delicate social position.

Paul may be required to function in a dual role. This would be the case if on the one hand he had been asked by Jews who were part of his former congregations to speak to the situation in Rome, and on the other if this invitation did not issue from the entire church. Paul's claim to be an apostle to the gentiles may result in the receptivity of the gentile readers. An authoritative basis is required for this type of instruction to be accepted by people who do not know him personally. The dialogical style of the letter helps cast Paul in the role of a teacher.[33] His assumption of such a role, however, remains socially delicate.

PAUL, THE LAW, AND THE COVENANT WITH ISRAEL

This study has implications for Pauline theology. It clarifies Paul's understanding of the status of the Jews in relationship to God. His intertextual references indicate for Paul that the covenant with Israel has been and remains broken, placing Jews under God's wrath. Jewish reliance upon the law and upon identity as a Jew are attacked in Romans 2

---

to encourage the Roman believers to enter Paul's apostolic orbit" requires modification. It does not take into account the necessity of a sociologically appropriate basis from which Paul can offer instruction to the Roman Christians (*The Purpose of Romans: A Comparative Letter Structure Investigation* [JSNTSup 55; Sheffield: JSOT Press, 1991] 164). Jervis's letter structure investigation, while useful at many points, fails to include questions of epistolary content. This shortcoming is evident in her statement that "a comparative study of the opening and closing sections of Romans yields no evidence that Paul was concerned either with the doctrine or practice of his addressees" (ibid., 163). The content of the epistle contains ample evidence of Paul's concern in these two areas.

[33]Stowers discusses these issues and the dialogical style of the diatribe as an indication of the role Paul wishes to fill (*Diatribe*, 179, 181–82). In that study Stowers still correctly affirmed a Jewish Christian presence in Rome influencing the argument of the epistle (ibid., 183).

because they are based upon a false presupposition grounded in a covenantal relationship which no longer stands. Paul's indictment of the Jews and his view of them as God's people is coherent when its foundation in scripture is understood.

The apparent discontinuity between the law of Israel and the gospel of faith is bound up in Paul's larger purpose to show the continuity of Israel and the law in relation to Christ, faith and the church. While Paul does reject "the ethnocentricity of the law," that is certainly not the emphasis of the epistle.[34] In fact, in Paul's argument any discontinuity is between God's plan as it was intended all along and its misappropriation by the Jews who misunderstood the true nature of the covenant. The emphasis is on the continuity of the law of Israel and the faith of Jesus Christ. Relationship, rather than contrast, is the point Paul is making concerning the law and the gospel.[35]

THEOCENTRIC THEOLOGY

The demonstration of continuity and relationship in the plan of God as a defense of God's righteousness is grounded in intertextual references found in Rom 2:17–29 and elsewhere. This confirms a conclusion that Paul's theology, at least in Romans, is more theocentric than christocentric. There is no doubt that the "Christ-event is the turning point" which makes clear the requirement of faith for salvation.[36] It is the preeminent fact of immediate importance to Paul.

---

[34]Beker, "Echoes and Intertextuality," 68. Beker seems unwilling to acknowledge the subsidiary nature of the "discontinuous aspect." However, even the discussion of the law from 7:7–25 to which Beker points for illustration is not meant to contrast the law with the gospel. Rather it functions to illustrate the role of the law in God's plan progressing toward the gospel.

[35]Stendahl reaches the following conclusion: "Paul's doctrine of justification by faith has its theological context in his reflection on the relation between Jews and Gentiles, and not within the problem of how [people] are to be saved" ("Paul Among Jews and Gentiles," 26). Pattee, in answer to the opinion of Räisänen and Sanders, reaches a similar conclusion about Paul's emphasis upon the continuity of the law and the gospel in Paul's argument ("Stumbling Stone or Cornerstone?," 17–19).

[36]Beker, *Paul the Apostle: The Triumph of God in Life and*

However, the work of Christ—for Paul in Romans and elsewhere—is understood in the context of the larger plan and glory of God.[37] The discussion of justification variously as new life in Christ, freedom from slavery, and dying to sin and the law in Romans 5–8 exists only in service to the larger argument. While it may be of primary importance to Paul in his gospel message it is secondary in the argument of Romans.[38] Given the christocentric focus of Paul's mission and the theocentric focus of his overall theology it is enough to recognize that the two are intertwined.[39]

CONCLUSION

There are a number of conclusions to draw on the basis of the analysis of intertextual references in Rom 2:17–29 which forms the center of this research. This study has fur-

---

Thought (Philadelphia: Fortress, 1980) 362.

[37]Beker describes the theocentric focus beyond Romans as well: "Paul's gospel is rooted in a theocentric...worldview. Paul joins apocalyptic to this theocentric perspective. Consequently, the promises of the Old Testament have not been 'fulfilled' in the gospel of Christ and should therefore not be spiritualized. Rather, they are taken up in the gospel so as to evoke a new expectation and hope for their ultimate 'fulfillment' in the kingdom of God" (*The Triumph of God: The Essence of Paul's Thought* [Philadelphia: Fortress, 1990] 24). This is entirely in accord with the thrust and point of Romans. See also Beker, *Paul the Apostle*, 362–67; and Dunn, *Theology of Paul*, 28–29, 49–50.

[38]William S. Campbell in terms of the continuity of the epistle joins Noack in a slight overstatement about what is "current" and what is "backwater" in Romans (B. Noack, "Current and Backwater in the Epistle to the Romans," *ST* 19 [1965] 164). Campbell refers to chaps. 5–8 as "the problem" rather than the center of the epistle ("Romans III as a Key to the Structure and Thought of the Letter," *The Romans Debate*, 255). I do not understand these chapters as problematic but as secondary to the core of the argument. However, Campbell's understanding of the relative importance of these sections of Romans is substantially correct.

[39]Sanders states that "It is probably a mistake, however, to play off against each other 'theocentric' and 'christocentric' interpretations of Paul. It is doubtful that Paul could have made a clear distinction" (*Paul, the Law*, 41). Perhaps this is true, but in the past Paul's theocentric focus has too often been overshadowed by excessively christocentric interpretation.

ther developed and defined a methodology by which some of the gradations of Pauline intertextual citation and allusion may be differentiated. It constructs a category defined as intertextual reference which is more substantial than the broad category of intertextual echo. This category of reference involves those allusions which may previously have been overlooked wherein Paul is engaged in intertextual exegesis of mutually interpretive OT texts.

Application of this method to Rom 2:17–29 confirms Pauline intertextual exegesis of OT references as the basis for his conclusions in that passage. References from prophetic texts in Jer 7:2–11, 9:23–26, and Ezek 36:16–27 interpret the narrative texts of Deuteronomy 29–30 and Genesis 17. These texts provide Paul with a number of theological themes which form the basis for his argument in Rom 2:17–29 and which recur throughout Romans and its web of intertextual references.

The radical indictment Paul brings against the Jews is based in his intertextual exegesis. Jer 7:2–11 and 9:23–26 allow Paul to conclude that the Jews are guilty of covenant-breaking disobedience, bringing disrepute upon the name of God. This does not mean the covenant is entirely disavowed, but Paul concludes that circumcision alone is of no value in assuring Jews a privileged position before God.

Intertextual references also allow Paul to redefine Jewish identity. For Paul, Deut 30:6, Ezekiel 36:6, and Jer 9:26 reinterpret circumcision in Genesis 17 as heart circumcision. From Deut 29:29 and Ezek 36:16–27 Paul proposes a redefinition of a Jew as one who is one inwardly, whose circumcision is spiritual. Paul's references allow him to undermine Jewish assurance of a superior position before God. He defines a spiritual obedience based upon faith which can result in salvation for gentiles as well as Jews. This passage forms a necessary foundation for Paul's treatment throughout Romans concerning God's righteousness in dealing with both Jews and gentiles.

This research clarifies a difficult text that interpreters have often bypassed. It shows the process by which Paul has come to his conclusions. The prospects are good that this method can have similar results when applied to other texts where writers are dependent upon scripture as their theological foundation.

BIBLIOGRAPHY
PRIMARY AND REFERENCE WORKS

Bauer, Walter; William F. Arndt; F. Wilbur Gingrich; and Frederick W. Danker. *A Greek-English Lexicon of the New Testament and Other Early Christian Literature*. 2nd ed., rev. and augmented. Chicago: University of Chicago Press, 1979.

Brown, Francis; S. R. Driver; and Charles A. Briggs. *A Hebrew and English Lexicon of the Old Testament, with an Appendix containing the Biblical Aramaic*. Oxford: Clarendon Press, 1962.

Charles, R. H., ed. *The Apocrypha and Pseudepigrapha of the Old Testament in English*. 2 vols. Oxford: Clarendon Press, 1963.

Charlesworth, James H., ed. *The Old Testament Pseudepigrapha*. 2 vols. New York: Doubleday, 1983, 1985.

Colson, F. H., et al., eds. *Philo*. LCL. 12 vols. London: Heinemann, 1929–62.

Drazin, Israel. *Targum Onkelos to Deuteronomy: an English Translation of the Text with Analysis and Commentary*. New York: Ktav Publishing House, 1982.

Epstein, I., ed. *The Babylonian Talmud*. 18 vols. London: Soncino Press, 1978.

Etheridge, J. W. *The Targums of Onkelos and Jonathan ben Uzziel on the Pentateuch with the Fragments of the Jerusalem Targum*. New York: Ktav Publishing House, 1968.

Freedman, H., and M. Simon, eds. *Deuteronomy*. Vol. 7 of *Midrash Rabbah*. 3rd ed. Trans. J. Rabbinowitz. London: Soncino Press, 1983.

Hatch, Edwin, and H. A. Redpath. *A Concordance to the Septuagint and the Other Greek Versions of the Old Testament*. 3 vols. Grand Rapids: Baker Book House, 1987.

Kittel, R., et al., eds. *Biblia Hebraica Stuttgartensia*. 4th ed. Stuttgart: Deutsche Bibelgesellschaft, 1990.

Macho, A. Díez. *Neophyti I: Targum Palestinense ms. de la Biblioteca Vaticana*. 6 vols. Madrid: Consejo Superior de Investigaciones Científicas, 1968–79.

Martínez, Florentino García. *The Dead Sea Scrolls Translated: The Qumran Texts in English*. Trans. Wilfred G. E. Watson. Leiden: E. J. Brill, 1994.

Metzger, Bruce M. *A Textual Commentary on the Greek New Testament*. Stuttgart: United Bible Societies, 1975.

Moulton, W. F.; A. S. Geden; and H. K. Moulton. *A Concordance to the Greek Testament*. 5th rev. ed. Edinburgh: T. & T. Clark, 1978.

Nestle, E., and K. Aland, eds. *Novum Testamentum Graece*. 26th ed. Stuttgart: Deutsche Bibelstiftung, 1979.

Oldfather, W. A. *Epictetus*. LCL. 2 vols. Cambridge: Harvard University Press, 1925.

Rahlfs, Alfred. *Septuaginta*. Stuttgart: Deutsche Bibelgesellschaft, 1979.

Smolar, Leivy, and Moses Aberbach. *Studies in Targum Jonathan to the Prophets*. New York: Ktav Publishing House, 1983.

Stenning, J. F. *The Targum of Isaiah*. Oxford: Clarendon Press, 1949.

Strack, Hermann, L., and Paul Billerbeck. *Kommentar zum Neuen Testament aus Talmud und Midrasch*. 6 vols. München: C. H. Beck'sche Verlagsbuch Handlung, 1922–61.

Thackeray, H. St. J., et al. *Josephus*. LCL. 9 vols. London: Heinemann, 1926–65.

Wevers, J. W., ed. *Deuteronomy*. Vol. 3 of *Septuaginta: Vetus Testamentum Graecum*. Göttingen: Vandenhoeck & Ruprecht, 1977.

Ziegler, Joseph, ed. *Ezekiel*. Vol. 16 of *Septuaginta: Vetus Testamentum Graecum*. Göttingen: Vandenhoeck & Ruprecht, 1952.

———. *Jeremiah*. Vol. 15 of *Septuaginta: Vetus Testamentum Graecum*. Göttingen: Vandenhoeck & Ruprecht, 1957.

———. *Isaiah*. Vol. 14 of *Septuaginta: Vetus Testamentum Graecum*. Göttingen: Vandenhoeck & Ruprecht, 1967.

COMMENTARIES ON ROMANS

Achtemeier, Paul J. *Romans*. Atlanta: John Knox Press, 1985.

Althaus, Paul. *Der Brief an die Römer*. NTD 6. Göttingen: Vandenhoeck & Ruprecht, 1966.

Barclay, William. *The Letter to the Romans*. Edinburgh: St. Andrew Press, 1955.

Barrett, Charles Kingsley. *A Commentary on the Epistle to the Romans*. Black's New Testament Commentaries. 2nd ed. London: A & C Black, 1991.

―――. *Reading Through Romans*. Philadelphia: Fortress Press, 1977.

Best, Ernest. *The Letter of Paul to the Romans*. CBC. Cambridge: Cambridge University Press, 1967.

Black, Matthew. *Romans*. NCB. London: Oliphants, 1973.

Bruce, Frederick F. *Romans*. TNTC 6. Grand Rapids: Eerdmans, 1985.

Brunner, Emil. *The Letter to the Romans: A Commentary*. Philadelphia: Westminster Press, 1959.

Byrne, Brendon. *Reckoning with Romans*. Wilmington: Michael Glazier, 1986.

Cambier, Jules. *L'Evangile de Dieu selon l'épître aux Romains: Exégèse et Théologie Biblique*. StudNeot 3. Louvain: Desclèe de Brouwer, 1967.

Cranfield, C. E. B. *A Critical and Exegetical Commentary on the Epistle to the Romans*. ICC, 2 vols., 6th ed. Ed. J. A. Emerton and C. E. B. Cranfield. Edinburgh: T. & T. Clark, 1975.

Dodd, C. H. *The Epistle of Paul to the Romans*. MNTC. London: Hodder & Stoughton, 1954.

Dunn, James D. G. *Romans 1–8*. WBC 38a. Dallas: Word Books, 1988.

―――. *Romans 9–16*. WBC 38b. Dallas: Word Books, 1988.

Fitzmyer, Joseph A. *Romans: a New Translation with Introduction and Commentary*. AB 33. New York: Doubleday, 1993.

Harrisville, Roy A. *Romans*. Augsburg Commentary on the New Testament. Minneapolis: Augsburg Publishing House, 1980.

Heil, John Paul. *Paul's Letter to the Romans. A Reader-response Commentary*. New York: Paulist Press, 1987.

————. *Romans – Paul's Letter of Hope*. AnBib 112. Rome: Pontifical Biblical Institute, 1987.

Hendriksen, W. *New Testament Commentary. Exposition of Paul's Epistle to the Romans*. 2 vols. Grand Rapids: Baker Book House, 1981.

Hodge, Charles. *Commentary on the Epistle to the Romans*. 2nd ed. Philadelphia: Claxton, 1866.

Holtzmann, Oskar. *Der Römerbrief*. NTD. 2 vols. Giessen: Töpelmann, 1962.

Huby, J. *Saint Paul. Épître aux Romains. Traduction et commentaire*. VS 10. Ed. S. Lyonnet. Paris: Beauchesne, 1958.

Käsemann, Ernst. *Commentary on Romans*. Trans. and ed. G. W. Bromiley. Grand Rapids: Eerdmans, 1980.

Kertelge, Karl. *The Epistle to the Romans*. New Testament for Spiritual Reading 12. Trans. F. McDonagh. New York: Herder and Herder, 1972.

Krimmer, Heiko. *Römerbrief*. Bibelkommentar 10. Edition C. Neuhausen: Hänssler, 1983.

Kuss, Otto. *Der Römerbrief: übersetzt und erklärt*. 3 vols. Regensburg: Pustet, 1957–59, 1978.

Leenhardt, Franz J. *The Epistle of Saint Paul to the Romans*. London: Lutterworth, 1961.

Lietzmann, Hans. *Die Briefe des Apostels Paulus an die Römer*. HNT. Tübingen: Mohr- Siebeck, 1933.

Lyonnet, Stanislas. *Les Epîtres de Saint Paul aux Galates, aux Romains*. SBJ. Paris: Cerf, 1959.

——. *Etudes sur l'Epître aux Romains*. AnBib 120. Rome: Pontifical Biblical Institute, 1989.

Maillot, Alphonse. *L'épître aux Romains. Epître de l'oecuménisme et thélogie de l'histoire*. Paris: Le Centurion, 1984.

Meyer, Heinrich August Wilhelm. *Critical and Exegetical Handbook to the Epistle to the Romans*. New York: Funk and Wagnalls, 1884.

Michel, Otto. *Der Brief an die Römer*. KEK. 14th ed. Göttingen: Vandenhoeck und Ruprecht, 1978.

Morris, Leon. *The Epistle to the Romans*. Grand Rapids: Eerdmans, 1988.

Moule, Handley C. G. *The Epistle of St. Paul to the Romans*. The Expositor's Bible. London: Hodder & Stoughton, 1894.

Murray, John. *The Epistle to the Romans*. NICNT. 2 vols. Grand Rapids: Eerdmans, 1968.

Nygren, Anders. *Commentary on Romans*. Philadelphia: Muhlenberg, 1949.

Pesch, Rudolf. *Römerbrief*. Die Neue Echter Bibel, Kommentar zum Neuen Testament mit der Einheitsübersetzung 6. Würzburg: Echter, 1983.

Rolland, Philippe. *Epître aux Romains. Texte grec structuré*. Rome: Pontifical Biblical Institute, 1980.

Sanday, William and Headlam, Arthur. *A Critical and Exegetical Commentary on the Epistle to the Romans*. ICC. Edinburgh: Clark, 1958.

Schlatter, Adolf. *Gottes Gerechtigkeit. Ein Kommentar zum Römerbrief*. Stuttgart: Calwer, 1962.

Schlier, Heinrich. *Der Römerbrief: Kommentar*. HTKNT 6. Freiburg: Herder, 1977.

Schmidt, Hans Wilhelm. *Der Brief des Paulus an die Römer*. THKNT 6. Berlin: Evangelische, 1963.

224

Schmithals, Walter. *Der Römerbrief: Ein Kommenetar.* Gütersloh: Mohn, 1988.

Stuhlmacher, Peter. *Paul's Letter to the Romans: a Commentary.* Louisville: Westminster/John Knox Press, 1994.

Taylor, Vincent. *The Epistle to the Romans.* London: Epworth Press, 1956.

Viard, Andre. *Saint Paul, Épitre aux Romains.* SB. Paris: J. Gabalda, 1975.

Wilckens, Ulrich. *Der Brief an die Römer.* EKK 6. 3 vols. Neukirchen-Vluyn: Neukirchener Verlag, 1982.

Zahn, Theodor, and Hauc, F. *Der Brief des Paulus an die Römer.* 3rd ed. Kommentar zum Neuen Testament 6. Leipzig: Deichert, 1925.

Zeller, Dieter. *Der Brief an die Römer. Übersetzt und erklärt.* RNT. Regensburg: Pustet, 1985.

MONOGRAPHS AND ARTICLES: ROMANS 2:17–29

Aletti, Jean-Noël. "Rm 1,18–3,20. Incohérence ou cohérence de l'argumentation paulinienne?" *Bib* 69 (1988): 47–62.

———. "Romains 2: Sa cohérence et sa fonction." *Bib* 77 (1996): 153–77.

Barth, Markus. "Speaking of Sin (Some Interpretive Notes on Romans 1:18–3:20)." *SJT* 8 (1955): 288–96.

Cambier, J.–M. "Le jugement de tous les hommes par Dieu seul, selon la verite, dans Rom 2:1–3:20." *ZNW* 67 (1976): 187–213.

Carras, George P. "Romans 2,1–29: A Dialogue on Jewish Ideals." *Bib* 73 (1992): 183–207.

Derrett, J. Duncan M. "'You Abominate False Gods; But Do You Rob Shrines?' (Rom 2:22b)." *NTS* 40 (1994): 558–71.

Fridrichsen, A. "Der wahre Jude und sein Lob: Röm 2:28 f." *Symbolae Arctoae* 1 (1927): 39–49.

Garlington, Don B. "ΙΕΡΟΣΥΛΕΙΝ and the Idolatry of Israel." *NTS* 36 (1990): 142–51.

Goppelt, L. "Der Missionar des Gesetzes: Zu Röm 2,21 f." In *Christologie und Ethik; Aufsatze zum Neuen Testament*, 137–46. Göttingen: Vandenhoeck und Ruprecht, 1968.

Krentz, Edgar. "The Name of God in Disrepute: Romans 2:16–29 [22–23]." *CurTM* 17 (1990): 429–39.

Lafon, Guy. "La production de la loi. La pensée de la loi in Romains 2,12–27." *RechSR* 74 (1986): 321–40.

———. "Les poètes de la loi. Un commentaire de Romains 2,12–27." *Christus* 134 (1987): 205–14.

Lyonnet, Stanislas. "'La circoncision du coeur qui relève de l'Esprit et non de la lettre' (Rom.2:29)." In *L'Evangile, hier et aujord'hui. Mélanges offerts au professeur Franz-J. Leenhardt*, 87–97. Geneva: Labor et Fides, 1968.

Schlier, Heinrich. "Von den Juden. Röm 2:1–29." In *Die Zeit der Kirche*, 38–47. Frieburg: Herder, 1956.

Schweizer, Eduard. "'Der Jude im Verborgenen..., dessen Lob nicht von Menschen, sondern von Gott kommt.' Zu Röm 2,28 f. und Matt 6,1–18." In *Neues Testament und Kirche: fur Rudolf Schnackenburg [z. 60. Geburtsag am 5. Jan. 1974 von Freunden u. Kollegen gewidmet]*, ed. J. Gnilka, 115–25. Freiburg: Herder, 1974.

Snodgrass, Klyne. "Justification by Grace—To the Doers: An Analysis of the Place of Romans 2 in the Theology of Paul." *NTS* 32 (1986): 72–93.

Tobin, Thomas H. "Controversy and Continuity in Romans 1:18–3:20." *CBQ* 55 (1993): 298–318.

RELATED MONOGRAPHS AND ARTICLES

Aageson, James W. *Written Also For Our Sake: Paul and the Art of Biblical Interpretation*. Louisville: Westiminster/John Knox Press, 1993.

Adams, Edward. "Abraham's Faith and Gentile Disobedience: Textual Links between Romans 1 and 4." *JSNT* 65 (1997): 47–66.

Adna, Jostein; Scott J. Hafemann; and Otfried Hofius. *Evangelium-Schriftauslegung-Kirche: Festschrift für Peter Stuhlmacher zum 65. Geburtstag.* Göttingen: Vanderhoeck & Ruprecht, 1997.

Aldrich, Roy L. "Has the Mosaic Law Been Abolished?" *BS* 116 (1959): 322–35.

Aletti, Jean-Noël. "L'argumentation Paulinienne en Rm 9." *Bib* 68.1 (1987): 41–56.

——. "La Présence d'un Modèle Rhétorique en Romains: Son Rôle et Son Importance." *Bib* 71 (1990): 1–24.

Alt, Steven Scott. "Early Tannaitic Exegesis and Modern Hermeneutics: A Study of Paul's Exegesis of Scripture in Romans and its Repeatability in the Twenty First Century." M.A. Thesis, Regent University, 1997.

Aune, David E. *The New Testament in Its Literary Environment.* Library of Early Christianity 8. Philadelphia: Westminster Press, 1987.

——. "Romans as a *Logos Protreptikos.*" In *The Romans Debate: Revised and Expanded Edition*, ed. Karl Donfried, 278–96. Peabody, MA: Hendrickson, 1991.

——. "Charismatic Exegesis in Early Judaism and Early Christianity." In *The Pseudepigrapha and Early Biblical Interpretation*, ed. James H. Charlesworth and Craig A. Evans, 126–50. JSPSup 14. Sheffield: JSOT Press, 1993.

Badenas, Robert. *Christ the End of the Law: Romans 10:4 in Pauline Perspective.* JSNTSup 10. Sheffield: JSOT Press, 1985.

Bammels, E.; C. K. Barrett; and W. D. Davies. *Donum Gentilicium: New Testament Studies in Honour of David Daube.* Oxford: Clarendon, 1978.

Barclay, J. M. G. "Paul and the Law: Observations on Some Recent Debates." *Themelios* 12.1 (1986): 5–15.

Barrett, Charles Kingsley. "Boasting (καυχᾶσθαι, κτλ.) in the Pauline Epistles." In *L'Apôtre Paul. Personalité, Style et Conception du Ministère*, 363–68. BEThL 73. Leuven: Leuven University Press, 1986.

Barth, Markus. *The People of God.* JSNTSup 5. Sheffield: JSOT, 1983.

Bassler, Jouette M. *Divine Impartiality: Paul and a Theological Axiom.* SBLDS 59. Chico, CA: Scholars Press, 1982.

———. "Divine Impartiality in Paul's Letter to the Romans." *NovT* 26 (1984): 43–58.

Beal, Timothy K. "Ideology and Intertextuality: Surplus of Meaning and Controlling the Means of Production." In *Reading Between Texts: Intertextuality and the Hebrew Bible,* ed. Danna Nolan Fewell, 27–39. Louisville: Westminster/John Knox Press, 1992.

Behm, Johannes, "μόρφωσις." In *Theological Dictionary of the New Testament,* ed. Gerhard Kittel, trans. Geoffrey Bromiley. Vol. 4, 754–55. Grand Rapids: Eerdmans, 1967.

Beker, J. Christiaan. *Paul the Apostle: The Triumph of God in Life and Thought.* Philadelphia: Fortress Press, 1980.

———. *Paul's Apocalyptic Gospel: The Coming Triumph of God.* Philadelphia: Fortress Press, 1982.

———. "The Faithfulness of God and the Priority of Israel in Paul's Letter to the Romans." *HTR* 79 (1986): 10–16.

———. *The Triumph of God: The Essence of Paul's Thought.* Philadelphia: Fortress Press, 1990.

———. "Echoes and Intertextuality: On the Role of Scripture in Paul's Theology." In *Paul and the Scriptures of Israel,* ed. Craig A. Evans and James A. Sanders, 64–69. JSNTSup. 83. Sheffield: JSOT Press, 1993.

Bell, Richard H. "Extra ecclesiam nulla salus? Is there salvation other than through faith in Christ according to Romans 2.12–16?" In *Evangelium-Schriftauslegung-Kirche: Festschrift für Peter Stuhlmacher zum 65. Geburtstag,* eds. Jostein Adna, Scott J. Hafemann, and Otfried Hofius, 31–43. Göttingen: Vanderhoeck & Ruprecht, 1997.

Berkley, Timothy W. "OT Exegesis and the Death of Judas." *Proceedings, Eastern Great Lakes & Mid-West Bible Society* 14 (1994): 29–45.

228

Betz, Hans Dieter. *Galatians: A Commentary on Paul's Letter to the Churches in Galatia*. Hermeneia. Philadelphia: Fortress Press, 1979.

———. "Christianity as Religion: Paul's Attempt at Definition in Romans." *JR* 71 (1991): 315–44.

Beyer, Hermann W. "βλασφημέω." In *Theological Dictionary of the New Testament*, ed. Gerhard Kittel, trans. Geoffrey Bromiley. Vol. 1, 621. Grand Rapids: Eerdmans, 1964.

Bischoff, A. "Exegetische Randbemerkungen." *ZNW* 9 (1908): 166–72.

Blackwood, Andrew. *Commentary on Jeremiah*. Waco: Word Books, 1977.

Bloch, Renée. "Methodological Note for the Study of Rabbinic Literature." In *Approaches to Ancient Judaism: Theory and Practice*, ed. W. S. Green, 51–76. Brown Judaic Studies 1. Missoula: Scholar's Press, 1978. First published as "Note méthodologique pour l'étude de la littérature rabbinique." *RSR* 43 (1955): 194–227.

———. "Midrash." In *Approaches to Ancient Judaism: Theory and Practice*, ed. W. S. Green, 29–50. Brown Judaic Studies 1. Missoula: Scholar's Press, 1978. First published as "Midrasch." *Dictionnaire de la Bible*, Supplement 5, ed. L. Pirot and H. Cazeues, 1263–81. Paris: Letousey et Ane, 1957.

Boers, Hendrikus W. "The Problem of Jews and Gentiles in the Macro-structure of Romans." *Neot* 15 (1981): 1–11.

———. "'We Who are By Inheritance Jews; Not From the Gentile Sinners.'" *JBL* 111 (1992): 273–81.

Bonsirven, Joseph. *Exégése Rabbinique et Exégése Paulinienne*. Bibliothèque de Théologie Historique. Paris: Beauchesne et ses fils, 1939.

Borgen, Peder. *Bread From Heaven*. NovTSup 10. Leiden: E. J. Brill, 1965.

———. "Debates on Circumcision in Philo and Paul." In *Paul Preaches Circumcision and Pleases Men: and other essays on Christian Origins*, 15–32. Trondheim: Tapir, 1983.

Bornkamm, Gunther. "Paulinische Anakoluthe." In *Das Ende des Gesetzes*, 76–92. Munich: Kaiser, 1952.

———. "Gesetz und Natur: Röm 2:14–16." In *Studien zu Antike und Urchristentum*, 93–118. 2nd ed. Munich: Kaiser, 1963.

Bowker, John. *The Targums and Rabbinic Literature; an Introduction to Jewish Interpretations of Scripture*. Cambridge: Cambridge University Press, 1969.

Boyarin, Daniel. *Intertextuality and the Reading of Midrash*. Bloomington: Indiana University Press, 1990.

Brawley, Robert L. "An Absent Complement and Intertextuality in John 19:28–29." *JBL* 112 (1993): 427–43.

Bright, John. *Jeremiah*. AB 21. New York: Doubleday, 1965.

Brooten, Bernadette J. "Paul and the Law: How Complete was the Departure." PSBSup 1 (1990): 71–89.

Brown, Stephen G. "The Intertextuality of Isaiah 66.17 and 2 Thessalonians 2.7: A Solution for the 'Restrainer' Problem." In *Paul and the Scriptures of Israel*, ed. Craig A. Evans and James A. Sanders, 254–75. JSNTSup. 83. Sheffield: JSOT Press, 1993.

Bruce, Frederick F. "Paul and the Law of Moses." *BJRL* 57 (1974–75): 259–79.

Bultmann, Rudolf. *The History of the Synoptic Tradition*. Trans. John Marsh. Oxford: Basil Blackwell, 1963.

———. "αἰσχύνω." In *Theological Dictionary of the New Testament*, ed. Gerhard Kittel, trans. Geoffrey Bromiley. Vol. 1, 189–90. Grand Rapids: Eerdmans, 1964.

Byrskog, Samuel. "Epistolography, Rhetoric and Letter Prescript: Romans 1.1–7 as a Test Case." *JSNT* 65 (1997): 27–46.

Cambier, J.–M. "La Liberté du Spirituel dans Rom. 8.12–17." In *Paul and Paulinism: Essays in Honour of C. K. Barrett*, ed. Morna Hooker and S. G. Wilson, 205–20. London: SPCK, 1982.

Campbell, Douglas A. *The Rhetoric of Righteousness in Romans 3:21–26*. JSNTSup 65. Sheffield: JSOT Press, 1992.

———. "The Meaning of ΠΙΣΤΙΣ and ΝΟΜΟΣ in Paul: A Linguistic and Structural Perspective." *JBL* 111 (1992): 91–103.

———. "Romans 1:17– A Crux Interpretum for the ΠΙΣΤΙΣ ΧΡΙΣΤΟΥ Debate." *JBL* 113 (1994): 265–85.

———. "False Presuppositions in the ΠΙΣΤΙΣ ΧΡΙΣΤΟΥ Debate: A Response to Brian Dodd." *JBL* 116 (1997): 713–19.

Campbell, William S. "Salvation for Jews and Gentiles: Krister Stendahl and Paul's Letter to the Romans." In *Studia Biblica 1978. Vol. 3. Papers on Paul and Other New Testament Authors: Sixth International Congress on Biblical Studies. Oxford 3–7 April 1978*, ed. E. A. Livingstone, 65–72. JSNTSup 3. Sheffield: JSOT, 1980.

———. "The Freedom and Faithfulness of God in Relation to Israel." *JSNT* 13 (1981): 27–45.

———. "Romans III as a Key to the Structure and Thought of the Letter." In *The Romans Debate: Revised and Expanded Edition*, ed. Karl Donfried, 251–64. Peabody, MA: Hendrickson, 1991.

Carson, D. A., and H. G. M. Williamson. *It is Written: Scripture Citing Scripture. Essays in Honour of Barnabas Lindars*. Cambridge: Cambridge University Press, 1988.

Charlesworth, James H. "In the Crucible: The Pseudepigrapha as Biblical Interpretation." In *The Pseudepigrapha and Early Biblical Interpretation*, ed. James H. Charlesworth and Craig A. Evans, 20–43. JSPSup 14. Sheffield: JSOT Press, 1993.

Charlesworth, James H., and Craig A. Evans, eds. *The Pseudepigrapha and Early Biblical Interpretation*. JSPSup 14. Sheffield: JSOT Press, 1993.

Cohn-Sherbok, D. "Paul and Rabbinic Exegesis." *SJT* 35 (1982): 117–32.

Collins, John J. "A Symbol of Otherness: Circumcision and Salvation in the First Century." In *To See Ourselves As Others See Us": Christians, Jews, "Others" in Late Antiquity*, ed. Jacob Neusner and E. S. Frerichs, 163–86. Chico: Scholars Press, 1985.

Cosgrove, Charles H. "Rhetorical Suspense in Romans 9–11: A Study in Polyvalence and Hermeneutical Election." *JBL* 115 (1996): 271–87.

Crafton, Jeffery A. "St. Paul and the Law." *SJT* 17 (1964): 43–68.

Cranfield, C. E. B. "Paul's Rhetorical Vision and the Purpose of Romans: Toward a New Understanding." *NovT* 32.4 (1990): 317–39.

———. "Giving a Dog a Bad Name. A Note on H. Räisänen's *Paul and the Law*." *JSNT* 38 (1990): 77–85.

———. "'The Works of the Law' in the Epistle to the Romans." *JSNT* 43 (1991): 89–101.

Cranford, Michael. "Abraham in Romans 4: The Father of All Who Believe." *NTS* 41 (1995): 71–88.

Dahl, Nils Alstrup. *Studies in Paul*. Minneapolis: Augsburg, 1977.

———. "Romans 3:9: Text and Meaning." In *Paul and Paulinism: Essays in Honour of C. K. Barrett*, ed. Morna Hooker and S. G. Wilson, 184–204. London: SPCK, 1982.

Daube, David. "Rabbinic Methods of Interpretation and Hellenistic Rhetoric." *HUCA* 22 (1949): 239–64.

———. *The New Testament and Rabbinic Judaism*. Jordan Lectures in Comparative Religion 2. London: Athlone Press, 1956.

Davies, Glenn N. *Faith and Obedience in Romans. A Study in Romans 1–4*. JSNTSup 39. Sheffield: JSOT, 1990.

Davies, W. D. *Paul and Rabbinic Judaism: Some Rabbinic Elements in Pauline Theology*. 2nd ed. London: SPCK, 1955.

———. "Paul and the People of Israel." *NTS* 24 (1977–78): 4–39.

———. "Paul and the Law: Reflections on Pitfalls in Interpretation." In *Paul and Paulinism: Essays in Honour of C. K. Barrett*, ed. Morna Hooker and S. G. Wilson, 4–16. London: SPCK, 1982.

———. "Reflections about the Use of the Old Testament in the New Testament in Its Historical Context." *JQR* 74 (1983): 105–36.

———. *Jewish and Pauline Studies*. Philadelphia: Fortress Press, 1984.

232

―――. "Canon and Christology in Paul." In *Paul and the Scriptures of Israel*, ed. Craig A. Evans and James A. Sanders, 18–39. JSNTSup. 83. Sheffield: JSOT Press, 1993.

Diezinger, Walter. "Unter Toten Freigeworder: Eine Untersuchung zu Rom III–VIII." *NovT* 5 (1962): 268–98.

Dodd, Brian. "Romans 1:17– A Crux Interpretum for the ΠΙΣΤΙΣ ΧΡΙΣΤΟΥ Debate?" *JBL* 114 (1995): 470–73.

Dodd, C. H. *According to the Scriptures: The Sub-Structure of New Testament Theology*. London: Nisbet and Co., 1952.

Doeve, J. W. *Jewish Hermeneutics in the Synoptic Gospels and Acts*. Assen: Koninklijke Van Gorcum & Comp. N.V., 1954.

Donaldson, Terence, L. "'Riches for the Gentiles' (Rom 11:12): Israel's Rejection and Paul's Gentile Mission." *JBL* 112 (1993): 81–98.

―――. *Paul and the Gentiles: Remapping Paul's Convictional World*. Minneapolis: Fortress Press, 1997.

Donfried, Karl P. "A Short Note on Romans 16." *JBL* 89 (1970): 441–49.

―――. ed. *The Romans Debate: Revised and Expanded Edition*. Peabody, MA: Hendrickson, 1991.

Draisma, Sipke, ed. *Intertextuality in Biblical Writings: Essays in Honour of Bas van Iersel*. Kampen: J. H. Kok, 1989.

Dupont, Jacques. "Pour l'historie de la doxologie finale de l'épître aux Romains." *RBén* 58 (1948): 3–22.

Dunn, James D. G. "The Formal and Theological Coherence of Romans." In *The Romans Debate: Revised and Expanded Edition*, ed. Karl Donfried, 245–250. Peabody, MA: Hendrickson, 1991.

―――. "The New Perspective on Paul: Paul and the Law." In *The Romans Debate: Revised and Expanded Edition*, ed. Karl Donfried, 299–308. Peabody, MA: Hendrickson, 1991.

―――. "Paul's Conversion–A Light to Twentieth Century Disputes." In *Evangelium-Schriftauslegung-Kirche: Festschrift für Peter Stuhlmacher zum 65. Geburtstag*, eds. Jostein Adna, Scott J. Hafemann, and Otfried Hofius, 77–93. Göttingen: Vanderhoeck & Ruprecht, 1997.

——. *The Theology of Paul the Apostle*. Grand Rapids: Eerdmans, 1998.

du Toit, A. B. "Persuasion in Romans 1:1–17." *BZ* 33 (1989): 192–209.

Elliott, John K. "The Language and Style of the Concluding Doxology of the Epistle to the Romans." *ZNW* 72 (1981): 124–30.

Elliott, Neil. *The Rhetoric of Romans: Argumentative Constraint and Strategy and Paul's Dialogue with Judaism*. JSNTSup 45. Sheffield: JSOT Press, 1990.

Ellis, E. Earle. *Paul's Use of the Old Testament*. London: Oliver and Boyd, 1957.

——. "Exegetical Patterns in 1 Corinthians and Romans." In *Prophecy and Hermeneutic in Early Christianity: New Testament Essays*, 213–20. WUNT 18. Grand Rapids: Eerdmans, 1978.

——. *The Old Testament in Early Christianity: Canon and Interpretation in the Light of Modern Research*. Grand Rapids: Baker Book House, 1992.

Evans, Craig A. "Mishna and Messiah 'In Context': Some Comments on Jacob Neusner's Proposals." *JBL* 112 (1993): 267–89.

——. "Listening for Echoes of Interpreted Scripture." In *Paul and the Scriptures of Israel*, ed. Craig A. Evans and James A. Sanders, 47–51. JSNTSup. 83. Sheffield: JSOT Press, 1993.

Evans, Craig A., and James A. Sanders. *Paul and the Scriptures of Israel*. JSNTSup 83. Sheffield: JSOT Press, 1993.

Feuillet, André. "Loi de Dieu, Loi du Christ et Loi de l'Esprit. D'apres les épîtres paulieniennes: Le rapport de ces trois lois avec loi mosaique." *NovT* 22 (1980): 29–65.

——. "La situation privilégiée des Juifs d'après Rom 3:9: Comparison avec Rom 1:16 et 3:1–2." *NRTh* 105 (1983): 33–46.

Fewell, Danna Nolan, ed. *Reading Between Texts: Intertextuality and the Hebrew Bible*. Louisville: Westminster/John Knox Press, 1992.

Fields, Bruce L. "Paul as Model: The Rhetoric and Old Testament Background of Philippians 3:1–4:1. Ph.D. diss. Marquette University, 1995.

Fishbane, Michael. *Biblical Interpretation in Ancient Israel.* Oxford: Clarendon Press, 1985.

Fitzmyer, Joseph A. "The Use of Explicit Old Testament Quotations in Qumran Literature and in the New Testament." *NTS* 7 (1961): 297–333.

Fowler, Robert M. "The Rhetoric of Direction and Indirection in the Gospel of Mark." *Semeia* 48 (1989): 115–134

Fraikin, Daniel. "The Rhetorical Function of the Jews in Romans." In *Paul and the Gospels.* Vol. 1 of *Anti-Judaism in Early Christianity*, Studies in Christianity and Judaism 2, ed. Peter Richardson and David Granskov, 91–106. Waterloo, Ont. Canada: Wilfrid Laurier University Press, 1986.

Froelich, K. ed. *Biblical Interpretation in the Early Church.* Sources of Early Christian Thought. Philadelphia: Fortress, 1984.

Furnish, Victor Paul. *II Corinthians.* AB 32a. New York: Doubleday, 1984.

———. "On Putting Paul in His Place." *JBL* 113 (1994): 3–17.

Gagnon, Robert A. "Heart of Wax and a Teaching that Stamps: ΤΥΠΟΣ ΔΙΔΑΧΗΣ (Rom 6:17b) Once More." *JBL* 112 (1993): 667–87.

Gamble, Harry Jr. *The Textual History of the Letter to the Romans: a Study in Textual and Literary Criticism.* Grand Rapids: Eerdmans, 1977.

Garlington, Don B. "Role Reversal and Paul's Use of Scripture in Galatians 3.10–13." *JSNT* 65 (1997): 85–121.

Gaston, Lloyd. *Paul and the Torah.* Vancouver: University of British Columbia Press, 1987.

———. "Israel's Misstep in the Eyes of Paul." In *The Romans Debate: Revised and Expanded Edition*, ed. Karl Donfried, 309–26. Peabody, MA: Hendrickson, 1991.

Gerhardsson, Birger. *Memory and Manuscript: Oral Tradition and Written Transmission in Rabbinic Judaism and Early Christianity.* ASNU 22. Trans. Eric J. Sharpe. Uppsala: Almquist and Wiksells, 1961.

———. *Tradition and Transmission in Early Christianity.* ConNT 20. Lund: Gleerup, 1964.

———. *The Testing of God's Son (Matt 4:1–11 & Par): An Analysis of Early Christian Midrash.* ConBNT 2. Trans. John Toy. Lund: Gleerup, 1966.

Getty, Mary Ann. "Paul and the Salvation of Israel: A Perspective on Romans 9–11." *CBQ* 50 (1988): 456–69.

Given, Mark D. "Restoring the Inheritance in Romans 11:1." *JBL* 118 (1999): 89–96.

Goodspeed, Edgar J. "Phoebe's Letter of Introduction." *HTR* 44 (1951): 55–57.

Gorday, Peter. *Principles of Patristic Exegesis: Romans 9–11 in Origen, John Chrysostom, and Augustine.* Studies in the Bible and Early Christianity 4. New York: Edwin Mellen, 1983.

Gordon, T. David. "Why Israel Did Not Obtain Torah-Righteousness: A Translation Note on Rom 9:32." *WJT* 54 (1992): 163–66.

Green, William Scott, ed. *Approaches to Ancient Judaism: Theory and Practice.* Brown Judaic Studies 1. Missoula: Scholars Press, 1978.

———. "Doing the Text's Work for It: Richard Hays on Paul's Use of Scripture." In *Paul and the Scriptures of Israel*, ed. Craig A. Evans and James A. Sanders, 59–61. JSNTSup. 83. Sheffield: JSOT Press, 1993.

Grobel, Kendrick. "A Chiastic Retribution-Formula in Romans 2." In *Zeit und Geschichte: Dankesgabe an Rudolf Bultmann zum 80. Geburtstag*, ed. Erich Dinkler, 255–61. Tübingen: Mohr-Siebeck, 1964.

Grundmann, Walter. "δόκιμος." In *Theological Dictionary of the New Testament*, ed. Gerhard Kittel, trans. Geoffrey Bromiley. Vol. 2, 260. Grand Rapids: Eerdmans, 1964.

Guerra, Anthony J. "Romans 4 as Apologetic Theology." *HTR* 81.3 (1988): 251–70.

——. "Romans: Paul's Purpose and Audience with Special Attention to Romans 9–11." *RB* 97.2 (1990): 219–37.

——. *Romans and the Apologetic Tradition: The Purpose, Genre, and Audience of Paul's Letter.* SNTSMS 81. Cambridge: Cambridge University Press, 1995.

Haacker, Klaus. "Das Evangelium Gottes und die Erwählung Israels: Zum Beitrag des Römerbriefs zur Erneuerung des Verhältnis zwischen Christen und Juden." *ThBei* 13 (1982): 59–72.

Hafemann, Scott J. "Moses in the Apocrypha and Pseudepigrapha: A Survey." *JSP* 7 (1990): 79–104.

——. *Paul, Moses, and the History of Israel: The Letter / Spirit Contrast and the Argument from Scripture in 2 Corinthians 3.* WUNT 81. Tübingen: J. C. B. Mohr, 1995.

——. "The Spirit of the New Covenant, the Law, and the Temple of God's Presence: Five Theses on Qumran Self-Understanding and the Contours of Paul's Thought." In *Evangelium-Schriftausle-gung-Kirche: Festschrift für Peter Stuhlmacher zum 65. Geburtstag,* eds. Jostein Adna, Scott J. Hafemann, and Otfried Hofius, 172–189. Göttingen: Vanderhoeck & Ruprecht, 1997.

Hahn, Ferdinand. "Zum Verständnis von Römer 11.26a: '...und so wird ganz Israel gerettet werden.'" In *Paul and Paulinism: Essays in Honour of C. K. Barrett,* ed. Morna Hooker and S. G. Wilson, 221–36. London: SPCK, 1982.

Hanson, Anthony T. *The New Testament Interpretation of Scripture.* London: SPCK, 1980.

——. "Vessels of Wrath or Instruments of Wrath? Romans IX. 22–23." *JTS* 32 (1981): 433–43.

Harris, J. Rendel. *Testimonies.* 2 vols. Cambridge: Cambridge University Press, 1916–1920.

Harrison, R. K. *Jeremiah and Lamentations: An Introduction and Commentary.* TOTC 19. Downers Grove, IL: Inter-Varsity, 1973.

Harrisville, Roy A. III. "In the Footsteps of Abraham: The figure of Abraham in the Epistles of Saint Paul." Ph.D. diss. Union Theological Seminary, 1990.

Hartman, G., and S. Budick, eds. *Midrash and Literature*. New Haven: Yale University Press, 1986.

Hays, Richard B. *The Faith of Jesus Christ: an investigation of the narrative substructure of Galatians 3:1–4:11*. SBLDS 56. Chico, CA: Scholars Press, 1983.

―――. "'Have We Found Abraham to be Our Forefather According to the Flesh?' A Reconsideration of Rom 2:1." *NovT* 27 (1985): 76–98.

―――. *Echoes of Scripture in the Letters of Paul*. New Haven: Yale University Press, 1989.

―――. "On the Rebound: A Response to Critiques of *Echoes of Scripture in the Letters of Paul*." In *Paul and the Scriptures of Israel*, ed. Craig A. Evans and James A. Sanders, 70–96. JSNTSup 83. Sheffield: JSOT Press, 1993.

Heil, John Paul. *Romans–Paul's Letter of Hope*. AnBib 112. Rome: Pontifical Biblical Institute, 1987.

Hills, Julian V. "'Christ was the Goal of the Law...' (Romans 10:4)." *JTS* NS 44 (1993): 585–92.

Hofius, Otfried. "Paulus – Missionar und Theologe." In *Evangelium-Schriftauslegung-Kirche: Festschrift für Peter Stuhlmacher zum 65. Geburtstag*, eds. Jostein Adna, Scott J. Hafemann, and Otfried Hofius, 224–37. Göttingen: Vanderhoeck & Ruprecht, 1997.

Holtz, Traugott. "Die historichen und theologischen Bedingungen des Römerbriefes." In *Evangelium-Schriftauslegung-Kirche: Festschrift für Peter Stuhlmacher zum 65. Geburtstag*, eds. Jostein Adna, Scott J. Hafemann, and Otfried Hofius, 238–54. Göttingen: Vanderhoeck & Ruprecht, 1997.

Hooker, Morna D. "Adam in Romans 1." In *From Adam to Christ: Essays on Paul*. Cambridge: Cambridge University Press, 1990. First published in *NTS* 6 (1960): 297–306.

―――. "Paul and 'Covenantal Nomism.'" In *Paul and Paulinism: Essays in Honour of C. K. Barrett*, ed. Morna Hooker and S. G. Wilson, 47–56. London: SPCK, 1982.

238

———. *From Adam to Christ: Essays on Paul*. Cambridge: Cambridge University Press, 1990.

Hooker, Morna D., and S. G. Wilson, eds. *Paul and Paulinism: Essays in Honour of C. K. Barrett*. London: SPCK, 1982.

Hübner, Hans. *Law in Paul's Thought*. Trans. James Greig. Edinburgh: T. & T. Clark, 1984.

Huggins, Ronald V. "Alleged Classical Parallels to Paul's 'What I Want To Do I Do Not Do, But What I Hate, That I Do' (Rom 7:15)." *WJT* 54 (1992): 153–61.

Hvalvik, Reidar. "A 'Sonderweg' for Israel: A Critical Examination of a Current Interpretation of Romans 11.25–27." *JSNT* 38 (1990): 87–107.

Instone Brewer, David. *Techniques and Assumptions in Jewish Exegesis before 70 CE*. Texte und Studien zum Antiken Judentum 30. Tübingen: J. C. B. Mohr, 1992.

Jaubert, Annie. *La notion d'alliance dans le Judaisme aux abords de l'ere Chretienne*. Patristica Sorbonensia 6. Paris: Editions du Seuil, 1963.

Jervall, Jacob. "The Letter to Jerusalem." In *The Romans Debate: Revised and Expanded Edition*, ed. Karl Donfried, 53–64. Peabody, MA: Hendrickson, 1991.

Jervis, L. Ann. *The Purpose of Romans: A Comparative Letter Structure Investigation*. JSNTSup 55. Sheffield: JSOT Press, 1991.

———. "'But I Want You to Know...': Paul's Midrashic Intertextual Response to the Corinthian Worshippers (1 Cor 11:2–16)." *JBL* 112 (1993): 231–246.

Jervis, L. Ann, and Peter Richardson, eds. *Gospel in Paul: Studies on Corinthians, Galatians, and Romans for Richard N. Longenecker*. JSNTSup 108. Sheffield: JSOT Press, 1994.

Jewett, Robert L. "Romans as an Ambassadorial Letter." *Int* 36 (1982): 5–20.

———. "The Law and the Coexistence of Jews and Gentiles in Romans." *Int* 39 (1985): 341–56.

———. "Following the Argument of Romans." In *The Romans Debate: Revised and Expanded Edition*, ed. Karl Donfried, 265–277. Peabody, MA: Hendrickson, 1991.

Johnson, Luke T. "Rom 3:21–26 and the Faith of Jesus." *CBQ* 44 (1982): 77–90.

Juel, Donald. *Messianic Exegesis: Christological Interpretation of the Old Testament in Early Christianity*. Philadelphia: Fortress Press, 1988.

Karris, Robert J. "Romans 14:1–15:13 and the Occasion of Romans." In *The Romans Debate: Revised and Expanded Edition*, ed. Karl Donfried, 65–84. Peabody, MA: Hendrickson, 1991.

Käsemann, Ernst. "The Spirit and the Letter." In *Perspectives on Paul*, 138–66. London: SCM, 1971.

Kaye, Bruce N. "'To the Romans and Others' Revisited." *NovT* 18 (1976): 37–77.

Kee, Howard Clark, "Appropriating the History of God's People: A Survey of Interpretations of the History of Israel in the Pseudepigrapha, Apocrypha, and the New Testament." In *The Pseudepigrapha and Early Biblical Interpretation*, ed. James H. Charlesworth and Craig A. Evans, 44–64. JSPSup 14. Sheffield: JSOT Press, 1993.

Keesmaat, Sylvia C. "Exodus and the Intertextual Transformation of Tradition in Romans 8.14–30." *JSNT* 54 (1994): 29–56.

Kidner, Derek. *Genesis: An Introduction and Commentary*. TOTC 1. Downers Grove, IL: Inter-Varsity, 1967.

Klein, Günter. "Paul's Purpose in writing Romans." In *The Romans Debate: Revised and Expanded Edition*, ed. Karl Donfried, 29–43. Peabody, MA: Hendrickson, 1991.

Krause, Deborah. "A Blessing Cursed: The Prophet's Prayer for Barren Womb and Dry Breasts in Hosea 9." In *Reading Between Texts: Intertextuality and the Hebrew Bible*, ed. Danna Nolan Fewell, 191–202. Louisville: Westminster/John Knox Press, 1992.

240

Krieger, Linda. "Paul and Torah." In *Paul the Jew: Jewish/Christian Dialogue*, ed. Wilhelm Wuellner, 41–47. Berkeley: Center for Hermeneutical Studies, 1990.

Kugel, James, L. "Two Introductions to Midrash." In *Midrash and Literature*, ed. G. Hartman and S. Budick, 90–101. New Haven: Yale University Press, 1986.

Kugel, James L., and Rowan A. Greer. *Early Biblical Interpretation*. Library of Early Christianity 5. Philadelphia: Westminster, 1986.

Kümmel, Werner Georg. *Introduction to the New Testament*. Nashville: Abingdon, 1975.

Lamp, Jeffery S. "Paul, the Law, Jews, and Gentiles: A Contextual and Exegetical Reading of Romans 2:12–16." *JETS* 42 (1999): 37–51.

Lampe, Peter. "The Roman Christians of Romans 16." In *The Romans Debate: Revised and Expanded Edition*, ed. Karl Donfried, 216–30. Peabody, MA: Hendrickson, 1991.

Le Déaut, Roger. *The Message of the New Testament and the Aramaic Bible (Targum)*. Subsidia Biblica 5. Rome: Pontifical Biblical Institute, 1982.

Lindars, Barnabas. *New Testament Apologetic: The Doctrinal Significance of the Old Testament Quotations*. Philadelphia: Westminster, 1961.

———. "The Old Testament and Universalism in Paul." *BJRL* 69 (1987): 511–27.

Longenecker, Bruce W. "Different Answers to Different Issues: Israel, the Gentiles and Salvation History in Romans 9–11." *JSNT* 36 (1989): 95–123.

Longenecker, Richard N. *Biblical Exegesis in the Apostolic Period*. Grand Rapids: Eerdmans, 1975.

Lüdemann, Gerd. *Paulus und das Judentum*. Theologische Existenz heute 215. Munich: Kaiser, 1983.

Manns, Frédéric. "Un Midrash Chrétien: Le Récit de la Mort de Judas." *RevScRel* 54 (1980): 197–203.

Manson, T. W. "St. Paul's Letter to the Romans—and Others." *BJRL* 31 (1948): 224–40.

Marcus, Joel. "The Circumcision and the Uncircumcision in Rome." *NTS* 35 (1989): 67–81.

———. *The Way of the Lord: Christological Exegesis of the Old Testament in the Gospel of Mark.* Louisville: Westminster/John Knox Press, 1992.

Margerie, B. de. "'L'ancienne alliance n'a jamais été révoqée.' Réflexion sur la mutuelle immanence des deux alliances au sein de l'alliance éternelle." *RevThom* 87 (1987): 203–241.

Martens, John W. "Romans 2.14–16: A Stoic Reading." *NTS* 40 (1994): 55–67.

Martin, Lynn Larry. "The Righteousness of God in Romans: A Study in Paul's Use of Jewish Tradition." Ph.D. diss. Marquette University, 1991.

McDonald, J. I. H. "Was Romans XVI A Separate Letter?" *NTS* 16 (1969–70): 369–72.

McEleney, N. J. "Conversion, Circumcision, and the Law." *NTS* 20 (1973–74): 319–41.

McNamara, Martin. *The New Testament and the Palestinian Targum to the Pentateuch.* AnBib 27. Rome: Pontifical Biblical Institute, 1966.

———. *Targum and Testament. Aramaic Paraphrases of the Hebrew Bible: A Light on the New Testament.* Grand Rapids: Eerdmans, 1972.

Mesner, David Earl. "The Rhetoric of Citations: Paul's Use of Scripture in Romans 9." Ph.D. diss. Northwestern University, 1991.

Michel, Otto. *Paulus und seine Bibel.* Gütersloh: Bertelsmann, 1929.

Moiser, Jeremy. "Rethinking Romans 12–15." *NTS* 36 (1990): 571–82.

Moo, Douglas J. "Israel and Paul in Romans 7.7–12." *NTS* 32 (1986): 122–35.

Neusner, Jacob. *The Rabbinic Traditions about the Pharisees before 70* . 3 vols. Leiden: E.J. Brill, 1971.

——. "The Rabbinic Traditions About the Pharisees Before 70 A.D.: The Problem of Oral Tradition." *Kairos* 14 (1972): 57–70.

——. "The Use of Later Rabbinic Evidence for the Study of First Century Pharisaism." In *Approaches to Ancient Judaism: Theory and Practice*, ed. W. S. Green, 215–25. Brown Judaic Studies 1. Missoula: Scholar's Press, 1978.

——. *What is Midrash?* Philadelphia: Fortress Press, 1987.

——. "The Mishna in Philosophical Context and Out of Canonical Bounds." *JBL* 112 (1993): 291–304.

Neyrey, Jerome H. *Paul, in Other Words: A Cultural Reading of His Letters*. Louisville: Westminster/John Knox Press, 1990.

B. Noack. "Current and Backwater in the Epistle to the Romans." *ST* 19 (1965): 155–66.

O'Day, Gail R. "Jeremiah 9:22–23 and 1 Corinthians 1:26–31: A Study in Intertextuality." *JBL* 109 (1990): 259–67.

Pattee, Stephen B. "Stumbling Stone or Cornerstone? The Structure and Meaning of Paul's Argument in Rom 9:30–10:13." Ph.D. diss. Marquette University, 1991.

Pelikan, Jaroslav. *The Emergence of the Catholic Tradition (100–600)*. Vol. 1 of *The Christian Tradition: A History of the Development of Doctrine*. Chicago: University of Chicago Press, 1971.

Penchansky, David. "Staying the Night: Intertextuality in Genesis and Judges." In *Reading Between Texts: Intertextuality and the Hebrew Bible*, ed. Danna Nolan Fewell, 77–88. Louisville: Westminster/John Knox Press, 1992.

Piper, John. *The Justification of God: An Exegetical and Theological Study of Romans 9:1–23*. Grand Rapids: Baker Book House, 1983.

Porter, Calvin L. "Romans 1.18–32: Its Role in the Developing Argument." *NTS* 40 (1994): 210–28.

Porter, Stanley E. "The Argument of Romans 5: Can a Rhetorical Question Make a Difference?" *JBL* 110 (1991): 655–77.

Räisänen, Heikki. *Paul and the Law*. WUNT 29. Tübingen: J. C. B. Mohr, 1983.

———. *The Torah and Christ. Essays in German and English on the Problem of the Law in Early Christianity*. Publication of the Finnish Exegetical Society 45. Helsinki: Finnish Exegetical Society, 1986.

———. "Paul's Conversion and the Development of His View of the Law." *NTS* 33 (1987): 404–419.

Reid, Marty L. "A Consideration of the Function of Rom 1:8–15 in the Light of Greco-Roman Rhetoric." *JETS* 38 (1995): 181–91.

Rese, Martin. "Israel und Kirche in Römer 9." *NTS* 34 (1988): 208–217.

Ridderbos, Herman. *Paul: An Outline of his Theology*. Trans. John Richard De Witt. Grand Rapids: Eerdmans, 1975.

Rolland, Philippe. "L'antithèse de Rm 5–8." *Bib* 69 (1988): 396–400.

Ryan, Judith M. "The Faithfulness of God. Paul's Prophetic Response to Israel: An Exegesis of Romans 11:1–36." Ph.D. diss. Fordham University, 1995.

Sanders, E. P. *Paul and Palestinian Judaism: A Comparison of Patterns of Religion*. Philadelphia: Fortress Press, 1977.

———. "On the Question of Fulfilling the Law in Paul and Rabbinic Judaism." In *Donum Gentilicium: New Testament Studies in Honour of David Daube*, ed. E. Bammels, C. K. Barrett and W. D. Davies, 103–126. Oxford: Clarendon, 1978.

———. *Paul, the Law, and the Jewish People*. Philadelphia: Fortress Press, 1983.

Satran, David. "Paul Among the Rabbis and the Fathers: Exegetical Reflections." PSBSup 1 (1990): 90–105.

Schneider, B. "The Meaning of St. Paul's Antithesis 'The Letter and the Spirit.'" *CBQ* 15 (1953): 163–207.

Schreiner, T. R. "The Abolition and Fulfillment of the Law in Paul." *JSNT* 35 (1989): 47– 74.

244

Schrenk, G. "ἱεροσυλέω." In *Theological Dictionary of the New Testament*, ed. Gerhard Kittel, trans. Geoffrey Bromiley. Vol. 3, 255. Grand Rapids: Eerdmans, 1965.

Scott, James M. "Paul's Use of Deuteronomic Tradition." *JBL* 112 (1993): 645–65.

———. "For as Many as are of the Works of the Law are Under a Curse (Gal 3:10)." In *Paul and the Scriptures of Israel*, ed. Craig A. Evans and James A. Sanders, 187–221. JSNTSup 83. Sheffield: JSOT Press, 1993.

Segal, Alan F. *Paul the Convert: The Apostolate and Apostasy of Saul the Pharisee.* New Haven: Yale University Press, 1990.

Senior, Donald. *The Passion Narrative According to Matthew: A Redactional Study.* BETL 39. Leuven/Louvain: Leuven University Press, 1975.

Siker, J. S. "From Gentile Inclusion to Jewish Exclusion: Abraham in Early Christian Controversy with Jews." *JSNT* 35 (1989): 30–36.

———. *Disinheriting the Jews: Abraham in Early Christian Controversy.* Louisville: Westminster/John Knox Press, 1991.

Smiga, George. "Romans 12:1–2 and 15:30–32 and the Occasion of the Letter to the Romans." *CBQ* 53 (1991): 257–73.

Smith, Morton. *Tannaitic Parallels to the Gospels.* SBLMS 6. Philadelphia: Society of Biblical Literature, 1951.

———. "A Comparison of Early Christian and Early Rabbinic Tradition." *JBL* 82 (1963): 169–76.

Speiser, E. A. *Genesis.* AB 1. New York: Doubleday, 1982.

Stanley, Christopher D. *Paul and the Language of Scripture: Citation Technique in the Pauline Epistles and Contemporary Literature.* SNTSMS 69. Cambridge: Cambridge University Press, 1992.

———. "'The Redeemer Will Come ἐκ Ζιών: Romans 11.26–27 Revisited." In *Paul and the Scriptures of Israel*, ed. Craig A. Evans and James A. Sanders, 118–42. JSNTSup 83. Sheffield: JSOT Press, 1993.

Stegner, William R. "Romans 9:6–29 — A Midrash." *JSNT* 22 (1984): 37–52.

———. *Narrative Theology in early Jewish Christianity*. Louisville: Westminster/John Knox Press, 1989.

Stein, Robert H. "The Argument of Romans 13:1–7." *NovT* 31 (1989): 325–43.

Steiner, Richard C. "Incomplete Circumcision in Egypt and Edom: Jeremiah 9:24–25 in the Light of Josephus and Jonckheere." *JBL* 118 (1999): 497–505.

Stendahl, Krister. *The School of St. Matthew and Its Use of the Old Testament*. 2nd ed. Philadelphia: Fortress Press, 1968. First published as ASNU 20. Lund: Gleerup, 1954.

———. *Paul Among Jews and Gentiles and Other Essays*. London: SCM, 1977.

———. *Final Account: Paul's Letter to the Romans*. Minneapolis: Fortress Press, 1995.

Stockhausen, Carol Kern. *Moses' Veil and the Glory of the New Covenant: The Exegetical Substructure of II Cor 3:1–4, 6*. Rome: Pontifical Biblical Institute, 1989.

———. "2 Corinthians 3 and the Principles of Pauline Exegesis." In *Paul and the Scriptures of Israel*, ed. Craig A. Evans and James A. Sanders, 143–64. JSNTSup 83. Sheffield: JSOT Press, 1993.

Stowers, Stanley. *The Diatribe and Paul's Letter to the Romans*. SBLDS 57. Chicago: Scholars Press, 1981.

———. *Letter Writing in Greco-Roman Antiquity*. Library of Early Christianity 5. Philadelphia: Westminster Press, 1986.

———. "ΕΚ ΠΙΣΤΕΩΣ and ΔΙΑ ΤΗΣ ΠΙΣΤΕΩΣ in Romans 3:30." *JBL* 108 (1989): 665–74.

———. *A Rereading of Romans: Justice, Jews, and Gentiles*. New Haven: Yale University Press, 1994.

Strack, H. L., and G. Stemberger. *Introduction to the Talmud and Midrash*. Minneapolis: Fortress Press, 1992.

Taylor, John B. *Ezekiel: An Introduction and Commentary.* TOTC 20. Downers Grove, IL: Inter-Varsity, 1969.

Thielman, Frank. *Paul & The Law: A Contextual Approach.* Downers Grove, IL: InterVarsity, 1994.

Tobin, Thomas H. "What Shall We Say that Abraham Found? The Controversy behind Romans 4." *HTR* 88 (1995): 437–52.

Thompson, J. A. *Deuteronomy: An Introduction and Commentary.* TOTC 5. Downers Grove, IL: Inter-Varsity, 1974.

Trigg, J. W. *Biblical Interpretation.* Message of the Fathers of the Church 9. Wilmington, DE: Michael Glazier, 1988.

Tsumura, D. T. "An OT Background to Rom 8.22." *NTS* 40 (1994): 620–21.

Vermes, Geza. *Scripture and Tradition in Judaism.* SPB 4. Ed. P. De Boer. Leiden: E. J. Brill, 1961.

Vorster, Willem S. "Intertextuality and Redaktionsgeschichte." In *Intertextuality in Biblical Writings: Essays in Honour of Bas van Iersel*, ed. Sipke Draisma, 15–26. Kampen: J. H. Kok, 1989.

Wagner, J. Ross. "The Christ, Servant of Jew and Gentile: A Fresh Approach to Romans 15:8–9." *JBL* 116 (1997): 473–85.

Watson, Francis. *Paul, Judaism, and the Gentiles: A Sociological Approach.* SNTSMS 56. Cambridge: Cambridge University Press, 1986.

———. "The Two Roman Congregation: Romans 14:1–15:13. In *The Romans Debate: Revised and Expanded Edition*, ed. Karl Donfried, 203–15. Peabody, MA: Hendrickson, 1991.

Wedderburn, A. J. M. *The Reasons for Romans.* Ed. John Riches. Edinburgh: T. & T. Clark, 1988.

Weiss, Konrad. "διαφέρω." In *Theological Dictionary of the New Testament*, ed. Gerhard Kittel, trans. Geoffrey Bromiley. Vol. 9, 63–64. Grand Rapids: Eerdmans, 1974.

Wiefel, Wolfgang. "The Jewish Community in Ancient Rome and the Origins of Roman Christianity." In *The Romans Debate: Revised and Expanded Edition*, ed. Karl Donfried, 85–101. Peabody, MA: Hendrickson, 1991.

Williams, Philip R. "Paul's Purpose in Writing Romans." *BSac* (1971): 62–67.

Witherington III, Ben. *Paul's Narrative Thought World: The Tapestry of Tragedy and Triumph*. Louisville: Westminster/John Knox Press, 1994.

Wolde, Ellen J. van. *A Semiotic Analysis of Genesis 2–3. A Semiotic Theory and Method of Analysis Applied to the Story of the Garden of Eden*. SSN 25. Assen: Van Gorcum, 1989.

———. "Trendy Intertextuality." In *Intertextuality in Biblical Writings: Essays in Honour of Bas van Iersel*, ed. Sipke Draisma, 43–49. Kampen: J. H. Kok, 1989.

Workin, Joel. "Reflection on Paul and the Law." In *Paul the Jew: Jewish/Christian Dialogue*, ed. Wilhelm Wuellner, 35–40. Berkley: Center for Hermeneutical Studies, 1990.

Wright, N. T. "The Messiah and the People of God: A Study in Pauline Theology with Particular Reference to the Argument of the Epistle to the Romans." D. Phil. thesis, University of Oxford, 1980.

———. *The Climax of the Covenant: Christ and the Law in Pauline Theology*. Edinburgh: T. & T. Clark, 1991.

———. *The New Testament and the People of God*. Vol. 1 of *Christian Origins and the Question of God*. Minneapolis: Fortress Press, 1992.

———. "Paul, Arabia, and Elijah (Galatians 1:17)." *JBL* 115 (1996): 683–92.

———. *What Saint Paul Really Said: Was Paul of Tarsus the Real Founder of Christianity?* Grand Rapids: Eerdmans, 1997.

Index of Ancient Texts

252

254

256

Index of Modern Authors